HATRED, RIDICULE
OR CONTEMPT

THE MACMILLAN COMPANY
NEW YORK · CHICAGO
DALLAS · ATLANTA · SAN FRANCISCO

HATRED, RIDICULE
OR CONTEMPT

A BOOK
OF LIBEL CASES

JOSEPH DEAN

Reputation, reputation, reputation! O, I have lost my reputation!
I have lost the immortal part of myself, and what remains is bestial!
SHAKESPEARE: *Othello.*

THE MACMILLAN COMPANY
New York • *1954*

FOR MY MOTHER

CONTENTS

7

INTRODUCTION

WHAT is a libel? This book tells the stories of a variety of English libel cases, most of them tried in recent years. They range in quality from the momentous to the absurd. They cover many fields of activity, and exhibit human nature in every posture and disguise. But whether its special feature be the legal arguments, the controversial subject-matter, the character of the parties, or the foibles of the Judge, each case to a greater or less extent illustrates and embodies the law.

Law is complicated, because human life is complicated, and a very short Introduction cannot give an adequate summary of the English law of libel. But it may deepen the interest of each case for the reader (who is assumed not to be a lawyer) and help him to form an opinion on the skill with which it was conducted in Court or the value of the expressions of judicial thought which it provoked. A libel, then, in the language hallowed by centuries of repetition in the Courts, is the publication of any statement which exposes a man to "hatred, ridicule or contempt". A more up-to-date definition includes any matter which "tends to lower a man in the estimation of right-thinking members of society generally or to cause them to shun or avoid him".

And how easy it is to publish a libel! To take but two examples, almost every novel or short story is written around the characters of real people known to the author, and every day the Press is filled with the columns of critics and commentators, each of them pontificating upon some theatre of life in which men and women contend for fortune and success. The possibilities of libel are infinite. A single malicious or inconsiderate expression may ruin a reputation. Only a strong and comprehensive law can hold the ring in the battle of words, which are the potent weapons of everyday life.

The first purpose of the law must always be to prevent the cold war of words from turning into a hot war of swords. For this reason in England, as in most countries, libel has from the very beginning been a crime, and it is still both a crime and a civil wrong. The victim of a libel may either prosecute in the Criminal Courts or sue for damages in the High Court, or both. For a criminal libel the maximum penalty is a fine and two years imprisonment. But prosecutions are rare these days, as the Courts have decided not to entertain them unless the libel is sufficiently serious to be "calculated to provoke a breach of the peace". The first two Chapters of this book deal with interesting, not to say sensational, prosecutions for criminal libels, but most of the following cases were civil claims for damages, which may well be and indeed have often been so heavy as to penalise a defendant more savagely than the criminal law itself.

Libel holds the scales of justice between the protection of private reputation on the one hand and public freedom of speech on the other. Scales so weighted are not easily balanced. Reputation has many aspects—it involves the whole relationship of a man with his fellows—and different circumstances may require different safeguards. The moral obligation or public usefulness of plain speaking may also vary with the occasion. If it is always difficult to do justice, the reconciliation of these two contradictory interests demands an extra sensitivity.

In England this delicate duty is largely discharged by a jury. The Lord Chief Justice, Lord Goddard, said during his summing up in the Laski case ("Revolution by Violence"): "A man may in this country publish anything which twelve common people, that is to say twelve jurymen selected at random from a panel of jurymen, think it is expedient should be published; he may not write or publish anything which twelve of his countrymen think ought not to be published." This is even truer to-day. The Laski case, like most of the cases in this book, was tried before a special jury. Only bankers, merchants, occupiers of private houses of a substantial rateable value, and "esquires" were entitled to sit as special jurors. But special juries have since been abolished (except for certain commercial cases) and libel actions are now tried before an ordinary jury, upon which almost every householder is qualified to sit.

The parties are entitled to agree to trial by a judge alone (as was the practice during the war, when trial by jury in civil cases was largely suspended) but the plaintiff (the person bringing the action) usually demands a jury, in the belief that they will award him higher damages. And so the jury remains. "Every man in England," said Sir James Scarlett in his address to the jury in *Cooper* v. *Wakley* ("Surgery in 1828"), "is at liberty to publish what he pleases. God forbid that that liberty should be abridged! But that liberty would become the source of the most bitter tyranny that ever an unhappy country laboured under, unless in those instances in which that freedom is abused some constitutional tribunal did exist to correct it. That tribunal, Gentlemen, you are."

This, however, is not the whole story. The jury have great scope, but the Judge, besides exercising by his summing up and general control of the trial a considerable influence upon their verdict, also retains an overriding authority. It is here that intricate points of the law of libel arise. For while the jury are only concerned to answer questions of fact, the Judge must follow the law. All his pronouncements are subject to review by the Court of Appeal, which is composed of three Lord Justices of Appeal. The decision of the Court of Appeal may in its turn be upset by the House of Lords, sitting as the final Court, beyond which there is no appeal. This system envisages the possibility of disagreement among the Judges—the decision in each Court going by the opinion of the majority—and the pages which follow contain many examples of an interesting, and sometimes amusing divergence of views.

What, then, are the counterpoises which keep the law of libel in balance? To begin with, the Courts will withdraw a case from the jury if they believe that the publication complained of is "incapable of a defamatory meaning" either in its ordinary sense or in the sense which the plaintiff puts upon it in his "innuendo". This practice raises such interesting questions that a chapter —"Libel or no libel"—has been given to summarising some of the leading cases. The criterion by which everything is measured in English law is that figment of the legal imagination— "the reasonable man". What would a reasonable man think to be the meaning of this or that alleged libel? It is obvious, of course, that reasonable men may reasonably differ in their opinion, and that a statement may have both innocent and guilty meanings. It is also true that the judgments of reason may change with the times. A hundred years or more ago it would have been libellous to call a man a Liberal; to-day it is almost certainly a libel to accuse him falsely of being a Communist. To upset a jury's verdict is tantamount to saying that the jury was composed of twelve unreasonable men, and the Courts are reluctant to take this step. The humane object of the law is to steer a course as close as possible to normality, and in this sense the libel cases in this book form a kind of broken, distorted mirror of the age.

The defendant in a libel action has a number of defences open to him. If one fails, he may rely upon another. First and foremost, truth, or "justification", is an absolute answer to every libel claim. Truth is now also a defence to a prosecution for libel, so long as it is also proved that publication was "for the public benefit". The lines in Moore's poem have not applied for more than a century:

> "For oh, 'twas nuts to the Father of Lies
>   (As this wily fiend is named in the Bible)
> To find it settled by laws so wise
>   That the greater the truth, the worse the libel."

But it is one thing to "know" the truth of a libel, and quite another to be able to prove it in Court. Mere rumour is not evidence. And a person who passes on a libellous rumour makes himself a party to the original libel, and must, if he seeks to justify it, prove, not that the rumour existed, but that it was true.

It is for this reason that the editor and proprietors of a newspaper and the printers and publishers of a book are equally liable with the author for every libel they publish. It is only very rarely, as in "Bottomley's Last Case", that anyone through whose agency a libel has been distributed can escape liability.

But this joint responsibility enables an editor to have the best of both worlds. He may fight the case in person, while his paper is separately represented by the most experienced and expensive counsel. This technique was devised by Labouchère, the great editor of *Truth*, who thrived on libel actions and was said to have a post-box marked "writs" at the entrance to his office.

The defendant often prefers the less exacting defence of "fair comment on a matter of public interest". Everybody has a right to criticise, to express an honest and outspoken opinion, about "anything which may fairly be said to invite comment or challenge public attention". This right extends, as will be seen, to political and spiritualist meetings as well as dramatic and musical performances. The law insists that the critic does not misstate the facts, believes what he writes and has no malicious motive for writing it. It is then for the jury to answer the question: "Would any fair man, however prejudiced he may be, however exaggerated or obstinate his views, have said that which this criticism has said . . . ?"

Sometimes it is possible for the defendant to plead "privilege". The law recognises the right to make libellous statements on certain occasions. No action can be brought against a Member of Parliament in any circumstances for anything said in debate. It is the same with words spoken in Court by Judge, counsel or witnesses. Privilege also extends to fair and accurate reports of public meetings (in newspapers) and of parliamentary or judicial proceedings. It is hoped that all the cases recounted in this book fall within the latter category! The story of how privilege was extended to reports published by order of Parliament is told in "The Westminster Libel Shop". But the most important kind of privilege possessed by the general public arises where it is the

duty, legal, social or moral, or the special interest of one person
to give information to another who has a corresponding interest
in receiving it. Obvious examples are a reference for a servant
given by a late employer to a prospective employer, a complaint
made to a proper authority, or a statement about the financial
credit of a trader communicated between the members of a trade
protection society. In these cases it is for the Judge to rule
whether the occasion was "privileged" and for the jury to decide
whether the privilege has been destroyed by the personal malice
of the author of the libel. This procedure will be seen at work in
Lord Gladstone's trial ("The Reputation of the Dead").

Although by its Latin derivation it means "a little book", a
libel need not be in writing. Human malice or carelessness have
discovered many another way of injuring a man's good name.
The expression "statement" does not necessarily imply words,
and "publication" in the law of libel means nothing more than
showing it to some third person. In Monson's case, for instance,
the libel consisted in putting a wax statue near the Chamber of
Horrors—see "Visual Images". The libels on Mr. Plumb and
Mrs. Honeysett arose out of an improper use of photographs
("A Policeman's Feet"). It is possible, as Swift wrote, to

> "Convey a libel in a frown,
> And wink a reputation down."

To be strictly accurate, however, only a slander can be conveyed in this fashion. There is no essential difference between a
libel and a slander. They are the twin branches of the law of
defamation. But slander is a defamatory statement published by
word of mouth or in some other "fugitive medium", while libel
is a publication in writing or other permanent form. This distinction is an historical heirloom from days when different Courts
dealt with spoken and with written words. But it seems to
correspond with something in our national way of life, for, as
slander is only actionable under certain conditions, it means that

people can be much freer with their tongues than with their pens. At all events the distinction has survived the passing of the Defamation Act, 1952, which contents itself on this aspect of the law with providing that slanders broadcast by wireless or television are to be treated as libels.

The practical difference between libel and slander is that in a libel action the plaintiff never has to prove that he has suffered any damage. Once he has been libelled, damage is presumed by the law, and he is entitled to ask, not only for an injunction to prevent further publication of the libel, but also for "general damages", which are assessed by the jury. The tactical objective of the defendant is to conduct the trial in such a way as to persuade the jury to award the minimum damages. This he may do by pouring scorn on the whole proceedings, discrediting the plaintiff in the witness-box, suggesting he is only out for money, and so forth. But sometimes these tactics rebound, and the jury feel that a rich defendant can afford to pay.

The Judge naturally has some influence over the jury's award. In one case Lord Hewart indicated his view of the appropriate damages in these words:

> "Many years ago, in the good old days, a judge, having the task of summing up a clear case to the jury, as I have now, turned to the jury and gave a very low whistle. I myself have never been more tempted to follow that example than in the present case. . . . At present our currency knows no coin smaller than a farthing, and it may be that, while you regret that there is no smaller coin, a farthing may more than adequately represent the compensation due."

In that case the jury duly awarded the plaintiff one farthing damages. But juries are seldom so commandingly directed!

There have been many serious libels. Often the plaintiff has been forced into Court so that some disputed issue, upon which his livelihood depends, may be threshed out in public. (Could

there ever be a better case in point than "The Last Trial in Westminster Hall"?) Sometimes out of righteous indignation the
plaintiff wishes to penalise the defendant with substantial damages.
Sometimes he seeks compensation for the heavy financial loss
which a libel may have inflicted upon him. But often he is content to establish the falsity of the imputation and accept a public
apology, either refusing damages or stipulating for their payment
to a charity.

The fact remains that a libel action may have a purely financial
incentive, and there is a standing temptation to a certain kind of
person to sue rich Corporations. This book contains a number of
cases (the reader will recognise them for himself) in which the
action was a speculative gamble rather than the redress of a personal hurt. There is a still less scrupulous type of proceeding, akin
to blackmail, in which a writ is issued in the expectation that an
attractive sum will be paid up, either to avoid the cost and trouble
of fighting the action or for some other oblique motive. The lust
for damages has been the most degrading element in English libel
proceedings, and it is tempting to draw a comparison with France,
where honour is often satisfied with the award of a "franc sym-
bolique". In England, however, it is thought a dishonour for the
plaintiff to win only a "farthing damages", so much so that he is
usually left to pay all his own costs. The truth is that we are so
accustomed to the valuation of human reputation in £.s.d. that
we take its unavoidable crudity for granted.

These abuses of the system have been tackled by the Defamation Act, 1952. It will scarcely be possible in future for men of
the stamp of Hobbs and Bottomley to make a substantial (and
tax-free) living out of libel damages. Moreover, while accepting
the principle of the "Artemus Jones" type of case (that a man
may be innocently guilty), the Act has created a special machinery
to prevent the giving of unjustified damages. No one knows yet
how well this machinery will work.

Much of our public freedom of discussion is due to the fact
that the law of libel protects individuals alone, and not groups or

sections of the community. A man may write pretty much what he likes about capitalists or socialists, but very little of what he feels but cannot prove about any particular capitalist or socialist. During the passage of the new Act several attempts were made to extend the protection of libel to groups "distinguishable by race, creed or colour". Fortunately for the future of public debate these amendments were defeated. Groups have in fact been protected for centuries by the crime known as "seditious libel", a misdemeanour to which, like blasphemous or obscene libel, there is no reliable defence, except a refusal by the jury to convict. Prosecutions for seditious libels were once the mainstay of Governments, particularly during and after the Napoleonic Wars, before the modern freedom of political discussion was accepted.

A word about costs. Costs play an important part in the tactics of litigation. A successful party is normally entitled to have his costs paid by his opponent. This means he may recover something between one-half and three-quarters of his expenses— *may* recover, but *cannot* if his opponent is penniless. An award of "contemptuous damages", such as a farthing, is usually taken to mean that the action should not have been brought, and that is why no costs are given. Whatever the damages are, if the defendant has paid a larger sum into Court, which the plaintiff has declined to take out in settlement of the action, the plaintiff must pay the defendant's costs from the time when the money was deposited in Court. (See "Blackmail".)

The choice of cases in the following pages may be thought capricious, and their arrangement even more so. But the book is not meant to be either a history or a treatise. It is an unorthodox anthology. Several cases, such as Whistler's action against Ruskin and Oscar Wilde's prosecution of the Marquess of Queensberry, have been deliberately left out, as they are already so well known. The same consideration applied to the two most famous slander trials of recent years, the Tranby Croft and Talking Mongoose cases, and in the event the book makes only a passing reference to a single slander action. There are, of course, a host of important or interesting cases of which no mention has been made. Libel actions have had a great vogue. Since the war, however, their frequency appears to have declined.

No attempt has been made to take sides. That is left for the reader. An English libel trial gathers its peculiar and picturesque character from its cross-examining techniques and its compromise between abstruse legal learning and the rough-and-ready convictions of twelve "men in the street". How far has the alliance of these elements made for a just peace and harmony in our midst? One thing seems fairly clear: if the pen is mightier than the sword, in England at least the writ is mightier than the pen.

I

SALOME AND THE BLACK BOOK

Rex v. *Billing* (1918)

IT has been claimed for juries that they bring to the administration of the law a healthy popular prejudice which would not otherwise be there. Certainly there are times when the verdict of twelve citizens vindicates an impassioned public opinion and is received with cheers from the public gallery. The Court then has something of the air of a theatre after the fall of the last curtain. A great performance has been brought to a successful climax with the acquittal of the hero or the condemnation of the villain.

So it was with the trial of Noel Pemberton Billing, M.P., in May and June, 1918. This performance, however, though it abounded in tension and dramatic incident, lacked the dignity of true drama. Even Mr. Justice Darling could not spice it with the drawing-room comedy wit so intimately associated with his judicial personality. It was a melodrama, almost a farcical melodrama. But it played to a full Court and an excited country for six days, and served, like a Greek tragedy, as a purge of public fear, though it made no call upon pity.

It will be remembered that the spring of 1918 was the blackest of all the black seasons of the first Great War. The long winter's slaughter at Passchendaele was followed by the German counter-attack and the breaking of the Fifth British Army. The war was now in its fourth year, and it seemed as if some diabolical force was at work, frustrating every heroic effort. Somebody must be to blame: somewhere there must be a core of evil infusing poison into the leadership of the country. The people, credulous and frightened, thirsted for a scapegoat in the higher direction of affairs, and Noel Pemberton Billing, Independent Member of Parliament for East Hertfordshire and patriot by profession, put on the armour of St. George and set out in search of a dragon.

Already the editor of an aggressive journal called *The Imperialist*, he now founded the society of "Vigilantes"—"to promote purity in public life." "There is an influence," he declared later in his address to the jury, "a mysterious influence—which seems to have dogged our footsteps through the whole conduct of this campaign. . . . Gentlemen of the Jury, I assure you that there must be some reason for all the 'regrettable incidents' of this war."

Dragon or scapegoat, he had not been long in finding it. At the end of January 1918 *The Imperialist* had disclosed the unspeakable truth: the Germans were winning the war by the propagation of sexual vice. It was all the fault of Oscar Wilde.

"THE FIRST 47,000," declared the headline, and underneath it a sulphurous article introduced the elusive "Black Book" to the English public. "There exists," it said, "in the *Cabinet noire* of a certain German prince a book compiled by the Secret Service from the reports of German Agents who have infested this country for the past twenty years, agents so vile and spreading debauchery of such a lasciviousness as only German minds could conceive and only German bodies execute. The officer who discovered this book while on special service briefly outlined for me its stupefying contents. In the beginning of the book is a précis of general instructions regarding the propagation of evils which all decent men thought had perished in Sodom and Lesbia. The blasphemous compilers even speak of the Groves and High Places mentioned in the Bible. The most insidious arguments are outlined for the use of the German agent in his revolting work. Then more than a thousand pages are filled with the names mentioned by German agents in their reports. There are the names of forty-seven thousand English men and women. It is a most catholic miscellany. The names of Privy Councillors, youths of the chorus, wives of Cabinet Ministers, dancing girls, even Cabinet Ministers themselves, while diplomats, poets, bankers, editors, newspaper proprietors, and members of His Majesty's household follow each other with no order of precedence." Unprintable paragraphs followed this revelation, and at last the article ended with the sentence, "The story of the contents of this book has opened my eyes, and the matter must not rest."

It was not intended that it should. The officer who claimed

to have discovered the Black Book was in fact the author of the article and, as he said at the trial, he and Billing sat down to wait for a libel writ. But nothing happened. As an indecent publication the article might have amounted in itself to an obscene libel, which is a misdemeanour of the old Common Law. But no one had any interest in prosecuting. Since no one could know whether he was one of the 47,000, no one could say he had been libelled. Besides, the scoop was only a semi-domestic affair. The circulation of *The Imperialist* was confined to subscribers, and they were unlikely to take offence at the quality of its contents.

It so happened that at this time J. T. Grein, a well-known dramatic critic and impresario in his own right, had arranged to present Miss Maud Allan in two private performances—for subscribing members only—of Oscar Wilde's play *Salome*. Maud Allan, already known the world over for her own dance "The Vision of Salome", was to appear in the title role, which included the spectacular "Dance of the Seven Veils". A week or so later modest advertisements to this effect appeared in the *Morning Post* and the *Sunday Times*.

Here was damning evidence. A man with a German name presenting in private—and on Sundays—a play which had been banned by the Lord Chamberlain for public performance, featuring a dancer who had studied music in Germany, and written by a man whose crime was notorious—what more convincing proof could be found of the German plot to debauch the Kingdom? What better witness to the authenticity of the Black Book? Remember, too, the protective disgust of a British jury at any inkling of vice, and the easy mockery with which Courts of Law delighted in handling the innocent fancies of literature—how much more would they revel in the fœtid, sensual language of *Salome*! It was true that *Salome* had been first acted by Sarah Bernhardt in Paris in 1895, that the play had been on sale in every English bookshop for twenty years or more, and that the words had been sung time and time again in Covent Garden to the music of Richard Strauss. It had to be conceded also that there was little sign in *Salome* of the twin vices of the Black Book, but the catalogue of perversions was not exhausted—in 1918 sadism and masochism still had something of a dreadful novelty about them, and if the worst came to the worst something might be made out of incest. Even then it did not follow that an actress had the character of the part she played. But there was no need for too much subtlety. What with the state of the country, the horrors of sexual espionage, and decadent literature, outraged patriotism was sure to be vindicated.

Pemberton Billing, the apostle of purity, felt himself on safe ground. In the following number of *The Imperialist*, which had now become *The Vigilante*, he reprinted the announcement of the performance under an indecent heading which may be paraphrased as "The Cult of Sexual Perversions", and added the single sentence, "If Scotland Yard were to seize the list of these members"—the members who subscribed for tickets for *Salome*—"I have no doubt they would secure the names of several thousand of the first 47,000."

Miss Allan and Mr. Grein prosecuted Billing for criminal libel. Three indictments were preferred: the first charged him with an obscene libel contained in the paragraph heading, the second with a defamatory libel on Grein, and the third with a similar libel on Maud Allan. The third was taken first, and was the only one tried. It set out the whole paragraph, including the headline, and added the innuendo: "Meaning thereby that the said Maud Allan was a lewd and unchaste and immoral woman and was about to give private performances of an obscene and indecent character so designed as to foster and encourage obscene and unnatural practices among women and that the said Maud Allan associated herself with persons addicted to obscene and unnatural practices." To this indictment Billing pleaded not guilty, and further that all the defamatory matters alleged in it were true and published for the public benefit: the gist of his written plea was that *Salome* was an "open representation of degenerated sexual lust, sexual crime and unnatural passions" and its performance would attract many of the "easy victims of pressure" whose names were recorded in the Black Book, and would therefore be "highly deleterious and prejudicial to public morality and to the interests of purity in the public life of this country generally". This plea of justification scarcely covered the libel on Maud Allan personally, a fact which seems to have escaped the attention of the Court. From her point of view it might have been easier if the indictment charging an obscene libel had been taken first, since there can be no justification of an obscenity. But she naturally wished to clear herself of the foul slur cast upon her character.

The trial opened at the Old Bailey in May, 1918. Billing conducted his own defence and soon proved himself an unscrupulous advocate and filibuster. His first step was to object to be tried by Mr. Justice Darling. "My reason is that I have, in my position as a public man and as a Member of Parliament, on many occasions criticised your Lordship's administration of justice in this country: I have referred both in the columns of the Press and in a book I have written and on public platforms to the atmosphere of levity which your Lordship has frequently introduced into cases you have tried." The martyr of public purity was determined to set the jury and the public against the Judge. Before the trial was over Darling had been hissed from the back of the Court. But he swept this objection aside, remarking that he had not read the criticisms, and invited the defendant to leave the dock and conduct his case from the table in the well of the Court. To this offer Billing replied loftily, "It is quite immaterial to me, my Lord." It was only after it was explained that he might not be heard from the dock that he consented to leave it. The acoustics at the Old Bailey were notorious. As Darling recalled later in the trial, there was a story that a prisoner in that dock who had been given seven years collapsed because he added the sentence to the echo and thought he had received fourteen years.

What was the truth about Oscar Wilde's *Salome*, which still awaits its first public performance? Billing also stated in his plea of justification that the play was "an evil and mischievous travesty of a biblical story". Oscar Wilde had in fact followed the story told in the Gospels, except in one important particular: Salome's motive for demanding the head of John the Baptist on a charger. In the Bible she did it to please her mother Herodias, whose marriage to Herod, her dead husband's brother, John had condemned. In the play Salome is seized with a physical craving for Jokanaan, as John is called. But Jokanaan rebuffs her, and all her longing is to satisfy her thwarted passion. It is a short play, one act only, oppressive with its larded language and repetition of the metaphors of desire.

"Jokanaan," cries Salome, Princess of Judæa, "thy body is white like the lilies of a field that the mower hath never mowed . . . Neither the roses in the garden of the Queen of Arabia, the perfumed garden of spices of the Queen of Arabia, nor the feet of the dawn when they light on the leaves, nor the breast of the moon when she lies on the breast of the sea . . . There is nothing in the world so white as thy body." When Jokanaan rejects her, she reviles his body, and praises the blackness of his hair. Again he repulses her advances, and she eulogises the redness of his mouth. "I will kiss thy mouth, Jokanaan, I will kiss thy mouth." It is to fulfil this ambition that, oblivious of all things and persons else, she consents to dance before Herod, and when as her chosen reward she holds Jokanaan's severed head in her hands her ardour is unabated. "Ah! thou wouldst not suffer me to kiss thy mouth, Jokanaan. Well! I will kiss it now. I will bite it with my teeth as one bites a ripe fruit. . . . Thy body was a column of ivory set on a silver socket. It was a garden full of doves and of silver lilies . . . Thy voice was a censer that scattered strange perfumes, and when I looked on thee I heard a strange music . . . I love thee yet, Jokanaan, I love thee only . . . I am athirst for thy beauty: I am hungry for thy body; and neither wine nor fruits can appease my desire." And then she kisses him, and is killed by Herod's command, and the curtain falls.

Her love has destroyed both the lover and the beloved, and it might have been argued that, like so many of Oscar Wilde's works, the play had a moral ending. The ending, the Judge said, was the only good thing about it. (Darling was himself an essayist and the author of a good deal of mannered verse, but the judicial Bench is not always the best seat of literary criticism.) Ellis Hume-Williams, K.C., (later knighted) who was leading counsel for the prosecution and also, like Billing, a Member of Parliament, did not argue this point, but opened his case on the footing that in the whole play, unattractive though it might be, there was nothing but "the straightforward passion of a woman for a man", and none of the unnatural vice recorded in the Black Book. It was, he said, a perfectly innocent performance, and he called Miss Maud Allan into the witness-box.

For her the innocence was of an altogether higher kind. In a long and disagreeable cross-examination nothing was so helpful to Billing as her insistence that Salome's love for John was the awakening of her soul to the voice of God. This had been the theme of Maud Allan's own dance, "The Vision of Salome," and this was her interpretation of the play. "It is the spirit. It is the first pouring out of the spirit. It is not physical at all. The spiritual life of Jokanaan is pervading her, and she feels it." And so Billing naturally read on and on through the pages of musky metaphor. "Thy mouth is like a band of scarlet on a tower of ivory. It is like a pomegranate cut with a knife of ivory. The pomegranate's flowers that blossom in the gardens of Tyre, and are redder than roses, are not so red. The red blasts of trumpets that herald the approach of kings, and make afraid the enemy, are not so red. Thy mouth is redder than the feet of those who tread the wine in the wine-press. Thy mouth is redder than the feet of the doves who haunt the temples and are fed by the priests. It is redder than the feet of him who cometh from a forest where he hath slain a lion, and seen gilded tigers——"

Mr. Justice Darling: "Gilded tigers"—"Gilded tigers."

Mr. Justice Darling: "Go on.—'Thy mouth is like a branch of coral that fishers have found in the twilight of the sea, the coral that they keep for the kings. It is like the vermilion that the Moabites find in the mines of Moab, the vermilion that the kings take from them. It is like the bow of the King of the Persians, that is painted with vermilion, and is tipped with coral. There is nothing in the world so red as thy mouth.' Before we go any further——"

Hume-Williams: "Do not let us go any further."

Maud Allan: "She would not be the first woman who has asked to kiss a man's mouth."

Mr. Justice Darling: "But, gentlemen, that is hardly the question:

she is the first woman who has talked about the gilded tiger."

Maud Allan: "Not as an Oriental, I do not think. Besides, it is her fantasy. I think her imagery is very great. It is quite uncustomary for a Westerner to understand the imagery of the Oriental people."

Mr. Justice Darling: "You think that Oscar Wilde understood it?"

Maud Allan: "He may have understood it, and written it down. I do not understand Oscar Wilde, because I did not know the gentleman."

A woman and an artist may see the body as nothing but a revelation of the spirit. But to men—and lawyers and juries at that, who deal with a coarser clay—this interpretation is less compelling; and it is distrusted for its blurring of the categories. "It is every woman's privilege to fall in love," Maud Allan claimed, and the Court was with her. But when she went on to say that "Salome fell in love with the holiness and the beauty of this man", and added that the play was no more sexual than the current musical *A Little Bit of Fluff*, she forfeited the sympathy of the twelve reasonable men in the jurybox.

The Defendant was an expert in the art of ignorance. None knew better than he that, when a party appears in our Courts without solicitor or counsel, special consideration is always shown by the Judge. The litigant in person can often rush in where counsel fears to tread. Counsel cannot put his evidence into the mouth of his own witness, or cross-examine him if he dislikes what he has said, nor can he use his cross-examination of his opponent's witness as an occasion to make little speeches to the jury, or his own speeches to the jury as an opportunity to give evidence without oath or cross-examination. When Billing tried these and other forbidden gambits, he disclaimed all guilt: he was just a plain blunt Englishman, defending the cause of public purity, while counsel were concerned only with their fees. At other times he displayed an accurate knowledge of trial procedure. No sooner, for instance, had the evidence for the prosecution been completed than he submitted (as the Defendant is always entitled to do) that no case had been made out against

him, and therefore the Judge should direct the jury to acquit
him there and then. Billing quoted chapter and verse, reading
out extracts from *Odgers on Libel*, a textbook familiar to lawyers.
But Darling had no difficulty in rejecting his submission, and the
trial went on.

Interest in the finer points of law and literature soon subsided,
as the hunt for the Black Book began. On the Portsmouth Road
near Ripley in Surrey there is a lake cloaked around on all sides
by fir trees, and on the other side of the road an inn of pale vermilion brick called the Hut Hotel. To this dark retreat a Mrs.
Villiers Stuart, the first witness for the defence, stated that she
was taken one afternoon in a taxi from London by two army
officers and there, over a cup of tea, she was shown the Black
Book. It was, she said, about the size of that book—pointing to
Odgers on Libel. The two officers who showed it to her had since
been killed in Palestine, and it was hinted that they had been put
out of the way. Of the contents of the book the Judge, vainly
endeavouring to control the trial by the rules of evidence, would
allow nothing to be said, unless the book itself was produced or
good reason shown why it could not be produced.

But the Defendant was not to be baulked of his public scandal.
When the Judge objected to his questions, he said to the witness:

"Is Justice Darling's name in that book?"—"It is, and that book
    can be produced."
Mr. Justice Darling: "It can be produced?"—"It can be produced: it
    will have to be produced from Germany, and it can be, and
    it shall be. Mr. Justice Darling, we have got to win this war,
    and while you are sitting there we will never win it. My
    men are fighting—other people's men are fighting——"
Defendant: "Is Mrs. Asquith's name in the book?"—"It is in the
    book."
"Is Mr. Asquith's name in the book?"—"It is."
"Is Lord Haldane's name in the book?"—"It is in the book."

Mrs. Villiers Stuart was ordered to leave the box.

But from this moment the irrepressible Defendant dominated

the Court. The Judge and prosecuting counsel were frequently insulted. Abuse and hubbub succeeded each other. At one point Billing said to the Judge, "I can't help the gallery applauding, any more than you can help them laughing at your jokes."

Fantastic charges were made, or hints dropped, and on the next three mornings the hearing began with disclaimers by counsel on behalf of men and women in public life, who had been slandered from the witness-box and were left without redress. The only absolutely safe places for libel and slander are a Court of Law and the Houses of Parliament: what is said in these conclaves is sacrosanct.

Captain Spencer, the author of the two articles, was Billing's next witness. This was his story. He had been personal A.D.C. to Prince William of Wied, the German Mpret of Albania. The Prince had shown him the Black Book in the Palace of Durazzo in 1913 and 1914. He described it as "a list of names of people who might be approached and the method in which they could be approached, for the purpose of obtaining information". Then he wandered off into a long history about a mission which he had undertaken in the Balkans, and about divers plots and conspiracies in London and Rome. Sinister forces had thwarted his patriotic labours. An attempt was made by the military authorities to silence him, as he knew too much, and he found himself locked in a small hut outside Salonika with a man sitting on a small bed with his head in his hands, who got up in a few minutes, held out his hand and said, "Good-bye, old man; they are shooting me at three o'clock." Spencer was then visited by doctors, who told him he was supposed to be suffering from most unusual hallucinations, but really someone had his knife into him. The doctors put him in a room under an old Orphan Asylum, from which he escaped in the uniform of an R.A.M.C. orderly. After further medical examinations he was maliciously invalided out of the service, and appointed an examiner of aeroplanes. How much more entertaining the *via dolorosa* of a small-time secret agent than a mean and unpalatable libel!

The story did not grow clearer under cross-examination. The

witness had stated that he had seen the book three times and taken some notes. What had become of his notes?

"I put them in another book, in an Albanian book of Albanian personalities with their failings and vices."

"What did you do with your notes?"—"The whole thing was cabled for and given to Commander Cozens-Hardy, of Naval Intelligence."

"What did you do with these notes?"—"I put all the notes in the book, and everything in a trunk."

"Was it a trunk of yours?"—"It was a trunk I had left in Rome."

"Did you take them yourself from Durazzo to Rome, or was the trunk with you at Durazzo?"—"It was all I took out of Durazzo, with the exception of a tooth brush. It was all I took with me, this book, some letters."

"And a tooth brush?"—"And a tooth brush."

"What did you do with your notes when you got to Rome?"— "I put them in a small steamer box or trunk."

"What became of the steamer trunk?"—"I cannot trace it; I do not know."

"Did you lose it?"—"I do not know what became of it; I was ordered on special service; I do not know."

"What became of the trunk? Where did you leave it?"—"If you communicate with Commander Cozens-Hardy, you might find them."

"Do you say he found it?"—"He cabled, and got all the papers."

"Did you give them to the Ambassador in Rome? In whose care did you leave them?"—"This book?"

"The notes—in whose care did you leave them?"—"I did not leave them in any one's care."

"Then how did Commander Cozens-Hardy get them?"—"I do not know; it is hearsay evidence."

"You do not know he got them?"—"Yes, I know he got

them, because I saw them at his office at the Admiralty."

"Did you examine them?"—"I did not."

"Did he tell you he had got them?"—"He told me he had received what he was trying to get."

"Did he tell you he had your notes?"—"He did not specify notes; it was a packet of papers and books."

Few things are more exhausting than cross-examining an evasive witness. Judge and counsel made one final effort.

"When you put the notes in the box, where did you put the box?"—"I took three boxes with me. I left three boxes in Rome. I left one in New York going up to Canada; I left one box in Appleton, Wisconsin; and another box I kept with me and came to London."

"I do not care what you did with your army of boxes; what I want to know is what did you do with the box which contained these valuable notes?"—"It was one of the five boxes I had left behind. I left three behind me in Rome, one in Appleton, Wisconsin."

"Where did you leave these notes?"—"You must ask Commander Cozens-Hardy where he found them."

Perseverance proved a waste of time. The witness was just as evasive about what reports concerning the Black Book he had made to what authorities. But the Judge indicated that he would like to have Commander Cozens-Hardy called as a witness, and early on the third day of the trial Hume-Williams announced that, while the officer in question was out of the country, Admiral Hall, Chief of the Admiralty Intelligence Department, was in Court and was ready to give such information as his Lordship might require. But Billing, unashamedly sly, objected to the giving of other evidence while a witness was still in the box, and at the same time pressed for the absent Commander to be sent for. Strictly speaking, the Admiral could only be called, by way of rebutting evidence, at the conclusion of the defence, and so it was arranged for a telephone message to be sent to the Admiralty.

But when the time came, the Admiral was having lunch, and Darling refused to keep the Court and the jury waiting.

Captain Spencer stopped short of accusing Admiral Hall of being a German spy. Of the Admiral he merely said that, though he knew that British secret agents "got marooned on islands", he was "powerless".

"If a Secret Service agent finds out too much," he explained, "he is sometimes ordered to an island and kept there."

"And he is sometimes shut up as mad?" asked Hume-Williams. —"Yes."

"When he is not?"—"Yes."

"And that is an English system?"—"No, it is a German system, practised in England. It is Germany working in England."

"So that the people who are able to get Secret Service agents marooned by the orders of the British Government are in the German Service?"—"Yes, I think I told you that privately. Do you never remember meeting me at dinner, and my talking to you?"

"I? Never!"—"When I came back from Albania you met me at dinner at a house, and we had a conversation together."

"I never met you before in my life!"—"I quite expected you to say that."

"Because it is the truth!"—"You were never at the Clitheroes?"

Captain Spencer was a master of the retort outrageous. This particular brand was a favourite tactic in this trial. But the Judge put an end to the ludicrous exchange by saying, "I expect one or other of you will get marooned." Further cross-examination revealed nothing more damaging or surprising than the fact that Spencer had never sent the names of the 47,000 or any of them to Scotland Yard.

Captain Spencer's story was corroborated by a Lieutenant Galbraith, who had found the Captain sharing a basement room in a Salonika hospital with a Colonel who was there for putting his general under arrest. Moreover, though he had not seen

Spencer escape, he had seen him return, in the uniform of an R.A.M.C. orderly. All in all, there was a good deal of evidence that the Army had taken a certain view of the egregious Captain. But of the existence or contents of the Black Book no further evidence was forthcoming, beyond what Mrs. Villiers Stuart added when she returned to the witness-box.

A few days after the trial the Foreign Secretary said in the House of Commons that Spencer had not been entrusted with a mission in Albania in 1913 and had not on his return from the Balkans made any special confidential reports to the Foreign Office. In November, 1915, he was attached to the British Adriatic Mission, where he carried out his duties to the satisfaction of his immediate superior. At the same time a Berlin newspaper stated that Prince William of Wied had never heard either of Captain Spencer or of the Black Book, until he read reports of the trial. And that was all.

But Billing had more than one buckle to his shield. He called five doctors, two dramatic critics, a priest, Lord Alfred Douglas and even Mr. Grein.

Lawyers never cease to be surprised at the evidence of doctors. The first doctor stated that sadism was a congenital, hereditary disease, of which the victim might be unaware until something, such as watching a sadistic play, provoked in him an uncontrollable impulse. *Salome* was such a play—it was "an open display by physical means of several forms of sexual perversion". One form of sadism was lust for dead bodies. Oscar Wilde was "a well-known monster". It would have been impossible for him to have written *Salome* without "a close and intimate knowledge of sexual perverts". Indeed the probability was that "he had Krafft-Ebing in front of him all the time." (Krafft-Ebing, a Viennese professor of neurology, was the first doctor to delve deeply into the sexual aspects of cruelty and to name the new-found vice after the Marquis de Sade.) Furthermore Oscar Wilde could not have imagined the scenes or written them without sadistic pleasure. Nor could people with "any trace of perversion" in them watch the performance of such scenes without intense delight, and so undoubtedly they would become perverts themselves. The doctor then pointed out that the moon is

used in the play as a symbol of Salome's developing passion, and
he touched lightly upon the connection between the moon and
lunatics.

The Judge was obviously impressed by this evidence. He quoted
one of Salome's speeches, and asked the witness:

> "Does not that strike you as downright nonsense?"—"Exactly;
> I mean it would be if it were not a scene of sexual passion."
> "Is it the sort of thing that people say in lunatic asylums?"—
> "Yes, it is a pure example of sexual perversion." But when
> the doctor began to talk of fetishism, masochism, and
> incest, Darling said, "Is not this overdoing it a bit?" So the
> doctor played his last card: it had never crossed his mind that
> Billing's libellous headline was aimed at Miss Maud Allan
> personally, but on the other hand it was impossible for her
> to play the part as Oscar Wilde intended it to be played
> without being a sadist herself.

If all this was true, and Maud Allan knew it, the defence was
fairly made out. But, of course, the other doctors were not
exactly of the same opinion. Next came the King's Surgeon, who
had neither read nor seen the play. Billing began to ask him a few
general questions on the moral state of the nation, all of them
inadmissible. Finding his path barred, he displayed once more his
tactical sense. "Having regard to the fact that this Court does
not permit me to examine my witnesses," he exclaimed, "I will
sit down." After the surgeon came a consulting physician, who
had read the play and seen nothing in it from a medical point of
view. When a friend suggested it was sadistic, he read it again
from that angle and found that it was. But he agreed, as Maud
Allan had suggested, that you can read anything into anything,
even the phrase "Mary had a little lamb". The next medical
witness thought that all the works of Oscar Wilde should be
banned, except perhaps *The Ballad of Reading Gaol* (which shows
the good that imprisonment does to some, said the Judge)
and that the only meaning of the libel was a charge of Lesbianism.
Finally a G.P. appeared in the witness-box to add his general
condemnation to the rest.

None of the doctors had seen the play, and one may marvel at the ease with which they were able to state its effect upon an audience. But while the preliminary stages of the prosecution were being enacted at Bow Street, the performance had taken place in the Court Theatre in Sloane Square. The dramatic critic of the *Morning Post* called it "a bizarre melodrama of disease". His colleague on *The Stage* described it as "impure in its atmosphere, which is charged with a sickly voluptuousness. A decadent literary art could scarcely go further than the gaudy harlotry of the words in which *Salome* is set out." But neither of these witnesses saw anything indecent or unnatural in it, or in Maud Allan's performance.

Not so Father Bernard Vaughan, who denounced from the witness-box "this abomination which I look upon as constructive treason against the majesty and sanctity of God". Reminded by the Judge that he was not in the pulpit, he explained himself: Salome's dance had caused such terrible results to Herod, how could its representation fail to work evil? John had died for his Master—splendid!—but Herod became a murderer. "It takes us all our time to keep normal and straight and pure when we are standing in the rear of our animal passions; but when we give way to them and have them fanned, inflamed, we are ablaze with devouring flames. I do not think anyone can contradict that who knows human nature."

Here surely was the root of the matter. Ugly words denoting perverse practices added nothing to the reality. *Salome* is a play about sexual passion and nothing else, and as such it may be condemned. But how much else stands equally condemned by this criterion!

It was eighteen years since Oscar Wilde's death, but for Lord Alfred Douglas, doomed always to live in the shadow of a shade, nothing was too harsh or contradictory to say about his old friend. "I think he has been very much over-rated, but of course he was a good second literateur. I think he had a diabolical influence on everyone he met. I think he is the greatest force for evil that has appeared in Europe during the last 350 years. He was a man whose whole object in life was to attack and to sneer at virtue and to undermine it in every way by every possible means, sexually and otherwise. I do not think he ever wrote anything which had not got an evil intention, except perhaps a stray poem or two; but if you take the whole of his poetry, it is inspired by evil intention; the same of his plays and books. He was studying Krafft-Ebing when he wrote *Salome*, which he intended to be an exhibition of perverted sexual passion. I translated it into English. Of course, it was a farce really, because Wilde really wrote the play in English, translated it into French, and got a French author to correct his numerous blunders and mistakes; and he then asked me to translate it into English; and then when I finished my translation he revised it and put it back into its own original language. It was simply that he wanted to pose as a great French scholar. Naturally I regret very much that I had anything to do with the production of what I regard as a most pernicious and abominable piece of work. At the time I did it I was entirely under Wilde's influence, of course. Wilde used the changes in the moon as a sort of register of what was going on in the play; he got the idea from one of Maeterlinck's plays. Whenever he was going to do anything particularly horrible, it was always disguised in the most flowery language, and always referred back to Art. With those sort of people evil is their good; everything is topsy-turvy; physical is spiritual; spiritual is physical, and so on; it is a perversion, an inversion, of everything. Wilde was a man who made evil his good all through his life. He was the most conceited man that ever lived. I did not see all the perversity of the play when I translated it. I was not completely innocent, but I was more ignorant then. I think its performance ought to be stopped by any possible means, whether so-called legitimate means or otherwise. I do not hold with everything they call legitimacy in this country: in some things you have to go outside the law if you want to do things."

It was only to be expected that Hume-Williams would question this bitter and intemperate witness about his friendship with Wilde, but in so doing he played into Lord Alfred's hands. Lord Alfred's role was that of repentant sinner, and when a fulsome review of *Salome* which he had written in the *Spirit Lamp*, an Oxford undergraduate magazine of the 'nineties, was read to him, and he was asked if that was his opinion of the play, he was able to say: "It is exactly the same opinion as your witnesses now have about it. The only difference is I have escaped from the influence and your witnesses are still under it." When asked to identify a letter which he had sent to *Truth* at the time of Wilde's trial, he threatened to tear it up, and the Usher held it up to him outside his reach. When asked if he recognised Wilde's notorious "prose poem"—the letter which refers to Lord Alfred's "slim guilt soul" and went far to convict Wilde—he complained, with truth, that it was about the twentieth time that it had been read in a public Court. When the Judge was summing up, Lord Alfred called him "a damned liar", an interruption which was greeted with cheers. Lord Alfred was ejected. But on leaving the Old Bailey after the trial he enjoyed a momentary popularity and was "lionised" by the crowd.

Did Oscar Wilde turn in his grave when his once beloved friend gave evidence? It was generally supposed that he had been the ruin of Lord Alfred. Lord Alfred shared this view. Others, including the present Marquess of Queensberry, believe that the opposite was the truth. Does this bizarre interlude in Lord Alfred's long career of poetry and criminal libel cast any doubt on the Marquess's judgment of his uncle's character?

The fifth day arrived, and the interminable Billing, who never gave evidence himself, went on calling his witnesses. He called Mr. Grein, the prosecutor on the next indictment, who thought *Salome* was "a work by an English pen in the spirit of Eastern art", an opinion which Billing did his best to upset, despite the rule that each side must accept the evidence of its own witnesses. Finally, he put Mrs. Villiers Stuart back in the box. She let off the last squib. After revealing that the Black Book had found its way into the hands of a Prussian guardsman and was now reposing in the old British Embassy in Berlin, she said she *had* mentioned its existence at the time to a prominent public man. His name? Mr. Hume-Williams.

At the end of all the evidence the Judge decided that the sentence in the *Vigilante*—"If Scotland Yard were to seize the list of these members I have no doubt they would secure the names of several thousand of the first 47,000," was not defamatory, and therefore all the evidence about the Black Book was irrelevant.

He might have given that ruling four days before! The trouble was that these words appeared in the indictment as well as the plea of justification, and Darling had an unholy fear of the Court of Criminal Appeal. If he kept out evidence which that Court thought should have been put in, a conviction would be quashed. But now, perhaps, he believed no conviction was possible, and it was best to finish the trial as soon as possible. A simple question remained for the jury: was it true that to perform in Oscar Wilde's *Salome* was to take part in a cult of sexual perversion? Billing withdrew any suggestion of Lesbianism, and Darling compliantly directed the jury to regard the libel as though it could not bear that meaning. Nothing was left except the theme of passion and cruelty. But by this time the issues had been so confounded by the historical romances and contradictory evidence of the Defendant's witnesses as well as the flamboyant articulations of the Defendant himself that it was difficult to see the fire for the smoke. Hume-Williams made a valiant address, pointing out with truth that almost the only person of whose personal honour nothing disparaging had been said was Maud Allan. But he feared it was in vain. "If," he said, "you are going to return a verdict in this case which shall clear the character of Maud Allan, I confess it will take some courage. The Defendant has created a sort of atmosphere, by his friends in the gallery and his followers outside, calculated to intimidate the jury if he can do it."

As for Billing, he was on the crest of the wave. "I am a libeller," he declared, "I have libelled public men for the last two and a half years. I have libelled them in the columns of the Press; I have libelled them on public platforms; I have libelled them in the House of Commons." It made little difference what he said. He persisted in interrupting the Judge throughout the summing-up. No one knows why Darling tolerated his behaviour. Long sentences have been served for lesser contempts of Court.

After an hour and a half the jury returned a verdict of not guilty, and pandemonium broke loose in the Court.

Billing, who had returned to the dock on the last day of the trial, sat unmoved, while the Court was cleared and the Judge expressed the hope that *Salome* would never be performed again. (Both Oscar Wilde and his works now stood condemned by the law.) Then Billing dared to ask for his costs. "You have nothing to say, sir. You are discharged." And, white lipped, Mr. Justice Darling left the court. Billing was mobbed by the hysterical crowd outside.

And so this nightmare trial ended. "The proceedings in Court constituted nothing less than a libel on the nation," wrote the *Daily Mail*, "names and innuendoes were bandied about with a recklessness that was as unfair to the persons mentioned as it was prejudicial to a fair hearing of the case before the jury. Scenes were enacted of such gross unseemliness that the Court at times resembled a madhouse. There was hardly a moment when the Judge can be said to have been master in his own Court. He lost control of it almost from the start, was petulant where he should have been firm, and conveyed the fatal impression that there was something he was trying to hide. A weak judge, a feeble counsel and a bewildered jury combined to score for the defendant a striking and undeserved success."

A few days later, à *propos* of nothing, Darling remarked in Court, "I am quite content with what a learned judge said by way of consolation to a prisoner sentenced for a long period. He said, 'We must all be somewhere.' That is my view of my own position." And so for many another year he continued to grace the Bench with an excess of wit. Billing likewise made many more appearances in the Courts, each time with a diminishing popularity, and when he died in 1948 the country had forgotten both his callow chauvinism and the not unimportant part he had played as an aeroplane pioneer. Sir Ellis Hume-Williams wrote a book of reminiscences, but did not mention the case of The King against Noel Pemberton Billing. As for the Black Book, many believed it existed; some may still think so. In his final speech to the jury Hume-Williams suggested that the Germans might well have compiled a list of important people in England whom it would be desirable to approach, and indeed the evidence, such as it was, scarcely went even as far as this. According to another theory it was merely an inventory of potential customers for Mercedes cars. One thing is certain: the Black Book was like the vital witness in so many alibis—it never was and never will be found.

II

WINSTON CHURCHILL AND THE BATTLE OF JUTLAND

Rex v. *Lord Alfred Douglas* (1923)

THE Battle of Jutland was a Pyrrhic victory for the British Grand Fleet. Our losses in ships and sailors were heavy, and far greater than those we inflicted on the Germans. But the German Fleet never again emerged from harbour, until it sailed out after the Armistice to scuttle itself at Scapa Flow. England remained the mistress of the seas.

The battle was fought on the afternoon and through the night of the 31st May, 1916. The first news given to the British public was contained in a communiqué issued by the Admiralty on the evening of the 2nd June. It was drafted by Mr. Balfour, the First Lord, in consultation with the Admirals in Whitehall, and it made depressing reading. ". . . The battle-cruisers *Queen Mary Indefatigable*, *Invincible*, and the cruisers *Defence* and *Black Prince* were sunk. The *Warrior* was disabled, and had to be abandoned . . . the destroyers *Tipperary*, *Turbulent*, *Fortune*, *Sparrowhawk*, and *Ardent* were lost, and six others are not yet accounted for . . . The enemy's losses were serious. At least one battle cruiser was destroyed, and one severely damaged; one battleship was reported sunk by our destroyers during a night attack; two light cruisers were disabled, and probably sunk. . . ."

This communiqué came as a dreadful shock. It seemed so apparent that the British Fleet had got the worse of it. The demoralising effect of the announcement was not reduced by a second communiqué in the early hours of the following morning. To alleviate public anxiety the Prime Minister then called upon Mr. Winston Churchill to write an appreciation of the situation. Churchill had been First Lord of the Admiralty at the beginning of the War, but was no longer a member of the Government. Indeed he was now known to be in opposition to Balfour, and for that reason it was felt that an encouraging commentary written in his masterful English would have a refreshing effect not only at home but also on neutral opinion abroad. Mr. Churchill's summing up, in which he described the battle as "a definite step towards the attainment of complete victory", was officially circulated for publication. A week after the Battle of Jutland Lord Kitchener went down in the cruiser *Hampshire*.

Out of these facts Lord Alfred Douglas concocted the most extravagant libel of the century. It was in a sense a result of the Black Book case, for it was on that occasion that Lord Alfred had met Pemberton Billing and his chief witness, Captain Spencer, and this prime pair seem to have been the source and origin of the idea.

The idea was that Winston Churchill had conspired to manipulate the Jutland communiqués in such a way as to enable Sir Ernest Cassel to double his fortune on the American Stock Exchange. According to the plan of this supposed conspiracy the language of the first communiqué would be carefully calculated to cause a sharp fall in British stock on Wall Street, and Sir Ernest Cassel would buy. When later announcements restored the market, Sir Ernest would sell at a large profit. Lord Alfred declared that this manœuvre had been completely successful and Sir Ernest Cassel had cleared forty or fifty million pounds, out of which he gave Churchill a cheque for several thousand and a suite of furniture. Sir Ernest Cassel was a naturalised German Jew, and according to Lord Alfred this was but one of many outstanding victories secured by international Jewry. The death of Lord Kitchener was another.

Lord Alfred Douglas did not promulgate this astonishing myth until 1921, when he was editor of a magazine called *Plain English*. At that time Churchill was again a Member of the Government, and when the charges were first made he consulted the Attorney-General (Sir Gordon Hewart) who advised him to take no notice. Lord Alfred's attack subsided from lack of prosecution, but in 1922 the Editor of the *Jewish Guardian* wrote to the *Morning Post* a letter accusing Lord Alfred of inventing vile insults against the Jews. The *Morning Post* published it, and were sued by Lord Alfred for libel.

This action was tried in July, 1923. Lord Alfred was as truculent as ever in the witness-box. His charges against Churchill were not directly in issue in this case, but they were mentioned during his cross-examination as examples of his untrustworthiness. He insisted upon their truth, but his counsel refused to cross-examine Winston Churchill and the high officers of the Admiralty, who gave evidence for the *Morning Post*. Nor did he challenge the written evidence of Lord Balfour (as he now was). Lord Alfred secured a verdict for a farthing damages, and was deprived of his costs.

He was not in the least discouraged. He formed the "Lord Kitchener and Jutland Publicity Committee", and at its inaugural meeting in London made a long speech, which was reprinted in the *Border Standard*. He then ordered 40,000 copies to be printed as a pamphlet and arranged for their sale at 2d. each in the streets of the town. The pamphlet was headed "The Murder of Lord Kitchener" and "The Truth About the Battle of Jutland and the Jews". After repeating his old story about the financial plot and taunting Churchill with having taken no proceedings, he said: "If Mr. Churchill were editing a paper and if he printed in his columns about one-half, one-quarter, one-fifth of what I printed about him, I would have him round at Bow Street with his nose hanging over the edge of the dock to answer a charge of criminal libel within twenty-four hours . . ."

There was only one thing left to do. The prosecution of Lord Alfred Douglas was undertaken by the Director of Public Prosecutions. The trial took place at the Old Bailey in December, 1923, before Mr. Justice Avory. The Attorney-General (Sir Douglas Hogg, K.C., later Lord Hailsham) appeared for the Crown, and Lord Alfred was represented by his old friend Cecil Hayes.

Again Lord Alfred set out to prove the truth of his libels, and again the story of the Jutland communiqués was told, in still fuller detail, by almost every person who had been present.

Lord Balfour produced the original draft of the first communiqué, which he had written with his own hand. Churchill had nothing to do with it, and had not been near the Admiralty for months, until Balfour sent for him the following day.

> "Did you read the leading article in *The Times* on the Battle of Jutland?" Lord Balfour was asked in cross-examination. "Probably not."
> "Do you read *The Times*?"—"It is not the sort of journal I abstain from reading."
> "Was there not a general storm of indignation in the Press that a British victory was made to seem like a German one?" —"There was a strong attack made on me."
> "I am sorry——"—"It did me no harm," Balfour assured counsel.

Mr. Churchill (now out of Parliament altogether, having just been defeated at the General Election) followed Lord Balfour into the box. His memory of his visit to the Admiralty on the 3rd June, 1916, was absolutely clear. After agreeing to write the appreciation, he was furnished with an Admiralty stenographer. Admiral Brownrigg said: "Now, sir, cough it up," and he thereupon dictated the document. He took the typed copy to Lord Fisher, with whom he had had difficulties, but was then on good terms, and his Lordship said: "I think it is absolutely right." That was all. He knew nothing of the first two communiqués until they appeared in the Press.

Sir Ernest Cassel had been a great friend of Churchill's and also of his father, Lord Randolph Churchill. When Churchill returned from the Boer War and began to make money by his books, Sir Ernest agreed to invest his profits for him, and in fact he looked after his savings for many years. In 1905 Cassel furnished a small library for Churchill and in 1908 he gave him a cheque for £500 as a wedding present. Somehow or other this innocent association had been distorted into a criminal conspiracy. But no financial *coup* had been made or attempted. By 1923 Sir Ernest Cassel was dead, but his private secretary gave evidence later in the trial that he had neither bought nor sold any

British stock within months before or after the Battle of Jutland.

Nor indeed had there been a big fall in British Stocks in America between the first and subsequent Admiralty communiqués. The fall took place immediately after the Germans announced a great naval victory—a few hours before the first British communiqué. The issue of *The Times* the next morning contained the following short paragraph:

"New York, June 2.—On the Stock Market here a break of one to four points followed the announcement from Berlin of the naval battle in the North Sea, but later the statement from London of the facts started a rapid recovery, and a good part of the losses was made up before the close." And *The Times* later commented on the almost negligible effect which the news of the naval battle had caused to the stock and money markets.

Mr. Churchill was cross-examined most acrimoniously, but he rode the waves with ease, and from time to time his puckish wit came into play. When he was questioned about his quarrel with Lord Fisher over the Dardanelles project and asked: "Did Lord Fisher refuse to see you and resign?" "No," he replied, "he resigned and refused to see me."

It was suggested that his history of the War was really a history of himself. "Would you be surprised to know that in thirteen lines there are thirteen 'I's'?"—"It would be a very great pity if there were, and if you will show me the passage I will endeavour to cut out a few in the next edition." The Attorney-General then discovered ten 'I's' in five lines of Lord Alfred's pamphlet.

Cecil Hayes was constrained to admit, when he opened the defence during the third day of the trial, that with all his experience in cross-examining men with brains he had never had such an ordeal as when he tried to see what was behind Mr. Churchill's eyes and clever brain. "At one instant," he said to the jury, "he frowned like a sphinx, rasped out a bitter reply, and the next moment he would smile a blandishment almost large enough to swallow you all." But stripped of his charm and exquisite manners, continued counsel, Mr. Churchill was a professional politician, a species of which the best definition was that he must "have a hide like a rhinoceros, a skin like the chameleon, be short of memory, and have the cheek of the devil". He must also have "a front of brass"—this last was one of the expressions used by Lord Alfred.

The two witnesses for the defence were Lord Alfred Douglas himself and Captain Spencer. Lord Alfred tried to prove his case by repeating a series of things he had been told, but this hearsay evidence was not allowed, and true to form his Lordship became excited. He complained of gross and abominable unfairness. "I have not had a chance of putting my case to the jury."

Captain Spencer, who had by now acquired two criminal convictions and been deprived of his rank, and had been described by Lord Alfred himself in *Plain English* as unworthy of belief, likewise repeated his performance at the Pemberton Billing trial. He claimed that as a prospective candidate for Dundee in 1919 he had run into Churchill at a civic luncheon given to Lord Haig. Churchill said to him, "Hallo, what are you doing here?" to which Spencer replied, "I am going to turn you out of Dundee," (for which Churchill was then the Member of Parliament). Spencer alleged that in the conversation which followed Churchill admitted his part in the Jutland conspiracy. He claimed blood kinship with Churchill, and remembered meeting him in his mother's flat in St. James' Place in 1913.

"Do you know that Lady Randolph Churchill never had a flat in London at all, and never lived in St. James' Place since 1883?"—"I can only speak of the time I saw her there."

"How old are you?"—"I am thirty-three."

"So that you were not alive in 1883?"—"No. I really did not want to mention it, but I remember that when living in St. James' Place I once met Mr. Churchill coming out of Boodle's Club in rather an unfortunate condition. I think it was in 1915, just before I had brought over from America two machines upon which Mr. Churchill based the tanks, and for which I received £5,000 from the Government." Mr. Churchill joined in the laughter in Court, and later returned to the witness-box to say he had never been a member of Boodle's and never recalled visiting that Club.

Spencer's tribulations in the Mediterranean theatre of operations seemed to have been adjusted somewhat since the Black Book Trial. It now transpired that he had discovered Lenin's plot to assassinate the Russian Royal Family, but was told he had a "touch of the sun" and was carried off in an armed ambulance. He escaped by putting a Red Cross nurse's uniform over his pyjamas and riding on a bicycle to the United States Consul.

"And you told us yesterday that the American Consul sent you back," said the Judge, "—still in your pyjamas?"

The defence called one more witness, a Captain Brown, the Editor of the *Border Standard*, who simply said that he had been supplied by Lord Alfred himself with a copy of the speech which was later turned into a pamphlet. Captain Brown, however, distinguished himself by repeating the words of the oath at the top of his voice.

"Are you deaf?" asked the Judge. "No."
"We are not either."
"He comes from Scotland," Hayes explained.
"That," snapped the Judge, "is no reason why he should not behave himself properly."

Upon this note the case for the defence closed. Speeches by counsel and Mr. Justice Avory's summing-up followed, and then it took the jury eight minutes to pronounce Lord Alfred guilty. Avory sentenced him to be imprisoned in the second division for six months and thereafter to find a surety in £100 to keep the peace and be of good behaviour to all his Majesty's subjects, and particularly to Mr. Winston Churchill.

In prison Lord Alfred wrote a poem called "In Excelsis" (as a contrast to Oscar Wilde's "De Profundis") but his days of defamation were over. During the second World War he dedicated a sonnet to Mr. Churchill, and that great Englishman in acknowledging it sent the message: "Tell him from me that 'Time ends all things.' "

III

THE ORDAINMENTS OF THE THEATRE

Porteous v. *The Sunday Times Ltd. and others* (1921)

A DRAMATIC critic is allowed to make a large number of disagreeable observations on the performance of a famous actress. If he takes advantage of this privilege, he lays himself open to an equally caustic and no less dramatic criticism from behind the stage before the curtain rises on the second night—but he will not be called to account by the law. Should he suggest, however, that she acted like "a raging, frothing epileptic, rolling on the floor and biting her toenails", he has ventured beyond the legal limit. That, at least, was the view taken by Ethel Irving in late January, 1921, when she read Sydney Carroll's notice of her performance in *The Three Daughters of M. Dupont*.

This play by the French dramatist Brieux was an attack upon the French system of arranged marriages. Julie, one of the three daughters, is passionately devoted to children, but is married to a brute of a man who is only interested in comfort and social advancement. The climax comes when he tells his wife that he will never allow her to have a child. This announcement drives her into hysterics, and there is a violent struggle, in the course of which she bites his hand. The husband storms off the stage, and the wife, left behind muttering, falls on the couch and then to the floor, sobbing over the destruction of her life's dream. It was a powerful scene, and Ethel Irving, an actress who specialised in strong emotional parts, played it well. Such at least was the description of it by Douglas Hogg, K.C. (later Lord Hailsham), who represented her at the trial.

Sydney Carroll in the *Sunday Times* had given a different version:

"Despite the alleged dearth of English actesses, every now and again I am amazed by an altogether unexpected and natural performance. I go to the Garrick expecting nothing but the magnificent propaganda of Brieux against marriages made by French parents, and some brilliantly wearisome fireworks from emotional Miss Ethel Irving, and I find a study of a live character by Miss Edith Evans that makes Brieux a reality, and outshines the pyrotechnical artist.

"Under proper control Miss Irving is one of our finest comediennes. Lately I have found her art sadly undisciplined. The actress saved up all her forces for the third act, and then devastated us. It was not a storm of passion. It was a tornado. Every shred of reserve was scattered to the flies, and the woman who wants children from a husband who refuses them became a raging, frothing epileptic, rolling on the floor and biting her toenails. Now this is all very fine in its way, and the house deservedly responds, but it is not the true touch.

"By contrast Miss Evans, who has been putting in some astonishingly good work of late in widely different character parts, was Nature itself opposed to Theatricality. Her Caroline, the quiet elder sister of the trio, made me cry like a child. Not for months have I been so deeply affected in a playhouse. The restraint, the conviction, the finish of the portrait of this yearning, self-sacrificing, ugly, ill-dressed spinster was almost perfect. Mr. Leon M. Lion cleverly detailed with some over-elaboration and terrier-like emphasis the part of the old father. Mr. Kenyon jumped backwards and forwards on the stage like a demented panther, but had moments of genuine pathos and realism. Nearly everybody else in the cast save Mrs. A. B. Tapping had defective wigs or moustaches, over-acted, and seemed to think that because it was a French play they could shout and gesticulate in the accepted extravagant way of stage Frenchmen. That was why, perhaps, Miss Evans, with her natural, unforced, mute sympathy, made such an appeal to me."

Ethel Irving's action for libels contained in this criticism was heard in November 1921—long after *The Three Daughters of M. Dupont* had been taken off. Mr. Justice Darling presided. Patrick Hastings, K.C. (later Sir Patrick) appeared for the *Sunday Times* and Sydney Carroll was represented by Gilbert Beyfus (now Q.C.). The issue lay in the eternal battleground between the artist and the critic: was the criticism a fair comment? If it described what never took place, it was not fair comment, but a mis-statement of fact. Ethel Irving said that she neither frothed at the mouth, nor bit her toenails, nor acted in any other way as though she were having an epileptic fit. Indeed she did not even roll on the floor, "because as soon as I reached the floor the curtain came down, and if I rolled it would have fallen on me."

Patrick Hastings on behalf of the *Sunday Times* maintained that the criticism was not to be read literally.

"You became so hysterical," he asked her, "that you fell on the couch and then to the floor?"—"Yes."

"If a person did not like the play he would not like it any more because you overplayed the part?"—"I bit the man's hand: it was biting my toenails that I did not like."

"But you did not think it meant that the public would think you really sat on the stage and bit your toenails?"—"An epileptic might."

"Did you see that it said that Mr. Kenyon jumped backwards and forwards like a demented panther? Do you mean that that suggested that he was clothed like a panther and went down on his knees and wagged his tail?"—"That would be absurd. Mr. Carroll said that I became epileptic."

"You mean," the Judge intervened, "that he thought that you acted like an epileptic?"—"Yes; but I should not have bitten my toenails."

"Don't," said Hastings, "hang on to those toenails." But Ethel Irving insisted. "That is the point," she cried.

"If the author had wanted you to play the part of an epileptic you would have done so?"—"I would not."

The cross-examination was interrupted, as Ethel Irving wanted to keep an engagement. Darling said to Patrick Hastings, "I shall not let you off to see her act." Next morning Patrick Hastings renewed his attack on a different line. He asked her if she had seen the newspaper placards in the street: "Famous actress sues for Libel." No, she had not.

"It all helps, this sort of placard, doesn't it?"—"I don't think so—not that sort of advertisement."

"Has anybody thought the worse of you because of this criticism?"—"I don't know how many read the notice."

(Ethel Irving said that she was shown the *Sunday Times* by a friend, at which the Judge remarked, "It is usually a friend who draws one's attention to a thing like that.")

"Do your friends think the worse of you because of it?"—"My friends have avoided the subject; any one would who thought that a woman had made a disgusting exhibition of herself."

"What did you bring this action for—damages or an apology?" —"I want to show the public that I am not an incompetent actress."

"You want an opportunity of telling the public that the critic was wrong?"—"Yes."

"Do you want to call evidence that you are a good actress?" —"That I did not make an exhibition of myself."

"That you acted the part properly?"—"Yes."

"Can you conceive the possibility of persons thinking that such was the excess of your passion that you were like a person rolling on the floor?"—"I was not rolling on the floor."

"You were on the floor?"—"But not rolling."

"One critic said that you did a semi-sensible back fall from the sofa?"—"I don't think that I did that."

"Did you have a kind of acrobatic fall?"—"No."

"You went to the floor with a bump?"—"Not much of a bump."

"How did you go?"—"I followed the instructions in the book: I fell on the couch and from that to the floor."

"I think I remember," remarked Darling, "something about 'a poet's eye in a fine frenzy rolling'."

"Oh, but that was not on the floor," Hastings put in at once and continued his cross-examination: "At this time you had knocked the furniture about, and bitten your husband?"— "Yes."

"Don't you think that this criticism means that you exaggerated the part, and were excessively violent?"—"No, I think that a woman who could bite her own toenails would be assuming an immodest and revolting attitude."

"What does 'raging, frothing epileptic' mean in a dramatic criticism?"—"It suggests that I acted the part as a lunatic."

Mr. Justice Darling: "I thought that biting was a sign of madness."

Hastings: "She bit her husband."

Mr. Justice Darling: "Yes, but we haven't seen him."

Hastings: "Assuming that a barrister did not conduct his case according to instructions and made an ass of himself, would it be libellous to say that he acted like an ass?"—"I would not have minded if Mr. Carroll had said that I made an ass of myself."

"That is useful for the critics to know," exclaimed Hastings tartly. "What would you say, Mr. Hastings," his Lordship then asked, "if a barrister did not follow his instructions but bit his toenails in Court?"

The effervescent advocate had no answer to this one, and the Judge supplied his own, "I should call it contempt of Court."

Hastings then repeated his theme question to this witness: "Don't you think this action is all in the nature of an advertisement?"—"No."

And as a parting shot he asked, "None of the actors like critics?" To which came the very true answer: "Oh, yes; some like them very much."

Now it was Beyfus' turn to cross-examine on behalf of Sydney
Carroll. He read out a laudatory account by Sydney Carroll
of an earlier performance by Ethel Irving, but she had not read
it. Darling, ever on the search for the magic moment and seldom
failing to find it, said, "A friend would not send her that."
According to Ethel Irving the attitude of the critics towards
her had changed since she appeared in *La Tosca*. Mr. Grein,
Sydney Carroll's predecessor on the *Sunday Times*, had so
praised her earlier performance as Julie in this play that the criticism
had been published in booklet form. Beyfus was not the man to
miss this opening.

"You publish the good notices and when you get a bad one
you bring a libel action?"—"No."
"Did Mr. Grein not write of you: 'She lets herself go regardless
of all the limitations and ordainments of the theatre'?"—"I
don't know what that means."
"Mr. Grein goes on to say: 'She becomes the author's interpreter, and while interpreting she creates a being of spon-
taneous existence'?"—"That is better."
"What are the ordainments of a theatre?"—"I am afraid I
cannot tell you."
"Another critic writes of your performance as Julie: 'She
grows into a tiger-cat and the tornado ends in almost physical
violence'. The critics all seem to go to the Zoo for their
metaphors. Your husband was said to be like a demented
panther."
"And Mr. Leon M. Lion to act with terrier-like emphasis,"
observed the Judge.
"This play," said Hastings, "will have to be revived."

Ethel Irving was well supported. Lillah McCarthy had been
to the first night. She declared in the witness-box that "Ethel's
great emotional effects were produced by elimination and never
by exaggeration. When she fell, she did so as though she was
incapable of supporting her body: her limbs relaxed and did

not become contorted. A woman in great trouble would never behave as the critic had said Ethel had behaved—unless she had been to a night club."

Hastings: "Critics do say some strange things sometimes?"—"Am I to give my opinion of critics?"
"Do you know that a critic said of Sarah Bernhardt that 'she had a smile like a barmaid working a beer-handle'?"
Mr. Justice Darling: "Who was the critic?"
Hastings: "It comes from essays written by George Bernard Shaw on actresses."
Mr. Justice Darling: "Oh!"
Hastings added that Shaw had also written of Sarah Bernhardt in tragedy that she was "so made up, rouged and incarnadined as to resemble a pillar-box and to leave such an impression on the critic's mind that he wanted to post a letter."
"It would be like thrusting it down her throat," said Darling.
There was a short appearance in the witness-box by a surgeon experienced in epilepsy who testified that Ethel Irving's performance was nothing like an epileptic fit, and then came that dying race of titans, the actor-managers. Matheson Lang was the first. He said that a notice like that in the *Sunday Times* might well affect the mind of a manager in casting his next play. No doubt the criticism meant that she had over-acted the part. Darling intervened: "Have you ever played Hamlet?"—"Yes."
"That is a part which actors play very differently?"—"Yes."
"Are there not two schools of thought—one thinking that Hamlet was mad and the other that he was not?"—"Yes."
"Which view do you take?"—"My view is that he was not."
At which the learned Judge remarked sadly, "It was awkward about Polonius then."
Mr. Lang recalled that Irving and Edwin Booth played to-

gether in *Othello*, and that on alternate nights one played the Moor and the other Iago.

"Don't you know," Hastings asked him, "that each actor thought that the other played the part very badly?"—"I did not know that."

Beyfus later asked him: "What do you think of Mr. Carroll's criticisms generally?"—"I think highly of him as a critic."

"Did he speak well of you?"

The witness did not answer this insulting question, and was followed into the box by Arthur Bourchier, who was more than a match for Patrick Hastings.

"You have wanted to 'have a go' at the *Sunday Times* for some time?" Hastings asked him. "I have had many 'goes'."

"And Mr. Carroll?"—"He is a part of the *Sunday Times*, and I had my go at him long ago."

"When you heard Mr. Porteous (Ethel Irving's husband) say that there was a chance of a libel action against the *Sunday Times* and Mr. Carroll, you said the equivalent of 'What-ho!'?"—"I saw that in one of your plays," Bourchier replied blandly.

"Mr. Hastings' play?" asked Darling in surprise. "Yes, he sent me two plays."

"What part did you play?" went on the Judge. "I did not accept them, my Lord."

Douglas Hogg, rising with ponderous pleasure, uttered the words, "Now Mr. Hastings says 'Who-ho!'", and then resumed his seat. Hastings went on with his cross-examination. "Did you produce *Henry V*?"—"I did not write it."

"Do you always write your plays?"—"Not always: I should like to."

"*Henry V* was written by somebody else?"—"Yes."

Mr. Justice Darling (*to Hastings*): "You are not advocating the Baconian theory?"

The point of these questions was to prepare the ground for the letter which Mr. Bourchier had written to the *Sunday Times* in answer to Sydney Carroll's criticism of *Henry V*. As Bourchier said, when he was insulted, he liked to insult back. The letter showed no retreat from this doctrine. Among other courtesies it recommended Carroll for the First Class of the Ancient Dishonourable Order of Ananias. "In other words you call him a first-class liar?"—"Yes, straight from the shoulder."

Apart from sparring with the distinguished counsel and not quite so distinguished playwright who faced him, bewigged and gowned, in the glare of the grey, legal footlights of the Court, the gist of Bourchier's evidence was that Carroll's criticism of Ethel Irving was wholly destructive.

"What is destructive criticism?"—"If you said, 'you should not write plays,' that would be destructive, but if you went through one of my plays and pointed out where it could be improved that would be constructive, and would be very useful."

(This was Bourchier to Hastings, and not, as it might have been outside the Court, Hastings to Bourchier.)

Beyfus then took Bourchier through some of his dealings with critics. Bourchier had a way with critics. "When I produced *Macbeth*," he said, "I had difficulty in finding room for all the critics. On the occasion of the production of *The Morals of Marcus* I excluded all the critics, and the bookings next day were enormous."

This sparkling performance had now been going on for nearly two days, and the Judge said, "I have been wondering whether this piece is to be played to the end." "That is very difficult," said Hogg, "owing to the attitude of the other side: we have not received an apology." "We have not," said Hastings, "been asked for one." Nevertheless, learned counsel put their wigs together, and shortly afterwards announced that they had settled the action. Hogg said there was no ground for suggesting (as Bourchier had suggested in his letter) that Carroll, whose real name was Frederick Carl, was anything but an Englishman, there being not a drop of German blood in his veins. Hastings on his side read out one of those soothing, equivocal statements which have so often been drawn up in the dark passages outside the Courts: the criticism did not mean what in fact it said, but, if anyone thought it did, the Defendants willingly stated that there was no foundation for that belief and willingly expressed regret that the words could have been capable of such a meaning. Hogg added that Miss Irving had no intention of making money: any damages would have been given to a Theatrical Charity.

And so, after the discharge of these colourful cannonades, the state of armed truce between the critics and the stage was resumed, and neither side regretted having to pay the costs occasioned by the engagement.

IV

SERMONS IN TRANCES

Morris v. *Associated Newspapers Ltd. and another* (1932)

MRS. MEURIG MORRIS was a "trance medium". She did not
practise the black arts of spiritualism, conjuring up weird pheno-
mena in darkened rooms. She had never held a "dark séance"
in her life. Her manifestations of the unseen world took place at
spiritualist services during which, after the singing of hymns,
she fell into a trance in the full view of everyone present. She
was a frail and nervous little woman, but on these occasions she
was wholly transformed into the personality of her "control".
She had several "controls", but her most frequent and very
punctual visitor was a being called *Power*. *Power* was at different
times reputed to be Caiaphas, the High Priest of Jerusalem, and a
zealous bishop of several hundred years ago, but he resolutely
refused to reveal his identity. Be that what it was, whenever
Power took possession of Mrs. Morris, she seemed to grow in
height, her head fell back, her hands flew to where the lapels of a
man's coat would be, and she was delivered of a bombastic sermon in a booming masculine baritone. For a short while in the
early thirties of this century *Power* may claim to have been the
most famous preacher in the land.

This intriguing achievement was partly due to *Power's* ability
to hold forth in a high philosophical language, which was not
only unintelligible to most of his audience, but was also quite
beyond Mrs. Morris's own level of knowledge or understanding.
Mrs. Morris was the sixth daughter of a Worcestershire market
gardener, and her only education came from attendance at her
village school. She was born in 1899, and at the age of nineteen
she married a chemist's assistant, who was twenty-five years her
senior. She gave birth to a daughter, and in 1922 the little family
moved to Newton Abbot in Devonshire. Nothing so far had

occurred in Mrs. Morris' life to bring her into touch with learning or literature or spiritualism, except that she had always been
conscious of seeing people whom others did not see.   But at
Newton Abbot she was introduced into a spiritualist circle and
before long she was falling into trances.   By 1924 *Power* had
begun his new preaching career and was soon delivering his
sermons to large audiences all over the country.

   Mrs. Morris did not exploit this unexpected turn of events for
her own commercial advantage.   But after some years she met
Mr. Laurence Cowen, an elderly dramatist, whom she converted
to spiritualism.   Thereafter Mr. Cowen organised her public life.
He also used her mediumship to communicate with the late
Israel Zangwill and his own deceased wife and brother, from
whom, with the help of a control called *Annette*, he received an
entire new play.   Mr. Cowen had a flair for publicity, but the first
play to be written on the other side of the grave has not yet been
produced.

   Mr. Cowen also arranged for photographs, a gramophone
record (marketed at 4s. 6d.) and a Movietone News film to be
made of *Power* in action.   But his most effective venture was the
presentation of Mrs. Morris at the beginning of 1931 in a series of
Sunday services at the Fortune Theatre in London.   The unusual
nature of the programme attracted the interest of the *Daily Mail*,
which sent a correspondent to investigate and report the proceedings.   The correspondent showed initiative.   He not only attended
the services and witnessed the making of the film, but also interviewed *Power* as well as Mrs. Morris.   Finally he organised a
public test of *Power's* genuineness, and then produced a report,
which led to an emotional eleven-day libel action, interrupted
from time to time by psychic demonstrations.

   The sequence of events, to say nothing of their excitement, can
best be followed by setting out the *Daily Mail* reports at length.
The first exhibition at the Fortune Theatre took place on Sunday,
January 11th, 1931, and the first report appeared on the following
day:

WOMAN'S AMAZING SERMON IN A TRANCE

ON A THEATRE STAGE

SOPRANO THAT CHANGED TO BARITONE

"A small, slim young woman, in a voluminous gown of amethyst velvet, walked nervously on to the stage at the Fortune Theatre, Covent Garden, last night to play the leading role in one of the strangest dramas ever seen in London.

She sat in a chair, and beside her sat Vice-Admiral J. C. Armstrong, Lady (Conan) Doyle, Mr. Dennis Doyle and Mr. Laurence Cowen, the playwright, who built the Fortune Theatre, all of whom were taking part in the first of a series of spiritualist services which are to be held at the theatre.

While hymns were being sung and addresses given, this young woman, Mrs. Meurig Morris, who in one night has shot into fame as one of the leading trance-mediums of the world, sat nervously fidgeting with her handkerchief and gazing at the floor.

When she rose to read an invocation she uttered it in a small, high-pitched voice which was scarcely audible.

Then more hymns were sung and music was played. Suddenly this young woman sat bolt upright in her chair, and her face and hands were twitching. She rose and gripped a thin velvet scarf which was round her neck and threw her head back so that she looked like a Portia. She opened her mouth, and her voice, instead of a small, timid soprano, was a ringing baritone.

Then for more than half an hour she delivered, unhesitatingly and with her eyes closed, an astonishing sermon. She delved into the profoundest philosophy and intricate science. Raising herself periodically on her heels, gripping her scarf, and occasionally throwing her arms out to emphasise a point, she copied all the mannerisms of the pulpit.

Her voice rose and fell just like a minister's, and with academic assurance she took her audience into the realms of protoplasm, agnosticism, evolution, involution, and atheism. In her amazing discourse, she dissected a man's brain and his eye—all to prove that there is survival after death.

The spirit control, who she declares delivers these sermons through her, she calls *Power*, because he will not reveal to her who he is.

When *Power* had finished his discourse with a fine oratorical flourish Mrs. Morris's hands slipped from her scarf, her body

sagged and lost its Portia-like dignity and slowly she shrank back
into her former timid self . . ."

In its next issue the *Daily Mail* reported an interview with
Mrs. Morris, who was surrounded by spirits congratulating her
on the success of her first night. A few days later the correspondent gave an account of a meeting of Anglican clergymen
convened to discuss the growth of spiritualism. He arranged for
the clergymen to be invited by Mrs. Morris to hear one of
Power's sermons. All this public attention had an effect on the
second of Mrs. Morris' Sunday performances, which was described by the *Daily Mail* in these words:

DOORS RUSHED TO HEAR TRANCE SERMON
1,000 SHUT OUT OF THEATRE
POLICE CALLED
EXHAUSTION OF MRS. MORRIS

"A great crowd besieged the Fortune Theatre last night, and
attempted to break into the building when Mrs. Meurig Morris,
the young trance-medium, gave her second 'sermon' under
spirit control.

Queues began to form at three o'clock in the afternoon, and
all the doors had to be locked nearly half an hour before the
meeting was due to begin.

A queue of nearly 1,000 people stretched down Russell Street.
The crowd swept forward towards the doors, and police had to
be called to guard them; before they arrived, however, there was
a big rush, the doors were forced open, a commissionaire was
swept off his feet, and fifty people swarmed into the already
crowded theatre.

When it was announced that the theatre was full, hundreds of
people rushed round to all the doors and windows and attempted
to get in where they could, and some panes of glass were
broken . . ."

There followed a very similar account of the proceedings inside
the theatre. On this occasion *Power* obliged with a discourse on
the question "What is Reality?"

A crescendo of excitement was being reached. The *Daily Mail* returned to the subject on each of the next five days.

20th January, 1931.

A TALK WITH "POWER"

TRANCE TEST ARRANGED

SERMON THROUGH MRS. MORRIS

"I interviewed last evening *Power*, the mysterious spirit control said to make use of the young trance-medium, Mrs. Meurig Morris, for the delivery of sermons at the Fortune Theatre, Bloomsbury.

This is the first occasion on which a newspaper correspondent has had a direct interview with a 'spirit'—and interest is added to the occurrence by the fact that Mrs. Morris claims that nobody, not even herself, knows *Power's* identity.

I did not seek the interview. I am told that I must regard it as a great honour that *Power* himself asked that I should go to the house of Mr. Laurence Cowen, the playwright, at Harrow, and discuss with him arrangements for a test to which I am anxious to subject Mrs. Morris.

People who have heard Mrs. Morris are puzzled. What is this strange power which changes her so completely and enables her to talk on scientific and philosophic subjects about which she declares herself she knows nothing?

Is it telepathy? Is it hypnotism? Has she a peculiar sub-consciousness which at some time has photographed these sermons and is able to reel them off during a trance? What is the secret of her changed voice and manner?

These are questions which people are asking, and with a view to securing answers to some of them, I asked Mrs. Morris if she would submit to a test. I suggested that I should get some one who does not attend her sermons to select a subject for an address, seal it in an envelope, and deposit it in a safe place—not saying a word about it to a living soul.

Mrs. Morris told me she thought that *Power* would learn from the selector's mind the subject proposed and would give a sermon on it through her. She was quite willing, she said, to submit to such a stringent test—but *Power* was not so amenable as his earthly medium.

When I asked him through Mrs. Morris this evening if he would accept my challenge, he at once became dignified and declared that he could not agree to such a proposition, but he compromised.

'You must understand,' he said to me in his baritone voice, which sounded much louder in the confined space of Mr. Cowen's library, 'that we who have passed over, although we have gained more and more knowledge, are not infallible.

'I do not profess to be able to do what you want me to do. Even if I could, I would not. But this is what I will do. You or anyone else may select a subject for a sermon or a text from any part of the Bible and hand it to the child (Mrs. Morris) when she goes into trance at the meeting. Then I will immediately deliver a sermon on that subject.'

Then *Power* added, 'Had it not been for this brother (meaning me) I would certainly not have undertaken this test. I do not like it, but if it is going to do the cause some good, then I agree under the condition which I have laid down.

'The sermon which I am shortly to give to dignitaries of the Church should be a sufficient test, for then I am going to answer any questions they like to put to me.'

Power went on to say, in answer to another question of mine, that the child (Mrs. Morris) had been undergoing such a great strain as the result of the publicity which she had received since her first appearance in London that it was essential that she should not be overtaxed.

'Therefore,' he added, 'when you have this test I do not want a great concourse of people.'

I gathered from him that this meant that he did not object to the Fortune Theatre, which he described as 'The Temple'; he did not want to speak to thousands of people in a great place like the Albert Hall.

Throughout this extraordinary séance which lasted an hour and a half, Mrs. Morris stood up in Mr. Cowen's library and gripped the lapels of her sports coat just as she grips the stole on the dress which she wears at the theatre. She wore the same masculine expression which she wears during one of her Sunday services.

At the conclusion of the long séance, when Mrs. Morris and I were sitting alone in Mr. Cowen's library, she suddenly laughed and immediately went off into a trance again.

She began to stroke an imaginary beard and to tap the arms of her chair.

In a very broad Irish brogue she asked me how I was. For several minutes I had a discussion with an Irishman whom I could scarcely understand.

When Mrs. Morris came out of this second trance I asked her who our visitor had been. She said it was the spirit of an Irish priest who often controlled her. The reason she laughed before going into a trance, she added, was because she saw the priest standing by my side, bending over the notebook in which I was writing."

21st January, 1931.

UNTIED KNOT MYSTERY WHEN "POWER" MAKES TALK FILM
MICROPHONES CRASH
MRS. MORRIS'S ESCAPE
SPIRIT'S SPECIAL EFFORT

"Ghosts and 'spirits' are notoriously lovers of the dark, but not so that mysterious spirit *Power*, which is said to take possession of Mrs. Meurig Morris and enable her to deliver amazingly brilliant sermons.

Yesterday *Power* made a talking picture, and the scene in the British Movietone studio would have astonished even a Hollywood film producer.

When Mrs. Morris arrived, Mr. Laurence Cowen, the playwright, said the lights were much too strong, so it was decided to ask *Power* about it.

Mrs. Morris went into a trance in a small room, and Mr. Cowen and Lady Doyle talked to the spirit control. He said the lights were terribly bright, but he would try and give a message and would call up all the assistance he could.

A small band of spiritualists sang hymns to create the right 'atmosphere', and then a great flood of light was poured on

Mrs. Morris. As she was entering her second trance she waved trembling hands over her head and breathed heavily. Then she rose from her chair and delivered in the baritone voice which is said to be *Power's* a message on how the people of this earth can co-operate with those on the next plane.

While Mrs. Morris was speaking, the microphones which hung near her head fell to the ground. She was not in the least disturbed, however, and *Power's* voice went on booming out.

Mr. T. Scales, the production manager, said afterwards that he could not understand how the microphones could have fallen. The rope holding them, he said, had been tied in a double reef-knot and this knot had slipped.

Mr. Cowen quickly stepped in with the 'explanation' that the extra power which Mrs. Morris had required for this demonstration had been responsible for the knot untying. So an extra piece was added to the film, and Mr. Cowen told the world through the microphones—which had been tied up again—how *Power* had untied the knots in the rope.''

22nd January, 1931.

MRS. MORRIS HEARS "POWER"
TALK-FILM OF HER "IN TRANCE"

" 'Oh, I am so happy!' cried Mrs. Meurig Morris, the young trance-medium, when she sat in the British Movietone theatre yesterday and heard *Power*, her spirit control, delivering a message to the world through her . . .

'I have never heard him before,' she said to me. 'For nearly eight years he has been using my faculties to preach his wonderful sermons to the world. He has preached hundreds of sermons through me, and yet I have never heard his voice or known what he said, except from people who have listened to him.

'Now that I have heard him, I think he is wonderful. . . .'

Throughout the film Mr. Cowen is seen to be concentrating his whole attention on Mrs. Morris, and many people will no doubt declare that he is hypnotising her. Mr. Cowen told me, however, that his tenseness merely shows his anxiety for Mrs. Morris's safety.

'I have never been known to hypnotise anybody in my life,' he said and continued:

'But to convince the sceptics I will arrange, if you like, to stay away from the Fortune Theatre (where Mrs. Morris delivers her sermons). You can send somebody to guard me.

'The test to which you have asked Mrs. Morris to submit will demonstrate that both hypnotism and telepathy are impossible. I want you to select the text or subject for a sermon and take it on the stage to her after she has gone into trance.'

Already great interest has been shown in the *Daily Mail* test, which is to be held some time after next Sunday. Yesterday, so Mr. Cowen told me, 700 applications had been received for seats, although the theatre holds only 500 people."

23rd January, 1931.

TRANCE SERMON MYSTERY
"DAILY MAIL" TEST ON SUNDAY
SEALED TEXT FOR MRS. MORRIS

"The *Daily Mail* test of the genuineness of the mediumship of Mrs. Meurig Morris will take place at the Fortune Theatre on Sunday night . . .

Power has agreed, in an interview with me, to preach from any selected text. A text has been chosen by a member of the staff of the *Daily Mail*. This has been placed in a sealed envelope, and I shall hand it to Mrs. Morris when she goes into a trance on Sunday night. I shall not open the envelope until just before I walk on to the stage.

When Mrs. Morris is in trance she keeps her eyes closed. It will be interesting to note whether *Power* finds it necessary to use her eyes in order to see the text.

The meeting will be presided over by the Rev. C. Drayton Thomas, a Wesleyan minister, who is a member of the committee formed by clergymen and ministers of all denominations to investigate spiritualism."

24th January, 1931
SERMON IN A TRANCE
"DAILY MAIL" TEST FOR MRS. MORRIS
WHAT WILL "POWER" DO?

"Mrs. Meurig Morris, the young medium who has puzzled thousands of people by the extraordinary sermons she delivers when in trance, was yesterday sitting in the offices of the Fortune Theatre, Covent Garden, using a typewriter as efficiently as any girl in a City office. . . ."

The climax came on the 26th January, exactly a fortnight after the drama had begun. The contents bills of the *Daily Mail* all over the country announced in bold type:

> "TRANCE
> MEDIUM
> FOUND OUT"

The paper itself contained the following article:

POWER'S SERMON—JARGON
ONE TALK FOR ALL TEXTS
MRS. MORRIS LAST NIGHT
IS IT HYPNOTISM?

"I have discovered one thing definitely about Mrs. Meurig Morris, the young 'trance medium' whose sermons at the Fortune Theatre have been attracting so much attention.

Her sub-conscious mind is crammed with spiritualistic jargon which she can trot out and hang on any peg which may be given to her as a text or a subject for a sermon.

Last night she preached a sermon in a trance on a text which a member of the staff of the *Daily Mail* had selected from the Book of Proverbs. The text was:

'Where no counsel is, the people fall; but in the multitude of counsellors there is safety.'

Mrs. Morris launched straight away into one of her pseudo-scientific-philosophic-theological messages, and whenever she dragged in the words 'counsel' or 'counsellors' they were not material to her sermon, for other words could have been used.

I have heard three of Mrs. Morris's sermons, and at a private séance I had with *Power*, her spirit control, he talked to me a great deal about the other world; and on all four occasions the young medium used the same phrases—many of which are almost meaningless—but strung them together in different contexts.

It is now very obvious to me that Mrs. Morris could preach a sermon on any subject, provided she had the text read out to her, and she would use the same phrases every time.

Mr. Laurence Cowen, the playwright, says that Mrs. Morris can deliver sixty or seventy different sermons, but I have found out that the only difference is in the stringing together of the sentences and phrases.

So it was last night.

'When one gives counsel upon the earth plane or upon the plane beyond death, that counsel is according to the mind and according to the outlook of one's own opinion.'

That is how Mrs. Morris began her sermon on the text that had been chosen for her. She continued:

'But when you see that the outlook and the mind that manifests itself therein is but a state of development one must admit that this counsel shows a state of expression of divinity and of the growth of the soul.

I want to say that, although we have come to give our message, many will say to give counsel, to the children of the earth, yet at the same time we know that it depends upon you all whether you are ready to receive it. Being part of God, you must of necessity have all the attributes, have all the seeds, within you.'

This is the strain in which Mrs. Morris went on.

The one thing Mrs. Morris plays on all the time is the receptivity of the mind to the great truths of spiritualism. But what the sceptic wants is evidence that these 'truths' come from a spiritual world.

If Mrs. Morris's sub-conscious mind is a sea of spiritualistic jargon, as I have suggested, how has it got there?

I have discussed Mrs. Morris's mediumship with hypnotists and doctors who have seen her, and they declare that there is nothing in her performance when in trance that is not consistent with post-hypnosis.

Whatever may be the cause, it is the extraordinary metamorphosis of Mrs. Morris from timid femininity to aggressive masculinity that impresses people.

Last night the impressiveness of her appearance was enhanced when she turned round in trance and delivered her sermon to the curtains at the back of the stage.

The explanation of this, as given to me, is that *Power*, when he delivers a sermon on this earth, is also speaking to an audience on his own plane, and he often overlooks the people on the physical world.

To the sceptic, the agnostic, and even to tens of thousands of people with open minds, Mrs. Morris is an extremely clever woman. But her spiritualism is unconvincing."

Mrs. Morris continued to take part in the Sunday services, and the correspondent continued to report them. On the 2nd February, the *Daily Mail* wrote:

"*Power*, that mysterious spirit who comes down from his elevated plane every Sunday evening to the stage of the Fortune Theatre, replied last night to my criticisms of him through his medium, Mrs. Meurig Morris. His reply was quite well thought out because it left me as mystified as ever, but I am afraid he will not convince me, nor thousands of other people, of his spiritual identity, until he gives us some proof. And this, apparently, he will never do, because, as he says with an engaging frankness, he is not infallible. Then *Power* launched into an explanation of how he uses Mrs. Morris to deliver his sermons. I cannot do better than reproduce what he said: 'Not only is there the physical atomic structure, but around it as an exact replica is a body called the etheric body. This body plays a great part in the question of control. Some people's etheric bodies are more loosely woven together, and these are the individuals that can be used so well for control.' Mrs. Morris lifted her left hand to her head and explained in the baritone voice, which is said to be *Power's*, how the spirits enter the physical body. 'From the top of the head here,' she said, 'there is a large cone-like shape, and it is through this that the power is poured.' Discussing the possibility of hypnosis, *Power* asked, 'Who is the hypnotist? Considering that I have worked with this instrument for years and alone, surely it cannot be a being upon the earth.' I must pay a tribute to Mrs. Morris. When I saw her last night, she said, 'I do not mind your criticism, because it is honest.' Whether she is genuine or not, she is honest, and I feel certain that she goes into a trance. The whole question is, who or what is responsible for that trance."

But Mrs. Morris and her counsellors were not appeased, and on the 6th February her solicitors demanded an apology and withdrawal, to be given as much prominence as the article on the 26th January and to be accompanied by a contents bill calling attention to it, together with the payment of an agreed sum for the furtherance of the Spiritualist Movement. These requests were not met, and a writ for libel was issued on the following day.

Mrs. Morris claimed that the placard—"Trance Medium Found Out"—and the article, whether taken separately or together, meant that she was a deliberate fraud. The *Daily Mail* put up two defences. First they said that Mrs. Morris' spiritualist activities were a matter of public interest and that all they had written was fair comment upon them. Alternatively they asserted that all they had written was true. The action, which became a *cause célèbre* of spiritualism, was tried more than a year later before Mr. Justice McCardie and a special jury. Serjeant Sullivan, K.C. appeared for Mrs. Morris, and the *Daily Mail* was represented by Norman Birkett, K.C. (now Lord Justice Birkett).

Mrs. Morris was naturally the most important witness in the case, and it was apparent from the start that her evidence was going to be, both for herself and the Court, a nervous ordeal. She broke down while taking the oath, and the Judge ordered the first of a number of short adjournments for the relief of tension. When the Court reassembled, Mrs. Morris began to tell, in answer to the questions of her counsel, the story of her experiences.

The approach of each of her Controls gave her a different sensation. She described the sensation of the approach of *Power*. "I first of all see a great yellow light, which is like a searchlight, and it comes right over me. Then I feel myself getting very big.

I seem to grow tall and my neck begins to get big and instead of being myself I feel such a strong personality. I seem to be changing and getting bigger, and it is as I get bigger and feel this personality that I lose my own consciousness."

"Is that all?"—"Yes, that is all."

"Once you lose consciousness you do not know what happens?" —"No."

Mrs. Morris had been warned of the first advent of *Power* by another control known as *Sister Magdalen*, but the extraordinary thing was that in all the eight years of *Power's* visitations she had made no study of spiritualist literature and no enquiry into the relationship of her experiences with physical science or religion. Nor was she concerned to know *Power's* identity. She was content to be the passive and incurious vehicle of an unknown force. Serjeant Sullivan relied upon this fact to prove the authenticity of *Power's* sermons.

"Have you read books on science or philosophy?"—"No."

"Have you received any instruction in science or philosophy?" —"None."

"And until you commenced your manifestations, had you any association with persons of superior education?"—"No one."

"Was your husband an educated man?"—"I should say just ordinary."

"Had he a library?"—"No."

"And were his habits literary or otherwise?"—"Otherwise."

It was disclosed that his habits had been alcoholic, until his wife had converted him to spiritualism. Serjeant Sullivan then asked his last question in examination-in-chief: "In the course of your life, as far as you are aware, have you ever had access to the information that apparently may be given in your sermons?"— "No."

Why not? The cross-examination was bound to be long and exhausting—in fact it lasted into three days. But Birkett's first questions were directed to this matter of Mrs. Morris' contented ignorance. Her reading on her subject had been confined to the spiritualist weeklies. She had not even dipped into the works of Sir Oliver Lodge, though she was to call him as a witness.

"Then may I leave it, as far as you are concerned, with your answer to the jury, that despite all that you have done in the spiritualist movement, about which I will have to ask you, you have never taken the trouble to buy a single book about it?"—"I have never bought any spiritualist books." She said later that she wished to keep her mind perfectly clear, so as to be a pure channel of communication.

Birkett began to ask Mrs. Morris about her first Control, a small girl known as *Little Sunshine*, who had been a great friend of Mrs. Morris's own daughter. But one day *Little Sunshine* told Mrs. Morris that her child had been very naughty and caught a bad cold—a piece of sneaking which was not resented any the less because it was true. Mrs. Morris had just finished relating this domestic incident when the clocks struck four, and the Judge said, "Really the issues that we are embarking upon touch the great mystery of the secrets of life and death, and I think we had better adjourn now and reflect upon it until the morning." The first day of the trial was over.

The next morning opened with questions about another of Mrs. Morris's Controls, *Father O'Keefe*, an old Irish priest "with a very long beard and a thin face". When *Father O'Keefe* took possession of Mrs. Morris, she spoke with an Irish brogue, although, she said, "I have never heard an Irishman in my life." A later witness had heard *Father O'Keefe* say "Sure and begorra" several times.

The next Control to come under review was a Red Indian known as *The Squaw*, who "helps to magnetise my body and keep me fit for my services." *The Squaw* had "a band round her head, and it looked like a feather."

"The typical squaw of fiction?"—"I have never read any fiction about squaws, so that I do not know."

"Do these Controls," asked Mr. Justice McCardie, "come when you call for them, or do they come unexpectedly?"— "No; I do not have them just when I want them. They

come when they have a message or some purpose to come
for, not otherwise."

"*Power*," asked Birkett, "comes every Sunday night at the
starting of the second hymn, does he not?"—"I know that
he does, because that is his mission, to work with me."

"Absolutely like clockwork?"—"Yes."

"He has never failed?"—"He never failed."

"He preaches for forty-five minutes and goes away for a
week?"—"He does not go away for a week."

"Unless you have an engagement in the country?"—"I feel
his presence, yes."

"He will go to Brighton, to Birmingham or to Nottingham,
so long as Mr. Cowen has advertised that he will be there;
is not that right?"—"It is nothing to do with the advertising
at all."

The cross-examination ranged far and wide, and Mrs. Morris
was comforted in the witness-box by the occasional presence of
Sister Magdalen and *Little Sunshine*, who alone of her spirit friends
vouchsafed from time to time to talk to her while she was conscious. The others came only when she was in a trance and unable
to hear what they said, with the result that she could be deceived
about the messages conveyed, as she put it, "through her larynx."
The deceiving, it was suggested, was the work of Mr. Laurence
Cowen. But Mrs. Morris declared that her "helpers" would not
permit her to be exploited. As for the messages which *Power* had
delivered in public, Birkett asked of one of them: "There is
nothing in that which has not been said a million times, is there?"
To which Mrs. Morris replied: "Mr. Birkett, there is no new
truth in the world." But these inhabitants of another world, who
conversed with Mrs. Morris, could surely reveal truths of trans-
cendent importance? They seemed, however, to content themselves with large, ambiguous generalities and little messages from
dead relatives and friends.

Sister Magdalen spoke in broken English, and was believed to have been a French nun. Her presence in Court fascinated both Bench and Bar. "Is she here now?" asked the Judge. "She is here, and that is why I have been trying to get as near to her as possible."

Birkett: "Is she still here?"—"*Sister Magdalen* is here—*there*." And Mrs. Morris pointed to the empty air beside her.

"She has never moved from there?"—"She stands and watches me."

Mr. Justice McCardie: "Does she speak to you now?"—"No. I do not hear her always when I see her. I only hear her on occasions—I suppose when I am ready to receive it."

"Is not she speaking to you now?"—"No."

Birkett: "If *Sister Magdalen* spoke to me I could not hear it?"— "No. I have what they call a clairvoyant power."

"When she speaks to you she uses her own vocal chords?" —"I am able to hear it because I have the power."

"But she uses her own vocal chords when she speaks to you?" —"I suppose that she has vocal chords in the body that she has got; she is bound to have."

"I want to pursue this matter. She is in the Court now?"— "Yes, she is just *here*. I wish that you could see her."

"An ethereal shape?"—"Yes."

"How is she dressed?"—"In very deep purple."

"Velvet?"—"It is flimsy. I cannot describe it. She has been standing here and she is standing now."

"Is she stationary?"—"Yes, she is stationary, watching me."

After a time Birkett inquired once more about the unseen witness.

"Is she still there?"—"Yes, she is."

"You can tell, can you, that her frame looks like a physical frame—it is the same outline?"—"Yes, it is the same type of body as ours, but it is more ethereal. I cannot understand it at all."

"Subject to that, it is a human form wearing a purple gown?"

—"Yes, it is clothed in purple; it looks like a human form, yes."

"Can you see the face?" queried the Judge. —"Yes."

"You can see the face, the eyes and the lips?"—"Absolutely like I am looking at you."

"That is what I meant," Birkett resumed, "with your ordinary physical eyes you can see the form?"—"Yes."

"You can see the form of *Sister Magdalen* in the purple gown?" —"I have a clairvoyant power and I am able to see it."

Mrs. Morris was unshaken by the most searching questions. A quotation from one of *Power's* sermons was read to her: "If you had the greater vision you would find, not a physical body, nor a body that you term the astral body, but you would see that the body was likened just to a streak of light, a streak of light which would come like a streak of lightning."

"A streak of light could not wear a purple gown, could it?"— "You are muddling. My vision only enables me to see the next world. I have not got the greater vision that *Power* is speaking of. I just see them as she is here now."

"You claim before my Lord and this jury that you can see the invisible?"—"I claim that I can see it. It is not invisible to me, but it is invisible to you."

On the third day Birkett read out long extracts from *Power's* sermons. Mrs. Morris did not claim to understand them—she admitted that one passage did not "sound very sensible." "Do you mean to say," asked the Judge, "that you are now, and that you will go on, preaching or announcing things that you do not understand?"—"Yes, I will, because I must do my work that I have been called upon to do. I may not understand."

"Does that mean that you would allow yourself to be responsible for anything—whether through the trance condition or otherwise—that *Power* chooses to transmit through your lips?"— "I have perfect faith in them, perfect faith."

Suddenly Mrs. Morris, whose eyes had been filled with tears for some time, grew paler and stared straight in front of her. Her face worked and her hands were clenched. "The Christ!" she gasped. "The Usher had better stand by, but do not touch her," ordered the Judge, echoing voices from the back of the Court. "It is all right," said Mrs. Morris, dissolving into tears. The Judge and Serjeant Sullivan invited her to rest for a while, while Norman Birkett proffered a doctor. "No, I am all right now," she said, bursting into tears once more, "It was only a vision. The Christ came."

Mr. Justice McCardie adjourned the Court for a quarter of an hour, and the cross-examination came to an end, though Mrs. Morris was twice recalled on subsequent days. When the Court reassembled, the gramophone records were played. The jury heard both Mrs. Morris' natural voice and the stentorian voice of *Power*. Later on they were also shown the talking film.

Serjeant Sullivan then began to call his supporting witnesses. A variety of people testified to Mrs. Morris' sincerity, some of them spiritualists, others confirmed doubters and disbelievers. Many thought that *Power's* sermons had a high intellectual content. The tide of discussion flowed to and fro over the sea-wall which separates science from religion.

One witness told Norman Birkett that she could see the aura of his etheric body; at the next moment she informed him that the pineal gland at the top of his head was the vestigial remains of a third human eye.

Another witness described a conversation which he had held in French, through the mediumship of Mrs. Morris, with the French photographer, Lumière, who had died fifteen years before. Lumière gave him a chemical formula for the development of psychic photographs. This witness, when asked his occupation, disclosed that he was a Customs and Excise Officer. "Testing spirits?" enquired Birkett. "Yes, but not the spirits of which we are speaking now."

"I am so strong about *Power*," declared Mrs. Violet Tweedale, an authoress, who had attended séances with Balfour, Haldane and Gladstone, "because he is so splendid for the people and tells

them what they want to know. It is the people I care about, not
Power. *Power* is nothing to me."

"Surely you ought not to speak like that about one who has
passed over?"—"Why not?" came the answer. "We are exactly
the same five minutes after death as we are five minutes before it.
There is no greater reverence due to the dead than there is to the
living. They are as much alive as we are." The once Christian
Court of King's Bench may have been startled by this faith in the
immortality of the human soul.

Mrs. Morris had been examined by a number of specialists.
None of them had any doubts about her genuineness. In one
consulting room she fell into a trance and began to speak in the
rough Irish brogue of *Father O'Keefe*. "I said that I did not believe in spirits," said the doctor, who told the Court he was an
atheist, "and *Father O'Keefe* said, rather angrily, 'You will know
better one of these days,' and rapped me on the knee with a
masculine gesture." This doctor found that Mrs. Morris, while
in trance, was entirely insensitive to pinpricks, her pulse went up
from eighty-six to 130, and the left side of her face became
clammy and colder than the right. The doctor saw Mrs. Morris
then transformed into *Power*. He enquired whether *Power* had
any anxiety about the result of the pending action, and *Power*
replied that he would be present at the trial, which would mark
the beginning of a new epoch in the history of religion. This
doctor formed the opinion that Mrs. Morris was hysterical.
Power was not a discarnate entity, but a secondary, dissociated
personality, which inhabited Mrs. Morris' sub-conscious mind
and fed on language heard and read by Mrs. Morris from her
childhood. There was, however, no element of deliberate pre-
tence on Mrs. Morris' part.

On the other hand a lady doctor who also examined Mrs.
Morris in a trance state was given some astonishingly accurate
information about a confidential matter she was engaged in and a
particular patient about whom she was very worried. *Little Sunshine* prescribed chloroform for the patient's condition, which the
doctor found brought instant relief. "I can usually tell by a
person's face," said this witness, "whether he is honest and truth-
ful, or deceitful. A man's soul is written on his face and we can

tell his character by the curve of his lips and the look in his eyes."

"But have not some of the greatest deceivers been childlike and bland?"—"No, I don't think so," the doctor replied. "You have not," enquired Mr. Justice McCardie, "been much about these Courts?"

Lady Conan Doyle and Sir Oliver Lodge also gave evidence. "There are many grades of existence in the other world," declared Sir Oliver, "I have been told recently by the denizens of the other world that the state in which they first are is a world of illusion, where they get whatever they want. I put it to my boy Raymond: 'You live in a world of illusion?' and he said: 'So do you, Father.' . . . When I have discourses with people who have departed, I have found them very much the same as we are. They know a little more, but I do not accept all that they say as gospel."

One important witness—Mr. Laurence Cowen—was not called, although he was sitting in Court throughout the trial. This omission was heavily commented on by Norman Birkett for the defence and by the Judge in his summing-up.

Most of the witnesses for the defence said very little which tended to prove that Mrs. Morris was not what she thought herself to be. There was, however, the evidence of Mr. Cowen's charwoman, who had overheard what she took to be rehearsals of a play. One evening, for instance, when Mr. Cowen and Mrs. Morris were in the library of his house at Harrow, she heard a little child's voice say, "I so happy," and then the voice of Mr. Cowen: "I would like that a little louder, my dear," and the words were repeated until Mr. Cowen was satisfied. Employees of the Fortune Theatre had likewise heard *Power* and Mr. Cowen conversing in the Manager's Office. On one occasion the telephone rang. *Power* was heard to say: "It is a long time since I have heard the telephone," and then he kept quiet until the receiver was replaced. "I thought," said the witness, "that Mrs. Morris was keeping herself in practice for her public performances."

This was more than Mrs. Morris, who was sitting in the well of the Court, could bear. She burst into tears, and cried out, "It is so dreadful. It is so dreadful to say this sort of thing against me!" She was given a glass of water and helped, sobbing, from the Court.

A Harley Street surgeon who at the Judge's suggestion had examined Mrs. Morris' throat and vocal chords, pronounced them normal. The voice of *Power*, he declared, was the voice of Mrs. Morris greatly magnified.

An actress, Barbara Oakshott, said that with a little practice she could give a very fair imitation of Mrs. Morris in action, and she produced and played a gramophone record in which she said a few words in her own voice and then, in an assumed, deeper voice, part of the sermon recorded by *Power*. The actress had not been impressed by Mrs. Morris' performance, which she thought was all "done to cue", except when *Power* "dried up" in the middle of his sermon. But the sermon which this witness attended had been delivered on the previous Sunday—after the trial with all its stress and strain had begun.

The last witness was the *Daily Mail* correspondent, who told the Court that he no longer thought, what he had believed when he wrote the article, that Mrs. Morris' trance was genuine. Asked why he had been annoyed at the publication of the placard, which accompanied his article, he replied that it had the effect of ringing down the curtain in the middle of the act and cutting short his investigations. "Oh, I see," said Serjeant Sullivan, "Sherlock Holmes baffled!"

Was the jury also baffled? A verdict with heavy damages for Mrs. Morris might seem to set a seal of approval upon the spiritualist claims. On the other hand was there really enough evidence for a finding that Mrs. Morris, who on any score was a woman of strange and remarkable powers, was a deliberate deceiver, either of herself or the public? There was no evidence of hypnosis, and the case was argued by both counsel as turning on the question whether her trances were genuine or simulated. If they were genuine, and Mrs. Morris genuinely believed that *Power* was a spirit speaking from beyond the grave, it was immaterial whether the jury also believed it—her honesty was established. On this vital issue Mr. Justice McCardie appeared to entertain the gravest doubts, and there came a moment on the

second day of the summing-up when Mrs. Morris rose to her
feet, seized the lapels of her coat, and began to address the Court
in a deep voice: "Thou who art a brother judge, hearken unto my
voice——" "This really must be stopped," rasped the brother
judge testily, "Tell her to stop. She knows better. Let her stop!"
"I will say this——" continued the voice.

"Let her stop!" cried the Judge, "we have had this so often,
members of the jury, that we are all getting tired of it. You can
stop her perfectly well—you can take her out."

"Do not touch her till I have left the body," rejoined the
resonant tones of *Power*.

"Each day we have had these outbreaks of emotion"—Mc-
Cardie was very upset—"Either she should stay out of Court, or,
if she comes in, she should suppress these things. She can be taken
out now. Let the Usher take her out of Court. I do not want her
to stay here. The jury will see now why I say advisedly that I dislike every minute of this case." Mrs. Morris was then assisted
out of Court, and once more the proceedings were adjourned for
an interval.

Mr. Justice McCardie completed his summing-up without
further interruption. "For myself I say advisedly as a Judge that
as long as I remain a Judge I care not for all the incarnate or discarnate spirits in the world. As long as I remain on the Bench
I shall resolutely seek to reach for truth and I shall firmly advise
juries to reach for truth, no matter if ten thousand million discarnate spirits come around me. You have got to find out what
the truth of the matter is here. Sir Oliver Lodge says that we are
living in a world of illusion. Perhaps we are, but whether it is
an illusion or not, this Court is an illusion to which we must
conform. . . . You have got to give your verdict. . . ."

The jury took three hours to solve their dilemma. It was 6.30
p.m. when Judge, jury and leading counsel were reassembled in
the Court. The jury had written out their verdict on a slip of
paper: "We find for the Defendants (the *Daily Mail*) on the claim
of fair comment on a matter of public interest, but we do not
consider that any allegations of fraud or dishonesty have been
proved." Mr. Justice McCardie gave judgment on this verdict
for the *Daily Mail*, and relieved the jury from further service as

special jurors for five years. "That," he said with obvious thankfulness, "concludes this litigation."

But Serjeant Sullivan was not content with this result. The jury had reached a decision which neither the Judge nor counsel on either side had anticipated. For if the libel meant that Mrs. Morris was a fraud, and indeed the whole defence had been an endeavour to prove that she was, how could it be fair comment, when the charge of fraud had not been proved? If Smith takes Jones to Court and says, "You called me a liar!" and Jones replies: "Whatever I called you, you are a liar!" can the answer be, "Smith is not a liar, but Jones was entitled to say whatever he did say"? The result was unusual, for it is generally accepted in our Courts that a charge of fraud, if it fails, incurs the heaviest damages, and for this reason the charge is seldom made.

But in this case both the Court of Appeal and the House of Lords declined to intervene. Lord Buckmaster, giving judgment in the appeal to the House of Lords, declared that the jury's verdict must be taken to mean that no allegation of fraud or dishonesty was made either in the *Daily Mail's* article or in the words of the placard "Trance medium found out". This verdict, he thought, was not so unreasonable as to be perverse, and so it was allowed to stand. The resources of the "Meurig Morris Defence Fund", into which the collections taken at *Power's* services were poured, had been exhausted in vain.

Of the truth or falsity of the spiritualist creed Lord Justice Greer in the Court of Appeal observed that "there was a very great philosopher, a Scotchman, with a very bright style of writing, which is very rare in Scotch philosophers, who said of another school of philosophy to which he did not belong that common sense in dealing with metaphysical questions of this sort in these high regions was equivalent to common nonsense; and I think that everybody would agree that the tribunal which is a good tribunal for the determination of questions of libel or slander is not the tribunal which one would like to decide these very difficult questions."

V

VOCAL SINS

Wilson v. British Broadcasting Corporation and another (1934)
Reavely v. Colles and another (1936)

ONE evening in 1933 a retired schoolmaster tuned in to the B.B.C. to hear the *St. Matthew Passion* sung by the Bach Choir in the Queen's Hall. As he listened, he grew more and more irritated. The man who was singing the Evangelist, it seemed to him, had no control of his breath: he kept inserting the "intrusive H" in the middle of his vowels. It was a habit which the schoolmaster loathed, and after a time he took paper and pencil and made a mark for every occasion when he thought he detected the offending aspirate. At the end of the performance he had made more than 200 marks, and he wrote an exasperated letter to the *Radio Times*. The *Radio Times* published it under the title "Vocal Sins":

"I have just been listening to the broadcast of Bach's glorious *Passion* music. While, on the whole, the rendering was excellent, there was one glaring fault that simply ruined the performance of one of the singers, and I am amazed that the B.B.C. could engage anyone quite so incompetent in his breath control. The 'intrusive H' must have appeared *hundreds* of times. Thus 'Pilate's wife' became 'Pigh-highlet's wigh-highf'; 'Potter's field' became 'Po-ho-te-her's feeheeled'; 'High Priest' was turned into 'High-high Pree-heest'; 'Purple robe' into 'Purple ro-hobe'; 'to' into 'too-hoo', and so on throughout the entire performance.

"It was simply ghastly. It seems to me—much as I admire in broad outline the great work of the B.B.C., that in one respect they are sadly lacking. If they once made the rule that in no circumstances would they engage anyone who was guilty either of the 'intrusive H' or the tremolo—and rigidly enforced the rule— the standard of singing in England would be immeasurably raised in a few years. The two faults I mention are grave and

80

horrible and, I regret to say, widespread, and the B.B.C. has it in its power to cure the trouble."

The old schoolmaster sent a copy of this letter to Mr. Steuart Wilson, the singer concerned. Wilson, who had sung the part of the Evangelist about forty times, did not regard the criticism as either helpful or fair. For one thing he disagreed with the statement of the facts, and while the law allows the most outspoken criticism, provided that it is honest and given without ulterior motives, it denies that any criticism can be fair if the facts on which it is based have been wrongly stated. According to Wilson, though he sang a lengthened vowel in 107 instances where two notes fell on a single syllable, he had used the "intrusive H" in only two places, neither of them mentioned in the letter; and when he had done so, it was not his lack of breath control, but an intentional artistic effect. More than this, he did not think it fair to say that his performance had been "ruined" or was "ghastly", and he felt unable to ignore the suggestion that the B.B.C. ought not to broadcast his singing. So he sued the B.B.C. and the retired schoolmaster, and the result was a musical libel action, in which, as in most "genre" lawsuits, leading practitioners of the art in question were called to give evidence on opposite sides.

Wilson in his own evidence was not challenged to demonstrate his voice, and his cross-examination by Stuart Bevan, K.C., on behalf of the B.B.C., was a performance in words without music. The reader may judge who scored the advantage.

"He (the schoolmaster) said that, apart from the use of the 'intrusive H' your rendering of the part was in all respects all that could be desired?"—"That is what is called in *Alice in Wonderland* the 'best butter'. He said that it had ruined the performance."

". . . I venture to put it to you that you do exhibit, from time to time, the defects alleged in the letter?"—"I agree that I sometimes do use 'the intrusive H'."

"Do you approve of the use of the 'intrusive H'?"—"I approve of it when used artistically."

"You have said that in some 107 instances you used the lengthened vowel. When you are doing that, is it not difficult to prevent the 'H' slipping in?"—"That depends on how skilful you are."

"You have given several instances where Jean de Reszke taught you to use the 'intrusive H'. They were all in operatic music. Do you realise that what is permissible in Opera is not permissible in Bach or concert music?"—"I would not admit that for a moment."

"A good deal of license is allowed in opera?"—"A good deal of license is taken."

"I suggest that in Bach and concert music the 'intrusive H' is taboo and that all the great singers are agreed on it?"—"I do not quite know who sets up the taboo."

"De Reszke was an opera singer and taught opera?"—"Yes, but he taught the principles of singing."

"He had never sung at concerts?"—"I do not think so."

"In your examples the language used is either French or German?"—"Yes."

"Can you appreciate that while the stolid Englishman might tolerate the introduction of an 'H' in German, with which he is not very familiar, it would be quite different if he heard his own language distorted in the same way?"—"The stolid German seems to have stood it all right."

"Was not Caruso the best example of the 'intrusive H'?"— "He certainly used it a great deal."

"Were not his performances on the concert platform quite spoiled by his use of the 'intrusive H'?"—"I understand that he could fill the largest hall in any country in the world with an audience who had stood all day to get in."

"Do you agree that, if you go over all the great works on singing, you will find the same view expressed again and again with regard to the 'intrusive H'?"—"Primers of knowledge often fall a long way behind practice and performance. They are aiming at safety all the time."

"Is not the use of the 'intrusive H' bad style on the concert
platform, but accepted style in opera singing?"—"Music
cannot be divided into watertight compartments. Music
is music."

For Mr. Wilson many witnesses were called to show that the
"intrusive H" was not necessarily a sign of lack of voice control.
Other witnesses—music critics, opera producers and professional
singers—approved of its use—occasionally. Melba herself had
used it in Tosti's *Good-bye*. This part of the dispute turned on
a question of taste. "While it would not enhance the beauty of
English to the English ear," said a professor of voice production
at London University, "it might enhance the value of music to
the musical ear." "Do you know of anything," Stuart Bevan
asked another witness, "which gives rise to more conflicting
opinions than music and acting?"—"No," came the answer,
"except religion."

The defence admitted that the "intrusive H" might be used
voluntarily or involuntarily. But if it was used involuntarily, it
was due to lack of control; if voluntarily, it was bad taste. Dr.
(now Sir) Adrian Boult was the first witness called for the defence.
He spoke highly of Wilson's qualities as a singer, "but," he said,
"no singer is perfect, and Mr. Wilson has the defect of using the
'intrusive H' rather more often than he himself is probably aware
of. I do not think it a serious fault, but I can quite understand its
becoming irritating by its repetition." But Dr. Boult did not
think it had "ruined" the performance in question, and he admitted that on all the occasions he had conducted for Mr. Wilson
he had never mentioned the "intrusive H" to him.

Many other witnesses, including Dr. (now Sir) Malcolm
Sargent disapproved of the "intrusive H" in concert singing or
oratorio, and there were others again who had thought that Mr.
Wilson's breathing was at fault. One of these, Mr. Arnold
Perry, another conductor, had heard Wilson use an "intrusive H"
in the word "love" in Bach's Cantata. "I could not understand
why he did it if it was intentional," he said, "I thought the cause
of it was something defective in the breath control."

"If the word 'love' occurred seven or eight times," the witness was asked, "might not Mr. Wilson have introduced the 'H' into them to obtain variety?"—"One doesn't usually try to introduce variety into Bach in that way," was the reply.

The schoolmaster himself was unrepentant.

"Was it true that Mr. Wilson's performance was ruined?"—"To me it was."

"When you wrote the letter you were very irritated?"—"I was irritated when I heard the broadcast, but not when I wrote the letter."

"Is this a clear suggestion that the B.B.C., should not broadcast Mr. Wilson's singing?"—"You can take it as that—until he has corrected his fault."

"You made no inquiries from any musician before you charged Mr. Wilson with lack of breath control?"—"No."

"Did it occur to you that it was a very serious statement to make?"—"It was absolutely legitimate criticism."

"Did you not consider that, before making a charge of that kind, a layman would rightly take the advice of somebody skilled in the art?"—"No."

The reader who tries now to make up his mind about the just solution of this case is not in the same position as the jurymen at the trial. Unlike them he has not seen or heard the witnesses or listened to the Lord Chief Justice's summing-up. Therefore he can never know whether he would have reached the same conclusion, if he had been there at the time. On this occasion the jury decided that the letter was not a fair criticism, and they brought in a verdict for £2,100 damages against the B.B.C., and the retired schoolmaster.

The case of the "elusive H" may be compared with a libel action which another singer, a Captain Cuthbert Reavely, brought two years later against *The Times*. The source of this

dispute was the criticism published by *The Times* of a performance of Mendelssohn's *Elijah* in the Albert Hall. Although
Mendelssohn's music was played and sung, the work was not
produced as an oratorio, but as a pageant or spectacle, with the
addition of scenery, costumes, acting and even special sound
effects. *The Times* critic disliked it intensely and said so with
some spirit. "To butcher a masterpiece to make a spectacle," he
wrote, "is a proceeding that can be justified on no artistic principle, though it may happen that occasionally the end may vindicate the means. For it is possible that one finished product
may become the raw material of a further product, and Mr. T. C.
Fairbairn has in some other productions shown that a pageant
may not be wholly incompatible with the claims of music. But
so much can hardly be said of his production of *Elijah*. . . ."

In this production Captain Reavely played the part of King
Ahab. The only line he had to sing was, "Art thou Elijah? Art
thou he that troubleth Israel?" But, having sung that line, he
was obliged, in the dramatised version, to remain on the stage for
nearly an hour, mutely signifying his part in the historical struggle
between King and Prophet. *The Times* critic summarised the
dramatic effect of this situation by observing that "the conflict
between Elijah and Ahab, which is felt as a clash between good
and evil in the narrative of the oratorio, is stultified by the physical
appearance of a King who can only make gestures of impotent
annoyance". Nor had Captain Reavely's singing of his line
made a favourable impression. He was described with others
as being "unsteady in their declaration".

Captain Reavely complained of these two passages. He stated
in his innuendo that they meant "that he was a man whose
physical appearance rendered him wholly unsuitable to take the
part, whose lack of ability as an actor was such that he could only
make impotent gestures, whose declamation was unsteady, and
who was wholly unfit to be engaged to take such or any similar
part." *The Times* naturally pleaded fair comment. The case was
tried in a day before Mr. Justice Swift and a special jury. F. H.
Lawton appeared for Captain Reavely; Sir William Jowitt, K.C.
(now Lord Jowitt), Valentine Holmes (now Sir Valentine Holmes,
Q.C.), and John Senter (now Q.C.) for *The Times*.

Captain Reavely's strongest objection was to the reference to his "physical appearance". When he entered the witness-box he pointed out that the clothes which he wore as Ahab were so magnificent that anyone would look wonderful in them. He generally played parts of a virile and dramatic character, he said. His counsel in opening the case, while conceding the right of *The Times* critic to dislike a performance and say so, denied that he was entitled to belittle an actor by insulting references to his "physical appearance". It occurred at once to the Judge that the critic might only have been referring to the fact that Ahab was present on the stage for so long a time without any more lines to sing, and when he suggested this, counsel agreed it would not have been so bad if *The Times* had said "presence" instead of "physical appearance", but added that his Lordship probably had a charitable mind. "I believe that everybody who reads *The Times* has a charitable mind," retorted Mr. Justice Swift.

During the cross-examination of Captain Reavely by Sir William Jowitt it began to appear that this production of *Elijah* had been a somewhat Philistine achievement. Yes, *Elijah* was an oratorio which Mendelssohn himself used to conduct in this country. The *Oxford Dictionary* defined an oratorio as "a form of extended musical composition, of a semi-dramatic character, usually founded on a Scriptural theme, sung by solo voices and a chorus, to the accompaniment of a full orchestra, without the assistance of action, scenery or dress." Captain Reavely accepted that as a fair definition, and agreed that one school of musical thought might hold that a dramatic representation of an oratorio spoiled the music. He agreed also that this production of *Elijah* involved an alteration of the order of Mendelssohn's music, the introduction of two ballets and the putting of some new words in Elijah's mouth. "There is a reference," remarked Sir William Jowitt acidly, "to a theological college founded by Elijah on the banks of the Jordan. There is nothing in the Bible about that."

Captain Reavely was questioned about the stage effects. "One of the things in the oratorio and the Bible is: 'Behold, there is a sound of an abundance of rain.' I suppose you had someone splashing water about to give that effect?" The answer was that a strip of film sound track had been used.

"In the oratorio the chorus simply records the fact that fire came down. I suppose in the pageant there was some kind of firework?" A stage chariot had in fact been designed to take Elijah to heaven, but was afterwards discarded.

Such questions as these prepared the way for the admission that there might be "some old-fashioned people" who found their imagination more stimulated by the simple words and music than by mechanical sound effects.

Captain Reavely agreed that in a spectacular representation of the oratorio Ahab was bound to be a central figure. He was wearing a magnificent head-dress. Yes, he knew the expression, "All dressed up and nowhere to go." Ahab was all dressed up. What did he do all the time he was on the stage? He had to act. Did not Elijah make severe comments about Ahab, and all Ahab could do was to listen in silence to what Elijah had to say? All the more reason for dramatic art. But Ahab could only make gestures of annoyance? Yes, but they were not impotent—he could influence Queen Jezebel and the crowd by signs. Anyone, said Captain Reavely, reading the article in *The Times* would consider him wholly inadequate both physically and histrionically.

Immediately after his remark about Ahab's gestures *The Times* critic had written: "Nor is it possible to be consistently realistic, and we have a company of angels standing on the floor looking up to Elijah on Mount Horeb, with the chorus of Orientals sitting quietly and unobservantly next to them, waiting to sing 'Holy, Holy, Holy'."

"Do you happen to know," enquired the Judge, "whether any of the angels have brought a libel action?"—"Not so far as I know, my Lord," Captain Reavely replied.

When Captain Reavely had finished his evidence, Sir William Jowitt invited the Judge to say that there was nothing for *The Times* to answer. "I confess," said Mr. Justice Swift, "I cannot see anything," and turning to the jury: "Can you?" The jury could not, and they at once returned a verdict for *The Times*.

VI

THE REPUTATION OF THE DEAD

Rex v. *Hunt* (1824)
Regina v. *Ensor* (1887)
Wright v. *Lord Gladstone* (1927)

"Rest, injur'd shade! Shall Slander squatting near
Spit her cold venom in a dead man's ear?"

—COLERIDGE.

"If the dead are not to be censured, it is only pronouncing
history a libel, and the annals of Britain should grow as
civil things as the sermons at St. James'."

—HORACE WALPOLE.

SHOULD the living be free to write what they like about the dead?
Personal pride and piety alike demand that ancestors—or at any
rate immediate ancestors—should not be exposed to public
scorn. Though a man may boast that his great-great-grandsire
was hanged for stealing sheep, an attack on his father or grandfather is almost an attack on himself, and one to which there is
no defence, except a riposte in kind. Hence no doubt the un-
dignified, but not unknown, spectacle of two otherwise sane
people abusing each other's dead parents.

A natural scruple respects the old tag *De mortuis nil nisi bonum*,
and civilisations, like individuals, may to some extent be judged
by the respect, or lack of it, in which they hold the memory of
those who have gone before them. All tradition, perhaps, is
based upon respect for the dead.

On the other hand nothing is more in the public interest than
that the truth about people, dead or alive, should be told and
known, especially about people whose influence has been felt on
thought or affairs. A false picture of the past may distort a whole
society, a fact which scarcely needs emphasis to-day.

Here, as in everything else, the law is faced with a conflict of

88

interests, and has to decide within its limited powers where to draw the dividing line. In the result the law of England now frowns ruthlessly upon the slightest libel on the living, but only occasionally takes notice of a libel on the dead. In the eighteenth and early nineteenth centuries the position was rather the other way about. In an age when criticism was generally more out-spoken, in spite of political prosecutions, but tombstones recorded in exorbitant detail the overwhelming virtues of the deceased, there was more sympathy for the view that with death the time for free comment (if it ever existed) had ended, and not, as to-day, just begun.

Witness the prosecution of John Hunt in 1824 for a libel on King George III. George III died in 1820, after sixty years on the throne and ten years of blindness and insanity, and his death was followed, amongst other things, by a commemorative poem called "A Vision of Judgment", written by Southey, the Poet Laureate. This poem was a fulsome panegyric in the style of contemporary monumental masonry. It described the passage of the lunatic king into heaven—after a friendly chat with Washington and an appearance before the Father of Lies, who found nothing against him. It was the kind of poem expected of the Poet Laureate on such an occasion, and had only one peculiarity: it was written in "hobbling hexameters", as for example:

> "O'er the adamantine gates an Angel stood at the summit.
> Ho! he exclaimed! King George of England cometh to
>   judgment. . . !
> Oh what a change was wrought! For now the corruptible
>   put on
> Incorruption; the mortal put off mortality. Rising
> Rejuvenescent he stood in a glorified body, obnoxious
> Never again to change, nor to evil and trouble and sorrow,
> But for eternity form'd, and to bliss everlasting appointed."

Byron was as much disgusted with the sentiments of this work as with the metre in which they were expressed, and proceeded to make fun of both in a poem of his own which he similarly called "The Vision of Judgment" and wrote under the name of

"Quevedo Redivivus". But no one was deceived or intended to be deceived about the identity of the author—the preface to Southey's poem contained an attack on Byron, a compliment which Byron now returned. There was much ill-feeling between these two poets, since Southey had once been, what Byron remained to the end, a revolutionary liberal, but had changed his opinions and now supported the established order. Byron in *his* "Vision of Judgment" followed the story of Southey's poem, but introduced Southey himself into it. While George III is undergoing the formalities for a visa to paradise, Southey is carried by a devil to the gates of heaven, where he is obliged to give a satirical account of his life and begin a recital of *his* "Vision of Judgment", with startling results:

> "Those grand heroics acted as a spell:
>   The angels stopped their ears and plied their pinions;
>   The devils ran howling, deafen'd, down to Hell;
>   The ghosts fled, gibbering, for their own dominions—
> (For 'tis not yet decided where they dwell,
>   And I leave every man to his opinions);
> Michael took refuge in his trump—but, lo!
>   His teeth were set on edge, he could not blow!
> Saint Peter, who has hitherto been known
>   For an impetuous saint, upraised his keys
> And at the fifth line knocked the poet down;
>   Who fell like Phaeton, but more at ease,
> Into his lake . . ." (Such was Byron's judgment on a Lake Poet!)
>   "All I saw farther, in the last confusion,
>   Was that King George slipp'd into heaven for one;
>   And when the tumult dwindled to a calm,
> I left him practising the hundredth psalm."

Byron's burlesque appeared in an ill-fated quarterly called *The Liberal*. Byron was living at the time in a large villa at Pisa and had installed Leigh Hunt on the ground floor as editor of the new magazine. It was intended that Shelley and the rest of the coterie of exiled liberals should also contribute poems and articles. But

Shelley was drowned very shortly afterwards, and Byron fell out with Leigh Hunt, who had brought his wife and seven children with him, all of whom Byron soon detested. *The Liberal* lasted for four quarterly numbers only. But these were published in London by Leigh Hunt's brother John, and so it came about that there was within the jurisdiction of the English Courts only one person responsible for the publication of "A Vision of Judgment", and John Hunt stood in the dock alone.

As a matter of fact John and Leigh Hunt owed their friendship with Byron to a previous prosecution for criminal libel. They were joint editors of *The Examiner*, and in one number they presumed to refer to the Prince Regent as "a fat Adonis of fifty". The consequence was a sentence of two years for each of them—in separate prisons. While John Hunt passed an uneventful term in Ilchester, Leigh Hunt in the Surrey Gaol decorated his cell with a trellis of roses, the ceiling being painted with blue sky and clouds and the window fitted with Venetian blinds. In this penitential arbour he received visits from Byron and other friends of liberty, and continued to edit *The Examiner*.

It could hardly have been expected, even in those days of sensitive government, that Byron's "Vision of Judgment" should find its way into the Court of King's Bench. Though it contained some strictures on the late King's reign, it was obviously a harmless lampoon. Indeed the Law Officers of the Crown (whose especial duty it was to prosecute any offence against the Sovereign) did not see fit to take notice of it. But there existed a society, called *The Constitutional Association*, which was more concerned about the dignity and reverence due to kings, even dead kings, than the king himself, and, since under English law any private person may prosecute another, the secretary of this Association prosecuted John Hunt.

The indictment was a formidable document, and must have taken a tedious half-hour for the Clerk of the Court to read. There were ten counts, each setting out a different verse of Byron's offending poem, and each woven in the same weighted tissue of words. In the first count it was said with some prolixity that John Hunt "being a person of a wicked and malicious disposition and wickedly and maliciously contriving to injure defame disgrace and vilify the memory and reputation of his late Majesty George the Third the Father of our Sovereign Lord the now King and of divers other the descendants of his said late Majesty members of the Royal Family of this Realm and also contriving and intending to cause it to be believed that his said late Majesty was a bad King guilty of misrule and a protector of tyrants and that his death was unlamented and unregretted even by those who attended his burial and thereby to disturb and disquiet the minds and destroy the comfort and happiness of our said Lord the now King and other the said descendants and to bring them into public scandal infamy disgrace and contempt with and amongst all the subjects of this Realm . . . with force and arms falsely wickedly maliciously and unlawfully did print and publish and cause to be printed and published in a certain printed book called 'The Liberal' certain false scandalous malicious and defamatory libel of and concerning his said late Majesty and also of and concerning his reign death and burial containing therein amongst other things the following false scandalous malicious and defamatory matter of and concerning his said late Majesty and also of and concerning his reign death and burial (that is to say)

'In the first year of freedom's second dawn
  Died George the Third (meaning his said late Majesty); although no tyrant, one
Who (meaning his said late Majesty) shielded tyrants, till each sense withdrawn
  Left him (meaning his said late Majesty) nor mental nor external sun.
A better farmer ne'er brushed dew from lawn.
  A worse king (meaning a worse king than his said late Majesty) never left a realm undone!
He (meaning his said late Majesty) died, but left his (meaning his said late Majesty's) subjects still behind.
  One half as mad—and t'other no less blind.
He (meaning his said late Majesty) died, his (meaning his said late Majesty's) death made no great stir on earth:
  His (meaning his said late Majesty's) burial made some pomp; there was profusion

> Of velvet, gilding, brass, and no great dearth
>   Of aught but tears—save those (meaning those tears) shed
>   by collusion.'

. . . To the great disgrace and scandal of the memory reputation
and character of his said late Majesty. To the great disquietude
and disgrace of our said Lord the now King and his laws. To the
evil example of all others in the like case offending and against the
peace of our said Lord the now king his Crown and dignity."

When the reading of the indictment was completed, prosecuting counsel rose to open his case. Solemn subjects must be
treated solemnly, was his theme. As there might be a danger of
the jury regarding the whole thing as trivial, the jury must be
shocked. "The author represented himself to be at the gates of
heaven," counsel complained, "and the transactions which he
pretended to have witnessed there he described with a degree of
levity and of impiety which was really astonishing. He fancied
himself almost in the presence of his Creator and he assumed a
tone fit only for a pot-house revel, which would certainly disgrace
the company of any gentleman. Such a publication, with honest
freeborn Englishmen, who, whatever might be their difference
of opinion on particular subjects, retained a reverence for Christian
worship, a solemn belief in eternity, and a solemn awe of the
sacred presence of the Creator—such a publication, so full of
ridicule, of levity and of impiety must ever stand condemned."
The case was accordingly treated with the utmost seriousness,
and no levity was allowed to mar the proceedings, not even
when the officer from Bow Street, called to prove the publication
of the poem, was asked, "Do you know what an hexameter
means?" and replied in all seriousness, "Why, you are hexamin-
ing me."

James Scarlett, the leading advocate of the day (later Lord
Abinger), represented John Hunt. He called no witnesses, but
made a long speech, pouring scorn on the prosecution as a squalid
endeavour to stifle the poetic license. More than that, he claimed
a constitutional right to say what one pleases of dead kings, and
himself gave an unflattering description of George III's reign,
justifying Byron's flippancies as historical comment. "I deny in

the strongest manner that it is a crime in any man to intend to
have it believed that a deceased king was a bad king, was guilty
of misrule, or was a protector of tyrants! If this be a libel, then
to say anything of the grandfather or ancestor of the King is a
libel. Gentlemen, his present Majesty is descended from Richard
III. We all know that Shakespeare had described Richard as a
tyrant and a murderer. Is this to be considered a libel?" As for the
charge that no one wept at the funeral, "Was a more absurd
indictment ever put upon the files of the Court . . . ? I remember that when Ministers were summoned to attend his funeral,
the universal opinion was that they would not continue in office
four-and-twenty hours. If that was their opinion also, I have no
doubt they set off with heavy hearts—that they considered the
event truly melancholy." Scarlett threw in a legal argument for
good measure. There could be no conviction in English law for
criminal libel, he argued, unless the writing tended to provoke a
breach of the king's peace. But as it was unthinkable that the king
would break his own peace, no one could be convicted of a libel
on the king, dead or alive!

But eloquence was in vain. · Chief Justice Abbott asked the jury
to decide whether the publication was "defamatory of his late
Majesty and calculated to disquiet the mind of his present Majesty,
and to bring his descendants into disgrace, contempt and scandal,"
and the jury returned a verdict of guilty.

What does "calculated" mean? The word occurs also in
many Acts of Parliament. Is a man guilty because he actually
intended the consequences of his act, or merely when the consequences are its natural result, though he may neither have intended nor foreseen them? Guilt or innocence of many a crime
turns upon this question, and sometimes it has been anwsered in
one way, sometimes the other. Scarlett took the point in 1824.
Before sentence was passed, he appealed to the full Court of
King's Bench for a new trial on the ground that the Chief Justice
had misdirected the jury in his summing-up, by not instructing
them that the prosecution must prove an actual, and not merely a
"constructive", intention to provoke the King. The Court
rejected the plea, and, although John Hunt swore in an affidavit
that neither he nor the author had the slightest intention of

wounding the feelings of his present Majesty and that the sole
design was to ridicule Southey's poem, the Court fined him £100
and ordered him to enter into sureties to be of good behaviour
for five years in a total of £2,000 and to be "imprisoned in the
custody of the Marshal of the Marshalsea till such fine be paid and
such securities given". John Hunt and his friends were able to
pay the fine and give the securities, and so he avoided the exactions
of that notorious prison. The trial had been held in January, but
the sentence was not delivered until June. Between those two
dates Byron had died in Greece and his body had been brought
back and buried in an English parish church.

But Scarlett had been right. Past authority supported him and
future authority was to agree with him. In 1887 a prosecution
for criminal libel on a dead man came before the great criminal
judge, Stephen, at the Cardiff Assizes. A popular, if impecunious,
local merchant had died, and his friends proposed to put up a
public statue in his honour. The statue was duly erected, but not
before a solicitor of the town had, in the local Press, suggested
the following epitaph for it:

"In honour of John Batchelor, a native of Newport, who in
early life left his country for his country's good; who on his
return devoted his life and energies to setting class against class,
a traitor to the Crown, a reviler of the aristocracy, a hater of the
clergy, a panderer to the multitude; who, as first Chairman of the
Cardiff School Board, squandered funds to which he did not
contribute; who is sincerely mourned by unpaid creditors to the
amount of £50,000; who at the close of a wasted and misspent life
died a pauper, this monument, to the eternal disgrace of Cardiff,
is erected by sympathetic Radicals.

Owe no man anything."

Here was the perfect test case. Nothing could have been more
likely to provoke that quaintly-worded outbreak known as "a
breach of the peace", since its appearance in the *Western Mail* had
in fact led to a direct and personal assault upon the author by the
outraged relatives, who then proceeded to prosecute him. Nevertheless Stephen directed an acquittal. "There must be a vilifying

of the deceased with a view to injure his posterity," he declared. "The dead have no rights and can suffer no wrongs. The living alone can be the subject of legal protection, and the law of libel is intended to protect them. . . . It is sometimes said that, as a man must be held to intend the natural consequences of his acts, and as the natural consequence of the censure of a dead man is to exasperate his living friends and reations and so to cause breaches of the peace, attacks on the dead must be punishable as libels, because they tend to a breach of the peace whether they are or are not intended as an indirect way of reflecting on the living . . . but the intent to injure the family is a fact requiring proof and necessary to be found by the jury, and not an inference . . . from the terms of the writing reflecting on the dead man. I am reluctant in the highest degree to extend the criminal law. To speak broadly, to libel the dead is not an offence known to our law."

If this is broadly true of the criminal law, it is wholly true of the civil law, and no one can sue or be sued for damages for impeaching the fair name of the dead. Libel deals with the settling of personal accounts between the living. But an affronted son may still have his remedy: he may challenge and provoke his father's enemy to the ordeal by trial. In the nineteen-twenties the second Lord Gladstone showed the way by his most vigorous vindication of his father.

A Captain Peter Wright, old Harrovian and Balliol man and during the 1914–18 War secretary and interpreter on the Supreme War Council, had published a book of essays. One chapter of this book contained a thumb-nail sketch of the Conservative statesman, Lord Salisbury. "To high literary powers he joined an acute scientific intellect," wrote Peter Wright. "His fastidious spirit was still further repelled by Liberalism, either in its members who worshipped God and Mammon with equal zeal, assigning to Mammon the inward service and leaving God to content Himself with the outward professions, or in its leader, Gladstone, who founded the great tradition since observed by many of his followers and successors with such pious fidelity, in public to speak the language of the highest and strictest principle, and in private to pursue and possess every sort of woman."

In a review of Peter Wright's book in *The Nation* the question was asked how a reputable publishing house could allow such a gross statement about Mr. Gladstone to appear. Peter Wright replied: "I referred to Gladstone's pursuit of women in his own level of life, and I had the best of reasons for so doing. Lord Milner, who was a young and active politician forty-five years ago told me that Mr. Gladstone was governed by his seraglio."

By this time Lord Gladstone and his brother had seen the book, and they wrote the following letter:

"*Mr. Peter Wright,*

Your garbage about Mr. Gladstone in 'Portraits and Criticisms' has come to our knowledge. You are a liar. Because you slander a dead man, you are a coward. Because you think the public will accept invention from such as you, you are a fool.

GLADSTONE.

I associate myself with this letter.

H. N. GLADSTONE."

Lord Gladstone (unknown at the time to Peter Wright) sent copies of this letter to *The Nation* and to Peter Wright's publishers. Peter Wright himself sent a copy to the *Daily Mail*, together with his reply:

"*My Lord,—I am in receipt of your Lordship's outburst dated July 22nd.*

I attributed to Mr. Gladstone the character of a hypocrite in matters of sex. I have evidence of his conduct as good as any that exists about events in the past. I wrote what I did write on the authority of the late Lord Milner. (Again he quoted Lord Milner's expression.) *This foible had considerable political effects. One affair turned Mr. Gladstone from being a friend of Turkey and an enemy of Russia, as he was in the 'fifties, into being a friend of Russia and an enemy of Turkey, as he was in the 'eighties.*

Mr. Gladstone's hypocritical character (which in no way detracts from his merits as a public financier) is the common, though it may not be the official, reputation of him that has descended to us. It was crystallized in Labouchère's famous epigram, 'that Gladstone might be caught playing cards with a fifth ace up his sleeve: but he would only explain that God had put it there.' This contemporary reputation is strikingly confirmed by the circumstances of the Parnell case as we now know them. Gladstone not only connived at Parnell's illicit relations with Mrs. O'Shea: but utilised them for his own political purposes. Parnell's sin was Gladstone's opportunity. As soon as the misconduct was made known and public in divorce proceedings, Gladstone was foremost in denouncing its immorality.

This hypocrisy in the case of another is more heinous than any hypocrisy in the case of himself. Strong temptations might excuse his own departure from his own avowed principles: no such excuse can be found in the case of another. Knowing he could commit the greater offence I do not find it difficult to believe he could commit the lesser.

These various considerations prompted the remarks about Mr. Gladstone at which you take offence. Thus based, my views are unshaken even by the impact of your Lordship's controversial language, which, if I may say so without impoliteness, must rather have been acquired by practice in your Lordship's pantry than by the exercise of your Lordship's talents for debate in the House of Lords.

PETER E. WRIGHT.

The Bath Club, Dover Street, W."

Lord Gladstone now carried his offensive into the Bath Club, on whose notepaper Peter Wright's letters had been written. He sent two letters to the Secretary:

"Dear Wilson Taylor,

Mr. Peter Wright appears to be a member of the Bath Club. In a book he made a foul charge against my father. He elaborated this in a letter to The Nation. . . . *He wrote on Bath Club notepaper.*

My brother and I wrote and told him that he was a liar and a coward, the law, in the case of a dead man, giving no remedy.

In a letter published this morning by the Daily Mail *he amplified his slander and his lies, not daring apparently to face us in Court. Again he writes on Bath Club notepaper. It seems to me that this is a matter for the Committee.*

Sincerely yours,

GLADSTONE.

I have this moment received a letter from Messrs. E. Nash and Grayson, Mr. Peter Wright's publishers, to say that when they accepted the work it did not contain the passage to which we take exception. Otherwise 'we should have declined to publish them'.

It appears they were put into a proof and when it went back to the printer the publisher did not observe them.

This shows the sort of man he is. I can tell you more about him—he is a foul fellow."

"My dear Wilson Taylor,

Many thanks for your letter. Of course, I do not wish to take part personally in any discussion or action of the committee with reference to P. W. I wrote to you because I was so indignant that the fellow was sheltering in my old Club, which, for my brother, myself and my wife becomes uninhabitable so long as it is polluted by his presence.

As an 'officer' in His Majesty's Army, he has accepted the description of a liar and a coward. By his baseless attacks on my father he has wantonly and deliberately insulted the fellow members of his club."

As a result of these letters Peter Wright was illegally expelled from the Bath Club—illegally because the Committee did not give him a hearing before reaching their decision—and for this wrong he obtained an injunction and £125 damages against the Club. The first of these two letters he made the subject of a libel action against Lord Gladstone. The action came on before Mr. Justice Avory and a special jury in January and February, 1927. Boyd Merriman, K.C., (now Lord Merriman) appeared for Peter Wright and Lord Gladstone was represented by Norman Birkett, K.C. (now Lord Justice Birkett).

The debunking of the Grand Old Man had shocked the country's memories, and the five days of the trial naturally attracted tremendous interest. It was really a prolonged scrutiny of Peter Wright's integrity as an author. In the witness-box he was obliged to disclose the full extent of his historical research. This was not, he declared, mere gossip, but let the reader judge for himself, as did the jury at the trial.

Peter Wright said that, while he was still at Harrow, he was told by Mr. James Haslam that Lily Langtry had been Gladstone's mistress, and in support of this charge he now produced a cartoon by Phil May headed, "We visit Mrs. Langtry," from a book called *Parson and Painter: Their Wanderings and Excursions among Men and Women*, by the Rev. Joseph Slapkins. This devastating piece of artistic evidence showed a man who closely resembled Mr. Gladstone, standing at a Stage Door and holding a bunch of Mr. Disraeli's favourite primroses.

Then Dr. Greatorex, a physician with a West End practice, had told Peter Wright of complaints by his women patients that Gladstone had tried to make their acquaintance in the street. Moreover as an Oxford undergraduate Peter Wright had heard from Walter Morison of Gladstone's relations with Olga Novikoff.

"Who," asked counsel, "was Olga Novikoff?" Peter Wright replied: "She was a very lovely Russian who was sent over by the Tsarist Government in the 'seventies for the special purpose of fascinating Mr. Gladstone, and she thoroughly succeeded." Lord Malmesbury had told him, Peter Wright explained, that the detectives who guarded Gladstone during the Fenian troubles complained that they were kept till the early hours outside Olga Novikoff's house, and yet were expected to be at early Divine Service.

But this was by no means all. A friend in Paris had told Peter Wright that a French actress called Brassine had had an intrigue with Gladstone, and Charlie Thomson, a well-known amateur steeplechaser, had mentioned that Mr. Gladstone had once tried to make advances to a lady whom he had left for a moment outside a shop.

Then there was Laura Bell, "the most famous courtesan of the nineteenth century," whose name had been connected with an orator and statesman "who was all things to all men and most things to most women". Even Lord Granville, Gladstone's own Foreign Secretary, had said, "I have known five of Queen Victoria's Prime Ministers, all of whom have committed adultery." An inference was also read into contrasting passages in Morley's life of Gladstone and Morgan's life of Morley concerning Gladstone's knowledge of the relations between Parnell and Mrs. O'Shea.

The whole thing was clinched, Peter Wright felt, by what

Lord Milner had told him. "After Lord Milner had used that phrase," Wright said, "I remember asking him about Mr. Gladstone's relations with Olga Novikoff. Lord Milner said nothing, but fell into his ordinary reserve." Here the Judge put a question:

"Were any other words used except 'being governed by his seraglio'?"—"I cannot remember."

"In connection with what matter," Merriman asked, "did Lord Milner use the phrase?"—"The change of relations between England and Turkey."

Apart from these reports from highly varied sources, Peter Wright relied in one instance upon the evidence of his own eyes, perhaps the most deadly piece of direct evidence with which a party has ever destroyed his own case.

"About fourteen years ago," he said, "I saw at Eastbourne a man named Cecil Gladstone whose resemblance to the statesman was unmistakable. I was told he was an illegitimate son, but I cannot identify my informant."

"Of what kind was the resemblance?" his counsel asked. —"Facial. I should say that he was a larger and inferior edition of Mr. Gladstone."

"Was he inferior in point of intellect?" asked Avory.—"He had not the distinguished air of the statesman."

This was the sum of Peter Wright's inside information. It was Norman Birkett's task to show, if he could, that the witness had been dishonestly indifferent to the truth or falsity of his charge against Gladstone. In a cross-examination which persisted into three days, he was able, not only to go far towards this objective, but also to make the forty-six-year-old Captain appear—by comparison with the Gladstone brothers, who were both in their seventies—both offensive and ridiculous.

"Do you regard yourself," was Birkett's first question, "as a serious journalist?"—"I try not to be dull."

"Does that mean that all serious people are bores?" snapped the Judge, and Birkett changed the adjective. "Do you regard yourself as a responsible journalist?"—"Certainly. The newspapers treat me as one, and I conclude that I am one. I speak the truth."

"Do you agree that the charge you make is about as horrible a charge as can be made?"—"No, because it has been made against innumerable great men."

"Is it a charge that Mr. Gladstone was a gross sensualist?"— "Yes, I think that that describes him."

"Is not a charge that a man is a gross sensualist one of the most horrible charges that can be made against him?"—"No, because it has been made against innumerable great men."

"Is it not a charge which reflects on all the women who honoured Gladstone with their friendship?"—"No, certainly not. He might behave very well at Carlton Gardens, but not elsewhere."

"Do you agree that it is a very grave charge of hypocrisy?"— "Oh, yes. That is what this charge is. It is much more a charge of hypocrisy than one of immorality."

"His religion, you intended to say, was a mockery?"—"No, Gladstone was not like ordinary people."

"Does it not mean that he was the rankest kind of hypocrite?" —"Yes, but, being a wonderful sort of man, he was a wonderful sort of hypocrite."

"Does it not follow from that that his professed religion was a simple mockery?"—"No, because he was such an actor and he threw himself so entirely into the part that he became it." One could not say, the Captain added, that Mr. Gladstone disbelieved what he said, and yet he acted in a way which was a complete contradiction of what he had said.

Birkett read the passage in Lord Rosebery's panegyric on Gladstone which referred to Mrs. Gladstone as having "for sixty years shared all the sorrows and all the joys of Mr. Gladstone's life, received his confidence, shared his triumphs, and cheered him in his defeats."

"Is this charge of yours that Mr. Gladstone was faithless to that wife of sixty years?"—"Yes, of course it is. Men who are very fond of their wives are often faithless to them."

"Do you regard immorality in a man as an ordinary thing?"— "No. I regard it as culpable."

"But not horrible?"—"No." The Captain agreed, however, that his charge, if made falsely, was a foul charge, though a person who made it falsely was not necessarily a "foul fellow". That, he said, was Lord Gladstone's bad English; "foul fellow" meant a dissolute person.

"If a person made a foul charge against you or your dead father what would you call him in your beautiful English?" —"I should call him intemperate." But Peter Wright admitted that a man who made a false charge without evidence, or without caring whether it was true or not, would be a liar.

Birkett continued to lay the foundations of his attack.

"Do you agree that a great degree of care is required in writing about the living when you are making serious charges?"— "Care to speak the truth? Yes, certainly."

"Do you agree that in the case of the dead who cannot speak for themselves a greater degree of care is required?"—"I think that the same degree of care is required for both."

"When a writer makes a serious charge against a dead man, would you regard that as a responsible task?"—"A serious writer ought to regard all he writes as a responsible task."

"A responsible journalist would regard it as his duty to verify the facts before making a serious charge against anybody?" —"Not if he thought that he knew them: otherwise he could never write anything."

"He might proceed upon information given to him without verifying a single thing if he had formed a decided opinion?" —"In this case my charge against Gladstone is one primarily of hypocrisy. If a man has formed that opinion, and the reason is there, why should he go through some process of verification? It would paralyse him."

The debonair self-assurance of some of these replies had made its impression on the Court. Birkett then began to investigate Peter Wright's sources. With regard to Lord Milner's phrase about Gladstone's "seraglio", Peter Wright alluded to T. P. O'Connor's obituary notice of Lord Milner for confirmation that Milner had used the expression. But what T. P. O'Connor wrote, referring to Milner as a young man, was this: "If Gladstone were mentioned—Gladstone was then in the zenith of the blind worship which he received from so many millions of his fellow citizens—the tall young scholar, straight apparently from the college hall, would answer with a laugh that you could not tell what Gladstone was going to do till you knew what the seraglio had decided: it was by this disrespectful word, said with a laugh, that the daring and sceptical youngster spoke of the devoted wife and daughter who looked after the domestic comforts of the great liberal leader."

But when this passage was read to him, Peter Wright remained unconvinced. "In the mouth of a man like Lord Milner, who was a great literary artist even when he was a young man," he said, " 'seraglio' could not mean wife and daughter." Even when he had read, at Birkett's request, a passage from the *Life of Dr. Johnson*, in which Boswell says, "We surely cannot but admire the benevolent exertions of this great and good man. . . . He has sometimes suffered me to talk jocularly of his group of females and call them his 'seraglio' "—even then Peter Wright was sure that, while Boswell might jest, Lord Milner would not.

"A literary artist might use the word jocularly?"—"Yes, but Lord Milner was not a jester, although he was sometimes ironical and sarcastic. At the end of his life he had not the wonderful style he had as a young man, but he spoke very precise English."

Birkett turned his attention to the little matter of Gladstone's putative bastard observed by Peter Wright in Eastbourne.

"Did you make any enquires about Cecil Gladstone?" he asked.—"I did not deliberately make enquiries. I should never write anything if I did."

"You believed what you heard and acted upon it?"—"I did."

Counsel handed up to the witness a birth and a marriage certificate, each stating that Cecil Gladstone was the son of William Gladstone, general merchant. Peter Wright now fell into the trap which Birkett set for him.

"So those two documents would appear to show the birth of Cecil Gladstone?" he was asked. "Yes, to William Gladstone."

"You want to emphasise the 'William' to the jury?"—"Yes: they both have the same Christian name and surname."

"You mean that William Ewart Gladstone was also a William?" —"Yes."

"The certificates would appear to show that Cecil Gladstone was the son of William Gladstone, a merchant?"—"A general merchant, yes, a very large category of people."

"Do you think that a Prime Minister is covered by that description?"—"I don't know that it does not. You are trying to show that Cecil Gladstone cannot be the son of the statesman, but I am not certain whether your proof is quite conclusive."

Cecil Gladstone's death certificate was next produced.

"Is the widow alive?"—"I don't know."

"Do you know whether she lives in Eastbourne now?"—"I do not."

"You have never made an enquiry about it?"—"No: I was only showing the process of thought by which I arrived at my conclusion."

"About what you were told by people whom you do not remember?"—"Whom I do not identify."

"Your words yesterday were 'Persons I cannot remember'," snapped Mr. Justice Avory, and Birkett went remorselessly on:

"You never from that day made any enquiry?"—"Certainly not."

"Do these documents influence your judgment at all?"— "They don't seem to be quite so very conclusive on your side, because, if Gladstone had an illegitimate son, this is rather the way in which he would deal with it. It does not seem completely to refute my view."

"In your view these documents are forgeries reeking with false information?"—"They might be."

"Given by a Prime Minister of this country?"—"If he had an illegitimate son; but he was not Prime Minister at the time."

"You think the certificates are full of false information?"— "Yes, by a Cabinet Minister who did not dare speak the truth."

Birkett now held up *Lodge's Peerage*, wherein it was disclosed that Cecil Gladstone's father William was Gladstone's first cousin, a fact which might not unnaturally account for the facial likeness. Wright was obliged to withdraw his accusation. Then came the inevitable question:

"Don't you think that you should be more careful before you make suggestions?"

Birkett, having made the killing as painful and protracted as possible, then held a *post mortem* on the incident. "When you saw the birth certificate, did it not seem to you that it was not usual for an illegitimate son to be registered in the name of his father?"—"It did not: but if a child were the illegitimate son of a statesman it would not be registered in his name."

"When I asked you whether a Cabinet Minister would be likely to be guilty of forgery and lying, your suggestion still was that Gladstone might have had something to do with it?"—"No, you were trying to suggest that because a man was a Cabinet Minister he could not speak an untruth, and I thought that that was a forensic trick."

"You now agree that the information on which you acted was quite unreliable?"—"Yes, but I thought I was right at the time."

Birkett next disposed of the French actress, Brassine, in a few short questions—all of which he then put into one omnibus question: "Apart from the fact that a man, now dead, told you as a lad of twenty that an actress twenty years before had an intrigue in London with Gladstone when he was seventy-two, you made no further enquiries?"—"No: why should I?"

After some further questions, Birkett said,

"Lord Milner is dead, Haslam is dead, Dr. Greatorex is dead, Morison is dead, Novikoff is dead, Laura Bell is dead, Sir Francis Burnand is dead, Labouchère is dead, and Lord Morley is dead?"—"Yes: and Gladstone was born six years before the battle of Waterloo."

"It is difficult when people are dead to get at the exact facts?"—"Nearly every character in history is dead; I don't know whether you have observed that, Mr. Birkett."

"Where is Charlie Thomson? Is he alive?"—"I don't know."

"Mrs. Langtry is alive, is she not?"—"Yes, she lives on the Riviera."

"Did you think that the charge you made might cause her grievous pain?"—"Yes, I am afraid it would; it is most annoying to think that I might cause grief to a living person. I am very sorry about it; more than I can say."

"Did you ever speak to Mrs. Langtry in your life?"—"No. I have seen her, of course."

On the next morning of the trial Birkett read a telegram which had been sent to him personally from Monte Carlo: "Strongly repudiate slanderous accusations by Peter Wright.

Lily Langtry." Peter Wright's counsel allowed this message to be put in as evidence, a gesture which was tantamount to dropping this charge also.

But Peter Wright would not yet admit defeat. When Birkett, turning to Madame Novikoff, said that he had all her correspondence with Gladstone in Court, and asked Peter Wright:

"Are you prepared to accept that in not one of those letters is there the faintest hint of impropriety?"—the reply was, "I should be perfectly certain of it where Gladstone was concerned."

"May I take it that had you known every word of the correspondence between Madame Novikoff and Mr. Gladstone it would not have made any difference to what you said?"— "No, because the very charge I made was one of hypocrisy."

"Do you know that physically she was most unattractive?"— "I certainly do not. I always heard the very opposite." (Later Merriman countered this suggestion by producing two photographs. The Judge said, "Can I take judicial notice of when a woman is seductive?" to which Merriman replied, "Your Lordship can take judicial notice of whether Mr. Birkett's question was well founded.")

Lord Gladstone had actually known Madame Novikoff and would be able to tell the Court about her, but Peter Wright dismissed his evidence in advance by calling him "the arch-humbug". And even if Lord Gladstone swore that his father knew nothing of the relationship between Parnell and Mrs. O'Shea, it would only be "a typical instance of Gladstonian humbug".

When the time came for Laura Bell to be discussed, Birkett produced another certificate—her marriage to Mr. Thistlethwaite, and asked, "Did you know that she had lived with her husband till his death?"—"He shot himself, poor chap," was the answer.

"Did you know that at the inquest his death was stated to be
accidental?"—"No, but it makes no difference to my opinion."

"Did you know she was a very religious woman when she
met Gladstone?"—"She combined preaching with being a
courtesan, which was one of the most remarkable things
about her," the witness responded, adding that Gladstone
had taught her the preaching.

Gradually Birkett wore his agile opponent down. He attacked
his motives.

"The offending sentence about Lord Gladstone is not essential
to your article on Lord Robert Cecil and the League of
Nations?"—"Digression is one of the arts of essay writing.
This is an essay, not an affidavit."

"It appears to be as unreliable," growled the Judge.

"Do you think it would be a cowardly thing to slander the
dead?"—"All history, as someone has said, is a register of
crimes and follies, and so nearly all history is a slander of
dead men. All history cannot be abolished for the benefit of
Mr. Gladstone."

"That," said the Judge, "is not an answer to the question. Is
your answer No?"

The answer was that it was not cowardly if the slanderer was
writing as a historian.

"You do not suggest that you were writing this essay in the
role of a historian?" Birkett asked, and he had really returned
to his first question of all.

But the cross-examination was not over. It was suggested that
Wright was a coward, not only for slandering the dead, but also
because of his reluctance to bring this action. This he denied.
Every libel must be "published", and before any action for
damages can be brought, the libeller must publish it to some one
other than the libellee. Peter Wright's explanation was that he
did not know Lord Gladstone's first letter had been published to
a third party until after he had published it himself by sending it

to the *Daily Mail* together with his reply—a step which naturally deprived him of any right to claim damages for it in a libel action. Some doubt was thrown on the genuineness of this explanation by a sentence which he had written in a letter to Lord Gladstone —"Weak and dull as my poor weapon of controversy is . . . I disdain to lift its point against so unworthy a descendant of so mighty a sire." This matter, however, was perhaps an unworthy one to be raised against the plaintiff. For when Lord Gladstone repeated his charges in his letter to the Bath Club and in the course of time Peter Wright issued his writ, Lord Gladstone pleaded, not only that his charges were true, but also, whether they were true or not, that they were published "on a privileged occasion" and therefore not actionable except upon proof of malice.

> Lord Gladstone, however, when giving his evidence, said that this defence was put in without his instructions. When asked whether he wished to stand by it (a question which Avory ruled out of order) he declared, "I wish that the case should be decided in its broad public aspect—to determine whether Captain Wright was justified in what he said and whether I was justified in using the words which I did in denouncing it."
> "Proceedings might have been taken on the first letter," the Judge muttered, "when no question of privilege would have arisen."
> "Does your Lordship seriously suggest that?" asked Merriman.
> "I never suggest anything in a Court of Law unless I suggest seriously," was Avory's testy answer. And Merriman was left to say, "Your Lordship has given an answer which the witness should have given. I cannot cross-examine your Lordship, and so I will leave it."

> Birkett now drew Peter Wright's attention to Gladstone's work for the rescue of women from the streets as a possible explanation of the many rumours which had been circu-

lated. In 1848 Gladstone had been one of the founders of the
Church Penitentiary Association for the Reclamation of
Fallen Women, and had contributed throughout his life to
this and similar charities. "If," asked Birkett, "a man spends
his time sincerely employed in the work of reclaiming fallen
women, so that he speaks to them in the street and visits
them in their homes, do you think that that is liable to mis-
conception?"—"There is," Wright replied, "a genuine
difficulty in the way of my answering that, and I cannot
do so."

Peter Wright felt very strongly about the terms of Lord Gladstone's letter to the Club. "Lord Gladstone first made a
charge of mendacity and then one of cowardice," he exclaimed, "Then he thought that that was not quite hot
enough to get me expelled from the Club, so he added a
charge of trickery, and thinking that that was not strong
enough he called me a foul fellow."

Birkett: "Did you think that he would write with indignation?"
—"Yes, but when one writes with indignation one should
take care to write the exact truth."

"When you are writing, with or without indignation, about a
charge which defames the memory of a great man you
should write with great care?"—"Not when you write a
book with a paltry circulation of 500 copies. A single
sentence in an obscure and unsuccessful book would not
have the serious result of a letter sent for the purpose of
getting a man expelled from a Club."

"Did you," asked Mr. Justice Avory, "expect your book to
be obscure and unsuccessful?"—"I did not expect it to have
any great success," was Peter Wright's answer, "I spoke of
Gladstone as a historical figure, as I would have done of
Wellington or Napoleon." He had no intention, he said, of
hurting Gladstone's family.

"Does this mean," the Judge asked, "that you now regret

and are sorry for having written this?"—"My Lord, I——"

"Do give me a direct answer to that question. You say that if you had had an opportunity you would have expressed regret. Are you sorry that you wrote it?"—"Yes, my Lord: but it is difficult to express it if Lord Gladstone does not retract the abusive language which he used. I do not regret it because it is untrue, but because it caused pain to his family. I would still express regret if they would retract the statement that I am a liar, a coward, and a fool. I regret that I hurt their feelings."

"Do you think it is any satisfaction to say to a person: I regret that I said what I did, but it is true?"—"I would say that I did not want to hurt their feelings."

"I hope," Merriman intervened, "your Lordship will ask the same question of the defendant."

Birkett continued to press Wright on this point, until the witness became annoyed and finally said, emphasising each word by striking the front of the witness-box: "I regret most emphatically hurting the feelings of Lord Gladstone and his family, and if they had given me anything of a chance I would have said so. I would say it now."

"Don't," said the Judge, "knock the furniture about."

When Peter Wright left the witness-box after ten-and-a-half hours under fire he had already lost the battle. The thing then turned into a rout. Birkett opened the defence with a scathing attack on the plaintiff, and then put the defendant into the witness-box. As Lord Gladstone had been from 1880 a Member both of the House of Commons and of the Government, and had lived with his father until his death in 1898, he was able to speak with personal knowledge of events and personalities which were known to Peter Wright only by hearsay. Lord Gladstone denied every charge absolutely.

There was no doubt that Mr. Justice Avory had taken an unfavourable view of the plaintiff from early in his examination. His questions were all, so to speak, one way.

To Lord Gladstone, however, he was nothing but helpful. Speaking of Labouchère's epigram, Lord Gladstone said, "It was a gibe, and to some extent a very very clever gibe."

Mr. Justice Avory: "Was he a jester?"—"Oh, very much so."

Merriman: "Sometimes the truth is spoken in jest and sometimes it is clothed in jest."

Mr. Justice Avory: "Is not Labouchère famous for having said during a debate in the House of Commons on a proposed new railway in the Lake District, that, in his opinion, no landscape was complete without a railway train in the distance?"

Merriman read to Lord Gladstone an article in *Vanity Fair* which hinted at an intrigue between Gladstone and Madame Novikoff, an article of which no notice had been taken, and asked: "Had not Mr. Gladstone the plainest cause to sue *Vanity Fair* for saying that his public conduct was influenced by his immoral relations with Madame Novikoff?" But the Judge nullified the question by observing: "If that action were tried before me I should have to consider whether the words were capable of any such meaning. The whole article is directed to the suggestion that Mr. Gladstone was improperly negotiating with a Russian agent" (and not carrying on a clandestine love affair). Merriman pressed the matter, and the Judge put in the question which normally would have had to wait for re-examination: "So far as you know, did your father ever see that article?"

When Lord Gladstone was asked what evidence he had for supposing that the Gladstone-Novikoff correspondence was complete, the Judge interrupted, "How can he answer that question?" But he could: anyone looking through the pile, he said, could see there were no gaps. What was more, as his father's private secretary he had opened all his correspondence without restrictions.

But with or without the hostility of the Judge counsel for

Peter Wright had virtually nothing to go on. Apart from the article in *Vanity Fair* and Mrs. O'Shea's assertion that Gladstone was always aware of her relations with Parnell, the most that was established by the cross-examination of Lord Gladstone was that on a number of occasions his father had been called a hypocrite—a charge which few Prime Ministers escape.

Lord Gladstone was supported by his brother, and after their evidence no one wished to dispute their honourable intentions. "We were the only sons living, and as soon as we had gone there would be nobody with our knowledge of the facts. It was our duty to force him into a Court of Law so that we might have justice done to our father."

Lord Phillimore, Lord Malmesbury, Lady Gwendoline Cecil and Mr. T. P. O'Connor also gave evidence. The latter, who had been a Member of the House since 1880, and was an intimate friend of Parnell's, threw light on that interesting period of Irish politics. In his opinion Gladstone neither knew nor thought of the Parnell-O'Shea liaison. Of the relations between Mr. and Mrs. Gladstone he said, that "the extraordinary solicitude with which Mrs. Gladstone watched the comings and goings of her husband was notorious, and there was evidence of it every day in the House of Commons and the Lobby. There was a special corner of the Speaker's Gallery where she was to be seen as inevitably as was Mr. Gladstone in the House whenever he had a great speech to make. Very often she was in the inner lobby waiting to take him home, and she would muffle him up if the weather were bad."

Peter Wright's publisher was called. He swore that he had no knowledge of the offending passage, which was inserted in the galley proofs. Merriman read to him some passages in other books which he had recently published. First of all there was an authoress who called herself "A woman of no importance" who had written:

"We have lately heard a good deal about Lord Beaconsfield's love affairs, but not much of Gladstone's. This is not fair, for he had quite a pretty taste in women—why should he have been less human than the rest of the world. . . ? I could tell some very illuminating stories if so inclined, but will only say that I have seen him indulging in little tender transports of love and rapture. I once accidentally surprised him kissing, quite a harmless little affair, but it impressed itself upon my memory, for she was pretty, soft and round, while he looked like a hungry hawk, with fierce eyes and beak pecking at her. He was a wonderful man, and in his old age distinctly amorous."

Then there was a book called *The Fall of Tsardom*, wherein it was written of Madame Novikoff: "She is well known and had many friends. . . . There was a time when Madame X was a greater power for Tsardom than she is to-day. . . . At the height of her fame she cast her spell successfully over no less a person than William Ewart Gladstone . . . but now her influence has waned and Tsardom has cast her off, but she is still with us."

The Judge objected to the reading of "this tosh", but he gave Norman Birkett in re-examination permission to read another passage from this book—so that the jury might know the kind of book it was. The words which Birkett read to an amused Court were these:

"In the half-lighted shades and the perfume-laden atmosphere, as her victim reclined at ease with his feet on the mantelpiece, she carefully displays her well-rounded arms and snowy neck, and whispers about that Bill in Congress as if her soul lay in its rejection."

The last witness for the defence was a surprise. Birkett called Mr. Charlie Thomson, the steeplechaser who had told Peter Wright the story of Gladstone's attempt to pick up a lady in the street. He had indeed told Peter Wright the story, and Peter Wright had asked him to send it in a letter to the Committee of the Bath Club, but on consideration he had written to Peter Wright, refusing to have anything more to do with it, partly because he thought it unfair to the memory of Gladstone, partly because the lady in question was of doubtful character and what she said might be open to suspicion. The case was complete.

At long last the time had come for "final speeches" and summing up. The issues and the state of the evidence were by now very clear. But Avory's summing up was needlessly partial: he took the bad as well as the good points against the plaintiff. On the issue of malice, for instance, which only arose if the jury rejected Lord Gladstone's defence of justification, he as good as directed a verdict for the defendant. "The mere fact that language was intemperate would not, in the absence of evidence that it was not used bona fide, be evidence of malice. If the defendant was actuated by righteous indignation or a desire to do his duty he would be protected even if his language was violent or excessively strong. They must bear that in mind in deciding whether the defendant was actuated by malice, i.e., a desire to do something other than that which it was his duty to do—namely, refute this calumny and vindicate his father's name." How this end could be furthered by an attempt to expel Peter Wright from his club the Judge did not explain. On the main question of justification it was perhaps unnecessary, in view of what had been demon- strated in the witness-box, for the Judge to emphasise his own opinion. But he stigmatised Peter Wright's case with one of his favourite alliterations: "If history is to be made of the tittle-tattle of the Upper Tooting tea-tables, you will no doubt consider whether it would not be better that history should not be made at all."

"Is not the man who slanders the dead a coward?" Avory continued. "Is not a man who makes a foul charge a 'foul fellow'? The plaintiff has chosen to put upon that expression an extrava- gant meaning—that he is a person of dissolute and vicious life— but the primary meaning of 'foul' is 'unclean', and a secondary meaning is that a foul fellow is one who uses scurrilous or abusive language or one who indulges in foul play. Shakespeare, whom the plaintiff would no doubt deem to be no less eminent than himself, wrote:

> 'Is't not enough thou hast suborned these women
> To accuse this worthy man, but, in foul mouth
> And in the witness of his proper ear, to call him villain?' "

The jury were out for two-and-a-half hours. At 7.15 p.m. the Court reassembled, and Avory said:

"I understand that you are agreed that the gist of the defendant's letter of July 27th is true?" To which the foreman answered, "That is so, my Lord."

"Then," said the Judge, "you need not trouble about the other matter (the question of malice)—that was only an alternative. This is a verdict for the defendant."

The verdict was greeted with loud applause. When this had been suppressed, the foreman of the jury announced: "We are of unanimous opinion that the evidence which has been placed before us has completely vindicated the high moral character of the late Mr. W. E. Gladstone."

Norman Birkett thanked the jury for these words, and as the Court rose a throng of friends and admirers pressed round Lord and Lady Gladstone and Mr. H. N. Gladstone and congratulated them on their family victory. The idol of the English Liberal tradition remained unfallen.

VII

LIBEL OR NO LIBEL

Sim v. *Stretch* (1935–6)
The Capital & Counties Bank Ltd. v. *George Henty & Sons* (1880–2)
Emerson v. *Grimsby Times & Telegraph Co. Ltd.* (1926)
Byrne v. *Deane* (1937)
Australian Newspaper Co. Ltd. v. *Bennett* (1891–4)
Broome v. *Agar* (1927–8)

In all legal systems a distinction is drawn between matters of law and matters of fact, and in the English system this distinction is of special importance, because matters of fact are generally decided by a jury, while matters of law are left to the Judge. In the eighteenth century the question whether anything was a libel or not was settled by the Judge as a matter of law. But ever since the passing of Fox's Libel Act in 1792 it has been the privilege of the jury to answer this question.

This feature of our system has important results. It ensures, for one thing, that the Judges do not set up, as they tried to do in the eighteenth century, a private and unpopular standard of right and wrong. Libel, which involves both the honour of citizens and their freedom of speech, is a delicate and personal branch of the law, which needs to keep in sympathy with public opinion.

But popular prejudice may be just as distorted as any bias on the Bench, and if juries were wholly uncontrolled they might give verdicts which were not only unjust in themselves but totally at variance with the principles of the law. Unless the Court is to abdicate its functions in favour of some sort of "People's Tribunal", a limit must be set to the powers of the jury. The Court has accordingly retained the jurisdiction to decide, as a matter of law, whether any words (or whatever may be the form of the alleged libel) are "capable of a defamatory meaning". If they are (in law) capable of a defamatory meaning, the jury is required to decide (in fact) whether they are defamatory of the person concerned. But if they are not capable of a defamatory meaning, the case should be withdrawn from the jury altogether, and if the Judge has wrongly left the decision to the jury the verdict will be upset by a higher Court.

A recent case may be given as an example. There was a quarrel between two neighbours in a Berkshire village about a housemaid called Edith, who had worked for each of them in turn. One of these neighbours, having succeeded in enticing Edith back, sent this telegram to the other: "Edith has resumed her service with us to-day. Please send her possessions and the money you borrowed also her wages." The result of this telegram was an action for libel and enticement. The jury awarded £25 for the enticement and £250 for the libel. The Judge thought the telegram was capable of a defamatory meaning, and so by a majority of 2 to 1 did the Court of Appeal. The House of Lords decided they were both wrong, and so the claim for libel was lost, with heavy costs. To say that a man has borrowed money from a domestic servant casts no slur either on his purse or his propriety.

This divided jurisdiction on law and fact has often led to points of considerable nicety, which raise the whole theory and meaning of libel. There have been many borderline cases in which the Judges disagreed on whether a thing was within the field of libel or not. Some of these cases are described in other chapters of this book. But to lawyers at any rate the leading case on this subject will always be *The Capital & Counties Bank* v. *Henty & Sons*, which was decided in the 'eighties of the last century.

The facts were simple enough. Hentys were a firm of Chichester brewers, who also owned a large number of inns in Sussex and Hampshire, to which they supplied their own brew of beer. They allowed their accounts with these inns to be settled from time to time with cheques which their tenants obliged their own customers by cashing across the Bar. Hentys paid these cheques into the Chichester branch of the Bank. But in 1878 a new manager arrived at this branch and refused to cash cheques drawn on other branches of his Bank by persons unknown to him. This was on any score a stupid decision, especially as the cheque which provoked it was only for £5 and only two other similar cheques for a total of £42 had been presented during the year. But the manager refused to give way, and when Hentys threatened to circulate their customers not to cash cheques drawn on the Bank, he replied, "I am quite indifferent as to your sending out orders to your tenants not to cash our cheques." Hentys thereupon sent to 137 of their customers and tenants occupying their public houses a printed notice in the following form:—

"Messrs Henty & Sons hereby give notice that they will not receive in payment cheques drawn on any of the branches of the Capital and Counties Bank."

This notice caused within a month a run of no less than £277,000 on the Bank. The Bank issued a writ against Hentys for libel, claiming £20,000 damages, on the ground that the notice was tantamount to saying that the Bank was insolvent or on the verge of insolvency. If this was what it meant, it was a serious libel. But Hentys denied that the notice had any such meaning, and they pleaded that in the circumstances they had a lawful interest in communicating it to their customers—it was, in other words, published on "a privileged occasion", and they were not liable, unless malice could be proved against them. They did not argue the point that, if it was a libel, the manager had authorised or consented to its publication and thereby destroyed any cause of action on the part of the Bank.

The case was tried in the first instance by Lord Chief Justice Coleridge and a special jury. The strongest argument for the Bank was, of course, the interpretation that a large number of its customers had put on the circular. But was this necessarily a reasonable interpretation? It might have meant a number of different things. Why should the only bad one be seized upon as decisive? Hentys had done something which they were entitled to do—that is, refuse to accept the cheques of a particular Bank—and there was no other way in which they could have expressed their refusal except by a written notice. But against this it was argued that the notice should have contained a statement of what had taken place between the Bank and Hentys, or at any rate should not have been left open to the inference of which the Bank complained. Whatever the intentions of Hentys may have been, they had in fact cast a most damaging reflection on the Bank.

It was a difficult question, and neither jury nor Judges could agree. The Lord Chief Justice thought that the circular might have a defamatory meaning and left the question to the jury. The jury could not agree and were discharged. The Bank was then anxious that there should be another trial before another jury, while Hentys contended that as the words were not capable of a defamatory meaning there was nothing for any jury to decide—and so Hentys were entitled to judgment. There was a succession of appeals, in each of which the same point was argued. The two Judges of the Common Pleas Division (a branch of the High Court which no longer exists) agreed with Lord Coleridge, but the Court of Appeal divided 2 to 1 the other way, and their decision was finally upheld by the House of Lords in 1882 by a 4 to 1 majority. In the result, then, the House of Lords decided that the notice could not be defamatory, and the Bank lost its action. Taking all the four Courts together, six Judges had supported this finding, while five were against it. Their judgments take up more than seventy closely-printed pages.

There have been many other cases of this kind, where a statement made by one party has done financial damage to another. As has been seen, the Court does not look at the damage, until it has decided the question of liability, and that turns upon the question of what can or can not be defamatory. But not every case is so difficult to decide. In 1925 a gentleman of the Grimsby fishing trade had arranged to be married on the afternoon of a particular day to a well-known Grimsby contralto. Unfortunately on the day before the wedding a full account of the ceremony appeared by a mistake in the local newspaper, and it was stated that, "The honeymoon is being spent in the South of England." When on the following morning the bridegroom went down to the fish market to put in a morning's work before the wedding, he found himself held up to ridicule and contempt. "You have soon got tired of the lady!"—was an obvious gibe. And so in due course he brought an action for libel against the *Grimsby Times and Telegraph*. But he did not get very far. The Court ordered his claim to be struck out as "frivolous and vexatious".

A case which provoked a more acute discussion was *Byrne* v. *Deane*. Mr. and Mrs. Deane were the proprietors of the Seaford Golf Club, of which Byrne was a member. Two gambling machines, known as "fruit" or "diddler" machines, had been kept for some years on the Club premises for the use of members. The machines were worked by putting in a coin and pulling a handle. If the machine stopped in a particular place it released more coins than had been put in. The proprietors of the Club did not own the machines but received a percentage of the profits which they made. But the machines were illegal under the Gaming Acts, and someone gave information to the police, as a result of which the machines had to be removed. Shortly afterwards there appeared on the wall where they had stood a piece of paper on which the following lines were typed:

> "For many years upon this spot
> You heard the sound of a merry bell
> Those who were rash and those who were not
> Lost and made a spot of cash
> But he who gave the game away
> May he *byrrn* in hell and rue the day.
> DIDDLERAMUS."

The proprietors, one of whom as secretary under the rules of the club controlled the posting of notices, did not put up this lampoon, but neither did they take it down, and Byrne sued them for libel, alleging that the words meant he had reported the presence of the machines to the police (which he had not) and was thereby guilty of underhand disloyalty to his club and devoid of all true sporting spirit. The action was tried without a jury by Mr. Justice Hilbery, who awarded him forty shillings damages and his costs.

But Byrne ran into unexpected difficulties in the Court of Appeal, to which the proprietors had recourse. Whatever the proprietors may have thought of the matter when the police complained to them about the machines, their counsel now argued the point that, as the use of the machines amounted to criminal gambling, it was the duty of a good citizen to report their presence to the police. Therefore to accuse Byrne of having informed the police was merely to say that he had done his duty as a good citizen; and that was no libel. It might be true that the charge would lower Byrne in the estimation of all clubmen, but the test of what is libellous is the opinion of "right-thinking members of society generally". Could this mythical consensus of opinion be permitted to regard it as dishonourable to put the law in motion against wrongdoers, and therefore as defamatory to say that a man had done so? "A difficulty in the case," said Lord Justice Greene during the argument, "is that the law requires a standard of duty which is different from that which a large number of people regard as being the proper standard. Can this Court regard any other standard than that which the Legislature has laid down?" Some crimes are offences against the moral law, while others are merely offences against Acts of Parliament, and carry no disgrace with them. But the Court for this purpose refused to draw any distinction between the two kinds of transgression.

Lord Justice Greer saw his way out of the dilemma. The lampoon in his opinion did not only mean that Byrne had told the police: it meant that he was disloyal because he had told the police. The charge of disloyalty was defamatory in itself, whether or not the reason given for it was a good or a bad one. In this way the Judge endeavoured to preserve the unity of the law. But he was not followed by Lord Justice Slesser or Lord Justice Greene, the other two judges of the Court, and so the appeal was allowed and Byrne lost his case. That was in 1937. To-day unfortunately hardly anybody is able to convince himself that the sentiments of a good citizen must necessarily coincide with the stipulations of Acts of Parliament or the rules and regulations which are made and unmade under them.

Thus the Court will not allow the jury to convict the defendant of libel, where the Court is certain that there was no libel. But the converse principle does not apply. If the jury acquits the defendant, the Court will never or hardly ever pronounce him guilty, however libellous his words may have been. It is the business of the plaintiff to make out his own case, and in order to do so he must satisfy both the Judge and the jury.

Two examples of this rule may be given. The first was a

dispute between two Australian newspapers which came in 1894 before the Privy Council, the supreme court of appeal for the British Empire. The dispute arose over the report of a boat-race between two oarsmen named Kemp and McLean. The Sydney *Evening News* announced that McLean had won the race, but from the account which followed this announcement it appeared that the race had really been won by Kemp. A rival journal, the *Australian Star*, in a comment upon the report in the *Evening News*, made the following observation:

"According to the Market Street Ananias, both Kemp and McLean won the boat-race yesterday. Poor little silly noozy."

In the ensuing libel action brought by the proprietor of the *Evening News* against the *Australian Star* the jury of four persons decided by a majority (English juries are not allowed to decide by a majority) that the words were not libellous. The Supreme Court of New South Wales ordered a new trial. But the Privy Council restored the verdict of the jury. It was a question for the jury to decide whether in the circumstances the word "Ananias" meant that the proprietor of the *Evening News* was a liar.

The second case was a slander action brought by a chauffeur against his former employer for calling him a "rotter" and accusing him of "joy-riding" in her car. Again the jury decided that the words were not defamatory, and this time the English Court of Appeal refused to order a new trial. Just as there are no words so innocent that they may not in certain circumstances be a libel on a particular person (for even words of praise may be spoken ironically), so there are almost no words so black that they must of necessity be intended and understood to convey their ordinary meaning. "One recalls," said Lord Justice Sankey, "the instance of the lady who in a West End drawing-room accused a noble Lord of being a thief, but when one is told that she said with a smile: 'Lord X, you are a thief, you have stolen my heart,' one recognises that to call a person a thief is not necessarily actionable."

VIII

DEAD OR ALIVE

Ralston v. Ralston (1930)
Utrillo v. Manson and another (1937–8)

On a first impression it might not be thought a libel to announce the death of someone who is still alive. To accuse even the toughest of human beings of being dead is scarcely likely—taking the usual definition of a libel—to bring him, or his memory, into hatred, ridicule or contempt. The hatred, ridicule and contempt may have been felt towards him already, and in that case they will be diminished, perhaps, rather than inflamed, by the good news of his death. Thus the libel, if it be one, appears to take away its own sting. Nor, by the other definition, is an announcement of death calculated to cause people to shun or avoid a man, except in the sense that they may cease their letters and visits. It is true that they may also cease to trade with him or to seek his professional services. But this misfortune will not turn a lie into a libel. A libel must be something which reflects upon human character. An action sometimes lies for a malicious falsehood, but a statement which affects a man's livelihood is not a libel, unless it also affects his reputation. Death of itself is a discredit to no man.

On further consideration, however, it is apparent that a false charge of being dead almost inevitably carries with it the implication that a living person is not the man he claims to be. For it makes him out as either a ghost or a fraud. An interesting case touching on this question came before Mr. Justice Macnaghten at Chester Assizes in 1930. There was no dispute about the facts. Mr. and Mrs. Ralston were a couple who married in 1894 and produced two children, but they parted in 1899 under a formal deed of separation. Mr. Ralston went to live at Valley, in Anglesey, while Mrs. Ralston moved to Ludlow, where, having always been interested in motoring, she established a garage. The concern prospered and after a time she formed it into a limited company, of which she was chairman and managing director and owned most of the shares. In 1929, while motoring with two friends in Anglesey, and acting on "information received", she visited a churchyard near her husband's home and found over one of the graves a tombstone bearing the inscription: "In loving memory of Jennie, the dearly beloved wife of W. R. Crawshay Ralston, of The Bungalow, Valley. Died 20th May, 1916."

Mrs. Ralston, whose first names were Edith Maud, was Mr. Ralston's only lawful wife. Her marriage was still in being, and Mr. Ralston was still paying her an annuity under the separation deed. The innuendo arising from this inscription might therefore be put in two ways, each of which was insulting to Mrs. Ralston. For either it meant that she was dead, in which case she was not Mrs. Ralston, or it meant simply that she was not and never had been lawfully married to Mr. Ralston. Mrs. Ralston accordingly sued her husband for libel.

At the trial she had no difficulty in convincing the Judge that the tombstone might be a libel on her, if the jury chose to decide that it was so. But for a wholly different reason the case never reached the jury. It was an old principle of English law that husband and wife must be treated as one person. This was the reason why for so long married women had no property rights. But another result of the principle was that neither husband nor wife could sue or prosecute each other, it being impossible to take proceedings against oneself. This particular rule was modified by the Married Women's Property Act, 1882, which gave to a wife the right to sue her husband—but only "for the protection and security of her own separate property". This provision of the Act was and is still in force, and as a result Mrs. Ralston had to prove that the libel might be harmful to her garage business. Her counsel argued strenuously that such a libel was likely to affect her credit and character as a trader, but Mr. Justice Macnaghten, after pondering the authorities, declared that "it cannot be said that chastity is a necessary qualification for the management or ownership of a garage". And so Mrs. Ralston lost her action. But her husband had, before the trial began, erased from the tombstone the statement that his Jennie had been his wife.

Although death is no discredit, the circumstances of it may, of course, be dishonourable. It would undoubtedly be a serious calumny to spread a false report that a man had committed suicide or was killed while running away from the enemy or driving to the danger of the public. It is little less offensive to suggest that he died of drink. This allegation was made in 1934 by a famous public art gallery about one of the most famous painters of this century. The painter was Maurice Utrillo, and the allegation appeared in the official catalogue of the paintings of the Modern Foreign School exhibited in the Tate Gallery in London. The words were these: "Utrillo became a confirmed dipsomaniac and at intervals throughout his life was placed under restraint. From 1919 to his death he was almost continually under supervision. He painted many pictures from picture postcards, which he sold to cabaret proprietors for the price of a drink. He died in 1934."

Utrillo was, and at the time of writing still is, alive. The mistake about his death, it was said later, was caused by the death in 1934 of a Spanish writer called Miguel Utrillo. "Utrillo" is a Spanish word meaning "little wineskin", and it was given to the painter as a child. The death of his namesake caused some confusion even in the French Press. Utrillo at the time took no proceedings in France, owing to the inadequacy of the French law of libel, but he issued a writ against the Director and Keeper of the Tate Gallery and the printers of the catalogue. As soon as the mistake was discovered, the catalogue was withdrawn, but the Gallery sought to defend the action.

The defendants pleaded that the words in the catalogue (except the mistake about his death) were true, and in support of this plea they put in a long list of "particulars" of the alcoholic exploits of Utrillo's earlier days. He was, they said, continually inebriated and saturated with alcohol, and when he could not procure alcohol, he drank lamp spirit, methylated, petrol, benzine, eau de Cologne and ether; he used to paint in the streets, with a bottle and a glass beside him, drinking incessantly and fetching more drink when the bottle was empty; he was frequently arrested for drunkenness and treated in alcoholic asylums and eventually certified a dangerous inebriate. The substance of these allegations was common knowledge in Paris and London, but they did not justify the libel, if Utrillo had since been cured of his vice. A man's past is not to be identified with his present. Counsel for Utrillo applied to "strike out the particulars"—so as to prevent the defendants from trying to prove them at the trial. But the Court of Appeal, before which the matter was brought, decided that the allegations were relevant, since the question of Utrillo's rehabilitation was one to be decided at the trial of the action.

This preliminary hearing had given considerable publicity to Utrillo's past life, but when the case next came before the Court a settlement was announced. The attention of the defendants had in the meantime been drawn to a book published in 1928, *La Legende et La Vie d'Utrillo*, in which it was stated that he had conquered the drinking habit, and after making enquiries the defendants had found this to be true. Moreover Utrillo had married in 1935 a fine and courageous woman who may claim with reason to have saved his life.

Utrillo desired only that his recovery should be recognised. He asked for a public apology, but no damages. The apology was now given by counsel for the defendants, who was glad to "make it plain to all who are present in Court, or who read this apology, that Monsieur Utrillo is alive and active in his old profession."

IX

ARTEMUS JONES AND HIS CONSEQUENCES

E. *Hulton & Co.* v. *Jones* (1908–9)
Cassidy v. *Daily Mirror Newspapers Ltd.* (1929)
Hough v. *London Express Newspaper Ltd.* (1940)
Newstead v. *London Express Newspaper Ltd.* (1939)

THE Law Reports are not much read by the general public. They have a dusty, technical and uninteresting look about them. Yet each reported case is only the statement of the Court's ruling, with reasons, upon some particular matter. Encrusted within these several hundred volumes of English literature, like fossils in a buried layer of earth, are tales both tragic and trivial, strange and commonplace. Each case is recorded under the names of the plaintiff and the defendant, however humble or illustrious they may be, and it happens from time to time that a man gains a gratuitous immortality from the novelty of the circumstances in which he went to law or the novelty of principle on which his claim was decided. So it was with Artemus Jones. Though Artemus Jones lived to receive a knighthood and a County Court judgeship and to be made a freeman of the City of London, his name will live in the libel action which he brought against the *Sunday Chronicle*, a case which established the rule that a writer may be guilty of libel without knowing the existence of the person he has libelled.

Thomas Jones has never been an uncommon name in Wales. When Thomas Jones, a Denbigh stonemason, christened his sixth son Thomas, there was really nothing that called for comment. But young Thomas, while still a boy, adopted the name of Artemus. It was an unusual name, and he and his father chose it for that reason. Indeed it was the most famous unusual name to be had. It had belonged to Artemus Ward, the American humorist, who enjoyed a tremendous vogue in England before his sudden death. Everyone read his articles in *Punch* and the whole of London flocked to hear his lectures, illustrated by a panorama, in the Egyptian Hall. There is no reason to think that his fame had not reached the Jones household in Denbigh. But where Artemus Ward took his name from is more obscure. His real name was Charles Farrar Browne. Washington had a general spelt Artemas Ward—St. Artemas was a Christian martyr of Roman times. On the other hand, research has revealed that an Artemus Ward was one of the original settlers in Waterford, Maine, Charles Farrar Browne's home town. However the name be spelt, it is safe to assume that part of the attraction was its unusualness.

Thus combining the commonest surname with the uncommonest Christian name, Artemus Jones advanced into the world of journalism. For a time he was a sub-editor on the *Sunday Chronicle*. Then he went to London and joined the *Daily Telegraph*. For six years he wrote Parliamentary sketches from the Press Gallery of the House of Commons, usually signed "T.A.J." —the initials of Thomas Artemus Jones. He published also a fair number of fully signed articles. In 1901, however, he put journalism behind him and was called to the Bar.

Seven years later, in July, 1908, the Paris Correspondent of the *Sunday Chronicle* was commanded to write a feature article upon the subject of Dieppe and its coming Motor Week. The Correspondent, wishing to give Dieppe a sprightliness and vivacity more real than apparent, invented a fictitious character. Humour lies in the extremes of incongruity, and, having been talking recently with a friend about Artemus Ward, he hit upon what he called the "fantastic hybrid" name of Artemus Jones. Neither he nor the then Editor had ever heard of Artemus Jones. But by this time that learned gentleman had acquired a busy practice on the North Wales Circuit. He was sitting in Court at the Chester Assizes, when a copy of the *Sunday Chronicle* was handed to him, and in an article headed "Motor-Mad Dieppe" he read the following words:

"Upon the terrace marches the world, attracted by the motor races—a world immensely pleased with itself, and minded to draw a wealth of inspiration—and, incidentally, of golden cocktails—from any scheme to speed the passing hour . . . 'Whist! There is Artemus Jones with a woman who is not his wife, who must be, you know—the other thing!' whispers a fair neighbour of mine excitedly into her bosom friend's ear. Really, is it not surprising how certain of our fellow-countrymen behave when they come abroad? Who would suppose, by his goings on, that he was a churchwarden at Peckham? No one, indeed, would assume that Jones in the atmosphere of London would take on so austere a job as the duties of a churchwarden. Here, in the atmosphere of Dieppe, on the French side of the Channel, he is the life and soul of a gay little band that haunts the Casino and turns night into day, besides betraying a most unholy delight in the society of female butterflies."

The comments of his fellow members of the Bar in the Circuit Mess that night are not on record, but we know that all round the Circuit Artemus Jones met the same faces and heard the same mocking, monotonous joke. Wherever he went, it was said at his trial, the libel pursued him, and it made his life a burden. He consulted a solicitor, who wrote to the newspaper, asking for an apology and damages. The newspaper denied that the article referred to him, but said they would put in a disclaimer, which they did, somewhat contemptuously, without showing it to Artemus or his solicitor. It ran as follows:

"It seems hardly necessary for us to state that the imaginary Mr. Artemus Jones referred to in our article was not Mr. Thomas Artemus Jones, barrister, but, as he has complained to us, we gladly publish this paragraph in order to remove any possible misunderstanding and to satisfy Mr. Thomas Artemus Jones we had no intention whatsoever of referring to him."

Artemus Jones was not satisfied with what his counsel Gordon Hewart (later Lord Chief Justice) called "a mere sarcastic postscript to the original libel", and so he issued a writ against E. Hulton & Co., the printers, proprietors and publishers of the *Sunday Chronicle*. The case was heard at the Manchester Assizes before Mr. Justice Channell and a special jury. Artemus gave evidence himself and called a number of witnesses from North Wales (but no one from the Bar) who either knew him or knew of him and thought he was the person referred to. In this they may be thought to have paid a doubtful compliment to their intelligence and charity alike. For if they were friends of Artemus, they should have known that he was not a churchwarden, did not live in Peckham, was not married, and indeed was obviously not the sort of person to play the part described, even allowing for "the atmosphere of Dieppe". There were only two things to associate Artemus with the article. One was his name, and the other was his previous connection with the *Sunday Chronicle*, which one of the witnesses remembered.

But the Courts must take the world as they find it, and there the evidence was, and it could not be gainsaid. Hewart offered to call a string of such witnesses, but the Judge said that if readers of ordinary intelligence understood the article as referring to Artemus Jones, it did not matter whether there were one or fifty of them. And so the plaintiff's case was closed. For the defendants the author of the article and the Editor of the *Sunday Chronicle* stated that they had never heard of Artemus Jones—the Peckham churchwarden was a figment of imagination. This evidence was not disputed. Mr. Edward Hulton also gave evidence. He had known Artemus Jones when he worked on the *Sunday Chronicle* and had given him letters of introduction when he left for London, but he had not read the article until after it was published. When he did so, he was struck at once by the name, but concluded from the substance of it that it could not possibly refer to the Artemus Jones he knew.

The Judge had made up his mind on the law from the very beginning of the case. It was clear that he was influenced unfavourably by the nature of the article. If a person chose to publish an article of this kind, he said fiercely, he did so at his own risk. The writer's actual intentions were irrelevant: would the ordinary reader think that the Peckham churchwarden was imaginary or a real person called Artemus Jones? The jury had no doubts. After only fifteen minutes they returned a verdict for the plaintiff with £1,750 damages, the foreman adding that they were quite unanimous.

But the legal argument had only just begun. Hultons took the case to the Court of Appeal, where they briefed Rufus Isaacs, K.C. (later the Marquess of Reading), to argue on their behalf. The argument turned on the familiar question of intention. There were two possible views. On the one hand libel had always been regarded as the publication of malicious untruths by one man about his neighbour. For such deliberate wrongdoing the law provided various penalties. How could a man be found guilty of defaming a neighbour whom he had never heard of and even believed not to exist outside his imagination? There seemed to be two strong objections: what he had written was not written about the neighbour at all, and in any event there was no element of malice about it. In a word, the necessary intention was lacking.

On the other hand there was an old maxim of the law that a man is presumed, until the contrary is proved, to intend the natural consequences of his acts. If the natural consequence of what he wrote was to lead reasonable people to suppose that he was referring to his neighbour, what difference should it make that he never meant to refer to him? The damage was done just the same: why should he not pay for it? As for malice, a man with honest motives could still be a libeller. It had never been a defence for an author to say that he did not think particular words were libellous or did not mean them to be so, or that he published them for the public benefit or his neighbour's own good, or because he believed them to be true. Whether words were libellous or not, and, if so, whether they were true, had always been questions for the Court. In the same way it was a proper question for the Court to decide whether words were a libel on the particular person who complained about them, no matter whom or what the author may have had in mind.

Such were the contending arguments. Counsel sought to support them with more general reflections. If, Rufus Isaacs pointed out, the plaintiff was entitled to succeed, then any number of Artemus Jones' might bring libel actions, so long as each could produce one witness to say he had read the article and thought it meant his friend. English law recognises no property in a name, and any other Jones might have taken the name of Artemus, for the same reason that both Thomas and the *Sunday Chronicle* had taken it, that it was so unusual as likely to be unique. If Artemus Jones succeeded, what would be the situation of authors in the future? It is almost impossible to write a novel without giving to some at least of the characters names that exist in real life. And even if the name be different, the description of the character with his address and occupation may very well coincide with the circumstances of a living person.

But Montague Lush, K.C. and Gordon Hewart, on behalf of Artemus Jones, brushed aside these remoter considerations. This, they said, was nothing to do with authorship: it was not even the author of the article who had been sued. Hultons were a company running a newspaper for profit. They had published an article which purported to be a factual account of a day in Dieppe. On the face of it the article was defamatory of Artemus Jones, if such a person existed, and they had taken no steps whatever to find out whether he existed or not. They were guilty of the grossest negligence. Let them take the consequences!

The three Judges of the Court of Appeal took time to consider their decision. After a difficult and important case has been argued judgment is often "reserved". In the traditional phrase "*Curia Advisari Vult*"—"The Court wishes to advise itself." Counsel then endorse their briefs "C.A.V.", and return, when the case next appears in the daily Cause List, to take the judgment and deal with any outstanding matters, and in particular, if they have won, to ask for costs. When a month later the Court of Appeal delivered their judgments in the case of Hulton *v.* Jones, Lord Justice Fletcher-Moulton was for Hultons, but Lord Chief Justice Alverstone and Lord Justice Farwell were in favour of Artemus Jones, and Hultons' appeal was therefore dismissed.

Hultons appealed to the House of Lords, the final appellate court. Unlike the Court of Appeal, the House of Lords did not find it necessary to take time for consideration. All four of their Lordships were unanimous in rejecting the appeal. The result, therefore, was that Artemus Jones received his £1,750 damages, and his costs in all three Courts were paid by Hultons.

Although many years later, when Lord Chief Justice, Lord Hewart declared that the case was of no importance at all, the consequences of the decision were all, and much more than all, that had been foreseen. As Lord Goddard has said, it "added a terror to authorship". Publishers became more libel-conscious. Novelists were at pains to state, on page one, that all their characters were fictitious and that any resemblance to a living person was the merest coincidence. Usually, no doubt, such an entry might discourage a jury from concluding that the gentle (or rather, reasonable) reader would think that X or Y was the object of the author's intentions. On the other hand, it might encourage such a finding, for no one who really thought he recognised an old friend in a book would be in the least dissuaded by the conventional note at the beginning. Indeed he would probably regard it as a blind.

But it was in Fleet Street that the decision wrought most havoc. There is no doubt that all three Courts which considered the case had been unfavourably impressed by the facetious nature of the article in the *Sunday Chronicle*. They said so in plain words, and to that extent they were out of sympathy with the newspaper and disposed to decide the issue in the manner in which they did. But although seven out of eight Judges agreed in the decision, they did not all agree in their reasons for it. The reasons were of the first importance, since they contained the principles which would govern the decision of similar cases in the future. The difference of opinion among the Judges was apparent in the judgments of Lord Alverstone and Lord Justice Farwell in the Court of Appeal. For Lord Alverstone it was enough that the libel might be understood by people to refer to Artemus Jones. Lord Justice Farwell, however, insisted that Artemus Jones could only succeed because the *Sunday Chronicle* had been utterly reckless in its use of names, not caring whether there was such a person as Artemus Jones or not; in the opinion of this Judge such recklessness was so inexcusable as to be treated as a deliberate intention to libel Artemus Jones. In the House of Lords the Lord Chancellor (Lord Loreburn) agreed with Lord Alverstone, but two of the other Law Lords, while agreeing with the Lord Chancellor, went out of their way to agree also with what Lord Justice Farwell had said. It was therefore difficult to know whether the law was the same for all cases of a similar kind, even when the newspaper could not be accused of recklessness. During the next thirty years there was a series of remarkable cases, in each of which a newspaper was sued for libelling a person it never knew to exist and never intended to refer to. In none of these cases was the newspaper reckless, though in each it was accused of negligence, which means in law a much lesser degree of carelessness. The results, as will be seen, were startling enough to recall Lord Mansfield's saying in the eighteenth century that "whatever a man publishes he publishes at his peril". Sueing a newspaper became an attractive proposition.

The first of these cases arose in 1928 when the *Daily Mirror* published in a gossip column the photographs of a man and a woman, and under it the words: "Mr. M. Corrigan, the race horse owner, and Miss 'X', whose engagement has been announced." Now this was an accurate statement. The Press photographer had seen the couple together on the racecourse at Hurst Park. Corrigan asked him to take the photograph and gave him the girl's name and address and permission for the engagement to be announced, and the girl did not say him nay. But Corrigan's real name was Cassidy, and he was, besides being a putative sometime General in the Mexican Army, also a married man. These facts were unknown to the *Daily Mirror* until Mrs. Cassidy served a writ upon them for libel.

The libel meant, it was declared in her statement of claim, that Mrs. Cassidy was a dissolute and immoral woman, who had imposed on her friends and acquaintances by pretending to be a respectable married woman, when in fact she was living in open adultery with her husband. At the time when Mrs. Cassidy brought her action she was not and had not for a long time been living with her husband. They had separated, but he still came to see her from time to time. When the action was tried, two friends of Mrs. Cassidy's testified that they had seen the man they knew as her husband visit her at her shop. These two friends also stated, after the manner of friends in this kind of libel case, that they had read the paragraph in the *Daily Mirror* and jumped at once to the conclusion that Mrs. Cassidy had deceived them.

It was argued for the *Daily Mirror* that the words did not bear the meaning which Mrs. Cassidy chose to give them, for they might just as well mean that Corrigan was intending to seduce the girl under a promise of marriage or to marry her after he had obtained a divorce. Moreover in their natural and ordinary meaning they were true—Corrigan and the girl *had* announced their engagement. Nevertheless the Judge ruled that the words *might* be defamatory of Mrs. Cassidy and the jury decided that they *were* defamatory of Mrs. Cassidy, and awarded her £500 damages.

An appeal was brought, and again the Court of Appeal divided two to one against the newspaper. A suggestion of negligence was made: it was hinted that the *Daily Mirror* was careless in taking Corrigan's word for it, since Corrigan was not a man of the highest reputation. But it is not always easy to make enquiries. A Press photographer can hardly be expected, when a man announces his engagement in the presence of his fiancée, to ask, "Are you married already?" If he does so, he may lay himself open to an action for slander. And if what the man himself says is not to be accepted, it may take a very long time to find out whether he is married or single, especially under another name. "If the decision of my brethren in this case is right," exclaimed Lord Justice Greer, the dissenting judge in the Court of Appeal, "it would be right to say that I could be successfully sued for damages for libel, if, having been introduced to two apparently respectable people as persons engaged to be married, I repeated that statement in a letter to a friend, on the ground that my words meant that a lady unknown to me, who was in fact the wife of the man, was not his wife and was living in immoral intercourse with him . . . I am afraid that for the future people will have to walk with wary steps through life and hesitate a long time before they accept the assertion of anyone, whom they have known as a bachelor, that he is in truth a single man."

In due course even the faithfully faithless friend so intimately associated with these cases was dispensed with. This step was taken in a case which arose out of a paragraph in the *Daily Express* in 1937. There was at that time a popular boxer called Frank Hough, and in an endeavour to enlighten the public about his domestic background the *Daily Express* wrote: "Frank Hough's curly-headed wife sees every fight. 'I should be more in suspense at home', she says. 'I always get nervous when he gets in the ring, although I know he won't get hurt. Nothing puts him off his food. He always gets a cooked meal at night, however late it is when he gets in.' "

Unfortunately the curly-headed lady was not Frank's wife, and the article caused a commotion where the real Mrs. Frank lived in Battersea. "The neighbourhood were all talking about it, one and the other, all looking at the papers and buying them, and there was a run on the *Daily Express.*"

Mrs. Hough brought proceedings, and, when the time came, two worthy neighbours appeared in the witness-box to support her claim. On this occasion, however, they did not suggest they had been misled by the article. On the contrary, they knew quite well that Mrs. Hough was Frank's lawful wife—they had been present at the wedding! But they were incensed on her behalf that anyone else should be credited with that honourable title, and they told her she ought to do something about it. Thus there was no evidence that anyone had understood the article to mean (as alleged in the innuendo set out in the statement of claim) that Mrs. Hough was "a dishonest woman falsely representing herself to be and passing as the wife of the said Frank Hough and that the said Frank Hough was not her husband and that she was an unmarried woman who had cohabited with and had children by the said Frank Hough without being married to him."

No matter, said the Court of Appeal. It was true that in the eyes of these two witnesses the article cast no imputation on their friend, but others might have read it differently. It was no more essential for any one to have understood the libel for what it was than it was necessary for any one to have believed it. The jury awarded Mrs. Hough fifty guineas damages.

And so it seemed that the road to damages was paved with good intentions, or rather with no intentions at all. But juries were growing wise. One day the *Daily Express* asked, "Why do people commit bigamy?" and supplied this answer:

"Harold Newstead, thirty-year-old Camberwell man, who was jailed for nine months liked having two wives at once. Married legally for a second time in 1932—his legal wife is pictured right, above—he unlawfully married nineteen-year-old . . . (left above). He said, 'I kept them both till the police interfered.' "

This was all true of a man who had been described at the Old Bailey the day before as a barman. There was, however, a ladies' hairdresser called Harold Newstead, also a Camberwell man and though aged twenty-four, said to look older, and he thought it proper at once to ventilate his wrong and vindicate his rights with a libel action. When his case was tried, evidence was given by a succession of ladies with magnificent coiffures, who stated that they had not taken up appointments in the belief that their hairdresser was languishing in gaol. The Judge left to the jury the following questions, given with the jury's answers:

"Was the *Daily Express* reckless or negligent in not publishing a fuller description of their man, to obviate any chance of confusion?"—"Negligent, but not reckless."

"Damages, if any?"—"One farthing."

"Would reasonable persons understand the words complained of to refer to Harold Newstead the hairdresser?" After long, long deliberations the jury could not agree and were discharged. Who then was entitled to judgment? If Lord Justice Farwell was right in 1909, judgment should be entered for the *Daily Express*, for unless it had been reckless it could not be liable, and, whatever the jury found, the *Daily Express* could hardly have been reckless, since what it had written was true. If Lord Alverstone and Lord Loreburn were right, recklessness and negligence were equally irrelevant, and Harold Newstead was entitled to an answer, from this or another jury. And so the Court of Appeal decided, though for the third time there was a dissenting voice, and an order was made for a new trial.

History does not relate whether Harold Newstead took his case to another jury, and won more, or less, or the same damages. But the acid views of the dissenting Judge, Lord Justice McKinnon, are on record: "We are encouraged and entitled to assume that any jury consists of twelve reasonable people . . . In this case the jury did assess the damages, if the words did defame the plaintiff, at one farthing . . . I suppose I am still entitled to regard them as twelve reasonable people, even if they failed to agree on a question which has virtually caused disagreement between my brethren and myself. I know, therefore, that twelve reasonable people have assessed the plaintiff's possible damages at one farthing. And on the facts proved I cannot conceive that any twelve reasonable people would arrive at a larger figure. It is said that we are bound to permit, if not to direct, a further trial of this case, and if another jury disagrees, yet another, and so on. That is in order that eventually some jury may answer 'No' to the first question, or answering 'Yes' to it, may give the plaintiff the farthing which one jury has already agreed upon, and which I am satisfied any reasonable jury would agree upon. I do not think we are constrained to adopt this course. For I think we sit here to administer justice, and not to supervise a game of forensic dialectics."

The difficulties created by these cases of " unintentional defamation" (and for every one that came to trial perhaps a hundred were settled out of Court) have been alleviated by the Defamation Act, 1952. Any person who has "innocently" libelled another may now make "an offer of amends" (which will consist mainly in the publication of a proper correction and apology) and if he does so, he will not be liable for damages. In this way it is provided that a reputation which has been accidentally injured will be restored, while it will no longer be possible to exploit such an injury by means of a "gold-digging action". But the conditions of "innocence" in this connection are fairly stringent. The author of the libel must have "exercised all reasonable care" and also must show, either that he did not intend his words to refer and knew of no circumstances by which they might be understood to refer to the person libelled, or that his words were not libellous on the face of them and he knew of no circumstances by which they might be understood to be libellous. The cases of which some account has been given in this chapter were responsible for this alteration of the law, but it is a moot point whether in any of them the publication was "innocent" within the meaning of the new Act.

X

TWO STOCKBROKERS

Blennerhassett v. *Novelty Sales Services Ltd. and another* (1933)
Canning v. *William Collins & Co. Ltd.* (1938)

STOCKBROKERS are the last people to be associated in the public mind with light-hearted fun and games. Yet the tradition of practical joking on the London Stock Exchange proved a serious impediment to the two stockbrokers who besought the Courts during the 'thirties to compensate their deeply affronted honour. They were both laughed out of Court, as though it was all a stockbroker's rag.

Consider first the case of Mr. William Lewis Rowland Paul Sebastian Blennerhassett. Blennerhassett was the only stockbroker of that name. But his name was a distinguished one, and he was well known in Throgmorton Street and the City generally. Suddenly, one afternoon in the summer of 1932, he found himself an object of ridicule. He returned to the Stock Exchange after lunch, and as he walked across the familiar, crowded hall he was met with jeers, ribaldry and laughter. The cause of this unexpected reception was soon made known to him. It was nothing other than an illustrated advertisement in the latest issue of the *Evening Standard*. "Beware of the Yo-Yo!" said the advertisement, and beneath this headline the following strange tale was recorded:

"Take warning of the fate of Mr. Blennerhassett, as worthy a citizen as any that ever ate lobster at Pimm's, or holed putt at Walton Heath. 'Sound man, Blennerhassett,' they said in Throgmorton Street, and 'nice people, the Blennerhassetts!' was the verdict over the tea-cups and in the local tennis club. But Yo-Yo got him and now . . . One day Blennerhassett brought his offspring to a shop to buy them two nice books, entertaining yet instructive. Near the book department they first saw the Yo-Yo being played. The tricks it could do in the hands of an expert! Up and down the string it spun and back and forth: round in fast flying circles: hopping and burring along the floor: lying still as a dead mouse and then suddenly returning to life—the embodiment of eccentric speed. Blennerhassett, ever responsive to the 'Gimmes' of his young, bought the children one each. At home that evening, with the deprecatory condescension so familiar in parents, he offered to give them the first lesson. Strangely enough the Yo-Yo was recalcitrant. It sulked. First it would and then it wouldn't. But the Blennerhassett blood was up. The dinner gong rang unheeded. The children suggested, implored, cried, but Blennerhassett kept on. He was determined to make that little devil on a string do its stuff. The nurse took the children to bed, Mrs. B. took herself to bed. But Blennerhassett toiled on at Yo-Yo. Came the dawn, and he was still there, dishevelled and wild-eyed, with the Yo-Yo string still dangling from his trembling fingers. They tried to part him from it, but it was no use, and eventually poor Blennerhassett was taken away.

To-day he is happy in a quiet place in the country and under sympathetic surveillance he practises Yo-Yo tricks. His old friends at Pimm's miss him at lunch and three-quarters of a certain golf foursome have had to find a stranger to make up their quorum.

So beware of Yo-Yo which starts as a hobby and ends as a habit."

It was the height of the Yo-Yo craze, and the ludicrous picture of Mr. Blennerhassett and his Yo-Yo was too much for the humourless stockbrokers. They gave him no peace. Mr. Blennerhassett found he could do no business that afternoon, and fled to his club. He found considerable excitement about the advertisement there. He ran into a City Alderman friend, a Member of the Committee of the Stock Exchange, who took a very serious view of it. Mr. Blennerhassett consulted his solicitors. A solicitor's letter was written and the *Evening Standard* published an apology. Nevertheless, Mr. Blennerhassett pursued the matter

and in due course came to Court, where he was cross-examined
by Sir Patrick Hastings, K.C.

"Can you tell me any book in the world, including the *Post
Office Directory*, *Who's Who*, and the *Stock Exchange Guide*,
in which there appears the name of Mr. Blennerhassett of
Throgmorton Street?"—"No."

"The name Blennerhassett is a very well-known Irish name,
is it not?"—"No. It is an English name."

"I am sorry, I thought that it was Irish, but I did not mean
to cast any aspersions on it. But don't you know that the
name Blennerhassett has been used as a humorous or comic
name for centuries?"—"I would not say for centuries. It
has been used by Gilbert in *The Bab Ballads*, and an American
author wrote a novel which is called by the name."

("Perhaps already you may know
Sir Blennerhassett Portico?")

"Do you not know that one of Mark Twain's humorous
stories concerns the adventures of a Mr. Blennerhassett?"—
"Yes."

Sir Patrick Hastings then asked about Pimm's Restaurant.
He described Pimm's No. 1 as a drink that "looked very
nice and tasted very nice, but afterwards sometimes made
one regret it, because it was stronger than it looked." Mr.
Blennerhassett had occasionally lunched at Pimm's, though
not on the day when the advertisement came out.

"If you wanted to make a joke about a man going to the City
and having lunch, there is no place which would strike you
so immediately as Pimm's?"—"I do not agree. If Throgmorton Street was mentioned, I should think of a restaurant
near the Stock Exchange."

"Were you in the habit of eating lobster at Pimm's?"—"I am
afraid I was."

"Have you ever played golf at Walton Heath?"—"No."

"Have you ever holed a putt anywhere?"—"No."

Sir Patrick Hastings then drew attention to the illustrations in the advertisement. The picture of "Mr. Blennerhassett", he said, showed that the gentleman had suffered a peculiar misfortune to the back of his head, which looked as if it had been eaten by mice. With him, said Sir Patrick, he had some singularly unprepossessing children. "What age do you think they are, speaking as a father?"—"About five or six."

"Have you any children?"—"I have a son."

"How old is he?"—"He is twenty-one."

But Mr. Blennerhassett insisted that there were things in the article besides the name and the mention of Throgmorton Street which pointed distinctly to him. Sir Patrick Hastings enquired about them.

"Have you," he asked presently, "any sense of humour?"— "You must ask other people about that."

"Are you suggesting that people could have thought that you had been taken away to what the Americans call a 'funny house'?"—"No."

"Do some funny scenes sometimes take place on the Stock Exchange?"—"When times are good and the Stock Exchange is in a pleasant mood there is any amount of ragging."

"Have you ever heard of a member having a newspaper under his arm and another member setting light to it and the whole house then exhibiting a certain degree of enthusiasm? Is not the Stock Exchange the home of practical jokes?"— "Very much so."

"If the name of a member of the Stock Exchange appears in the newspapers then they make a May Day of it?"—"They did."

But Blennerhassett added that the Stock Exchange had been

very depressed, and little joking had taken place of late. "You must have cheered them up?"—"I was the first joke that had happened for a long time."

After Mr. Blennerhassett's evidence a colleague testified that he thought the advertisement referred to Blennerhassett, and mentioned the fact that members of the Stock Exchange were not allowed to advertise. Sir Patrick Hastings seized upon this unwise remark.

"If you wanted to advertise yourself as a member of the Stock Exchange," he asked, "would you select a picture of yourself being escorted to a madhouse with a Yo-Yo?"

The next witness was the serious-minded Alderman who had associated the advertisement with Blennerhassett. This time Mr. Justice Branson asked a few necessary questions.

"Did you think that he had gone mad with a Yo-Yo?"— "No."

"Or had been taken to a lunatic asylum?"—"I knew that he had not."

"Or that he had got into this to advertise his business as a stockbroker?"—"No."

That was the case for the plaintiff, Mr. Blennerhassett.

The defendants now explained how the name of Blennerhassett came to appear in the advertisement. The author of the script had a small daughter who used to go each morning into her father's room, and say: "Will Mr. Blennerhassett have his trousers this morning?" Her father would say, "No," whereupon she discreetly retired, and returned with some other article of clothing, and asked whether "Mr. Blennerhassett" would have that. This game went on for as long as father allowed it, and that was the only reason why he chose the name "Blennerhassett" when he wrote the advertisement. He had, he said, never heard of the plaintiff, and had no intention of portraying any living person. He used the name to paint a picture of a stolid, rather didactic person being over-fascinated by a rather crazy game. The artist who drew the caricatures for the advertisement was equally ignorant of Mr. Blennerhassett or any other prominent stockbroker.

The special jury enjoyed an entertaining day, but they were not called upon to give a verdict. The Judge took it upon himself to decide that no reasonable person could have thought this imaginative advertisement told the story of a living person. He dismissed Mr. Blennerhassett's claim with costs.

A similar fate befell Mr. John Canning some years later. Mr. Canning was rung up one night, and when he lifted the receiver all that he heard were strange animal noises. A few days later an anonymous postcard arrived in his morning post, and on it he read the words, "Get back to your ruddy cage." Mr. Canning was at a loss. He did not understand these messages, until a friend asked if he had read a book called *People in Cages*. Mr. Canning promptly read it. It was a book which told a story about the Zoological Gardens. According to the blurb on the dust-cover, "The Zoo on a hot July afternoon makes a brilliant setting for the story and affords material for entertaining satire. 'What they keep in the cages is tame enough; the wild ones walk in through the turnstiles'—that was the Keeper's opinion. And a visitor sees even more significance in the comparison: 'We're all in cages ourselves and some of our performances must be very amusing to God.'"

One of the characters of this original work was—"a financier who is 'wanted' for taking risks with other people's money. He runs panic-stricken from cage to cage and turns to bluff it out with his pursuers like a wolf at bay." It so happened that the name of this financier was Captain John Canning.

John Canning duly sued the publishers of the book for libel. As always in this kind of case there were some points of resemblance and others of difference between the living Canning and the fictitious Canning. John Canning had served in the War and retired from the Army with the rank of Captain in 1922. Among his old regimental friends he was still known as Captain Canning. He was engaged in finance in the City of London. He was dark, powerful and broad-shouldered, and looked about forty. He had a sister named Mary. He had hunted at one time and was a Fellow of the Zoological Society. But, like Blennerhassett, he was cross-examined to show that libellous suggestions about stockbrokers were never taken seriously.

"I have never been to the Stock Exchange, but I have heard that in times when business is slack, the members have a rather reprehensible habit of ragging people?"—"Yes."

"Are the reasonable people who, we have been told, thought that the book referred to you, the people who rang you up at midnight and made growling and quacking noises down the phone?"—"I do not know who they were."

"Is it not the position that your friends on the Stock Exchange seized a heaven-sent opportunity for a little harmless banter?"—"I do not call it that. 'Captain Canning' in the book was making love to the doctor's wife and kissing her parlour-maid when he went to call."

"No one would think that of you?"—"No one who knew me, but I am continually making new acquaintances."

"This blackguard in the book had never been a Member of the Stock Exchange?"—"The book refers to finance and many people would connect the two."

"This must have been a perfect God-send to your friends in the Stock Exchange. It must almost have made up for the Slump?"—"Not quite that."

"I suggest that this is utterly and absolutely ridiculous, that this is a perfectly inoffensive novel with one character in it that does not bear the slightest resemblance to you except that the authoress has called him 'Captain John Canning'?" But Mr. Canning insisted that it was not inoffensive.

Once again the defendants had to explain how the accident occurred. The authoress had taken the name of Canning "out of a history book". "John was about as common a name as I could find," she added, "I looked into the London Telephone Book to see if there was anyone called 'John Canning' and there was no one."

Lord Chief Justice Hewart summed up, and the jury returned a verdict for the defendants. Mr. Canning, like Mr. Blennerhassett, was ordered to pay the costs of the proceedings. The conclusion must be that neither Mr. Blennerhassett nor Mr. Canning was as fortunate as Mr. Thomas Artemus Jones.

XI

VISUAL IMAGES

Monson v. *Tussaud's Ltd.* (1894–5)
Tolley v. *J. S. Fry & Sons Ltd.* (1929–31)

A SUBSECTION of the Defamation Act, 1952, lays it down that "any reference in this Act to words shall be construed as including a reference to pictures, visual images, gestures and other methods of signifying meaning". It may be wondered whether this does not stretch the meaning of "words" beyond their proper limits. The fact is, however, that libel and slander have never been limited to words, whether written or spoken, but since the Act, which makes certain alterations in this branch of the law, chooses to talk throughout about "words", it was necessary to make it clear that the changes are to apply equally to libel and slander by other means. A libel or a slander may be conveyed in any shape or form.

This Chapter tells the story of two libel cases, neither of which has anything in common with the other, except that in both cases the libel took the form of a "visual image" and arose, not from the nature of the image itself, but out of the circumstances of its publication.

Inside the old Madame Tussaud's waxworks exhibition in London a special turnstile led, on payment of sixpence, to the Chamber of Horrors. The Chamber of Horrors was devoted mainly to portraits of notorious murderers and models of the scenes of their crimes. But between the Chamber itself and the turnstile was an ante-room called the Napoleon Room No. 2, which contained, besides a recumbent effigy of Napoleon and relics of him and of the Duke of Wellington, portrait models of Mrs. Maybrick, the notorious poisoner, and of Pigott, who had committed suicide to avoid arrest on a charge of forging the Parnell letters. In this ante-room, at the beginning of January,

1894, was placed a wax figure of Alfred John Monson, the most talked about man in the country. For Monson had been tried in Edinburgh on charges of murder and attempted murder and released after the jury had brought in a verdict of "not proven" on both charges.

The wax figure was dressed in a brown knickerbocker suit, which he was supposed to have worn on the crucial day, and beside it was shown a gun labelled "Monson's gun". Also shown in this room was a figure of one Scott, who had been charged with complicity in the murder, but never found. The scene of the alleged crime had been Ardlamont House in Argyllshire and the case, which attracted tremendous interest, became known as *The Ardlamont Mystery*. At the same time that Monson's figure appeared in the Napoleon Room a model set was exhibited in the Chamber of Horrors itself, described as "Ardlamont Mystery: Scene of the Tragedy".

A rival waxworks exhibition, owned by another member of the Tussaud family in Birmingham, also exhibited a figure of Monson outside, but close to, its Chamber of Horrors, and advertised the fact in local newspapers with this announcement: "See the Chamber of Horrors (extra room, 3d.) and the instruments of torture—see Vaillant, the Anarchist, and Monson of Ardlamont. Admission to the Exhibition and Entertainment 6d."

The facts disclosed at Monson's trial were startling. For some three years he had been nominal tutor to a young man called Cecil Hambrough who was living with him and his family. This arrangement had resulted from an introduction between Monson and Hambrough's father, effected by a financial agent of the name of Loftus Tottenham. While young Hambrough was with the Monsons, Monson, Tottenham and Hambrough senior were engaged in a series of financial negotiations designed to raise money on the wealthy entailed Hambrough estates. In 1893 Monson, who had been bankrupted the previous year, made many attempts to insure his pupil's life, all of which failed as he had no insurable interest. But on August 4th, after Cecil Hambrough had signed an application form which Monson had filled in, two provisional policies of £10,000 each were issued by The Mutual Life Insurance Company of New York. Monson paid the first premium out of a cheque for £250 which he obtained from Tottenham as deposit on a supposed contract for the purchase of Ardlamont. Three days later Cecil Hambrough purported to assign the policies to Mrs. Monson and instructed the Company to deliver them either to her or to Monson.

The Monsons and Cecil Hambrough had taken Ardlamont House and its shootings for the summer. The estate could only be approached from Glasgow by water, and here on the following day, August 8th, arrived the mysterious Scott, ostensibly to inspect the boilers of a new yacht. That night Monson and Cecil Hambrough went out in a small rowing boat. The boat was sunk (it was found afterwards to have been flooded through a plughole which had been cut in its bottom) but Monson and Hambrough escaped with a drenching. The following morning Mrs. Monson and her family were despatched to Glasgow, and Monson, Hambrough and Scott went out shooting, Monson and Hambrough carrying shot guns. During that morning Hambrough was shot dead in a wood on the Ardlamont Estate. His death was certified as accidental, and it was not until application had been made for payment of the life policies, and two officials arrived to make enquiries, that suspicion was aroused and Monson was arrested and charged with the murder of Cecil Hambrough by shooting and his attempted murder by drowning.

The trial lasted for ten days, and much of it was taken up with the testimony of gun experts. Although there was ample evidence of motive and opportunity, certain points about the shooting appeared to be consistent with accident and inconsistent with murder. It was common ground that the fatal shot had been fired by Monson's gun, and a good deal turned upon whether the jury believed Monson's story that Hambrough had borrowed the gun that morning.

To return to the Tussauds' exhibitions, no doubt a verdict of "not proven" was less unequivocal than one of "not guilty", but it did not entitle anyone to make discreditable insinuations about Monson's connection with Cecil Hambrough's death. Such insinuations might be suspected from the placing of Monson's portrait near the entrance to the Chamber of Horrors—as much as to say, this man had a narrow escape! Monson at once issued writs for libel and applied for immediate injunctions (before the trial of the action) to stop these portraits being shown. The Court had no doubt that the exhibition amounted to a libel, and since both the Tussaud establishments disclaimed any intention of justifying it, they made an order for the injunctions.

The defendants then produced evidence that Monson had not only consented to the exhibition, but had contracted for a consideration of £100 to give Tussauds the brown knickerbocker suit and the gun, and also a sitting, so that his portrait might be improved. This evidence came from Loftus Tottenham, who had negotiated with the London Tussauds and given a receipt in these terms:

"Jan. 3, 1894. Received of Madame Tussaud & Sons (Limited) the sum of £50 on behalf of Mr. A. J. Monson for the 20-bore gun used at Ardlamont on August 10 last, a suit of clothes he was wearing on that date, and an undertaking to give Mr. John Tussaud a sitting for his portrait for a figure for this exhibition. The balance, £50, to be paid after the above sitting has been given.

B. Loftus Tottenham, on behalf of
A. J. MONSON."

But Monson, though he admitted that he and Tottenham had bought a gun for £4 10s. paid for by Tottenham in a shop at Charing Cross that morning (which became the "gun used at Ardlamont") denied that he had ever authorised any agreement of this kind. Certainly he repudiated it, and the cheque was returned—because, so Tottenham said, Monson thought a libel action would be more profitable. It was, in fact, decided in the end that there was no evidence that Tottenham had acted with Monson's authority. But the Court of Appeal cancelled the order for the injunctions, and the figure of Monson remained in its compromising position near the Chamber of Horrors until after his action—for damages, an injunction and the return of his suit— had been tried.

The trial took place a year later—in January, 1895—before Lord Coleridge, the Lord Chief Justice, and a special jury and lasted three days. Monson's reputation had not improved in the meantime. An action had been fought on the life policies and it was found that they were void by reason of false and fraudulent statements made by Monson in the application form. Moreover Monson had prejudiced his chances of getting heavy damages for the painful publicity, which he claimed that the waxworks exhibitions were inflicting on him, by himself publishing an account of the trial, called "The Ardlamont Mystery—Solved", with two pictures of himself. He also contracted to give lectures on the subject for a high fee. There was other material, too, on which Monson was open to cross-examination. Even his treatment of Tottenham, who had undoubtedly lent him a fair amount of money, was not likely to create a good impression with the jury. He had prosecuted Tottenham, who had been a Crown witness in the murder trial, for misappropriating some furniture left in his care, and Tottenham was sentenced to three months' imprisonment. Now Tottenham was brought from prison and gave evidence against Monson, vowing in the witness-box to prosecute him for perjury and theft as soon as his own sentence had been served. In the result the Lord Chief Justice summed up in favour of Monson on the issue of libel or no libel—"Did not the exhibition," he asked, "keep his memory green in no creditable sense?"—but he was no less disparaging to Monson concerning his claim for damages—the jury must consider whether he was a man who had a reputation to lose.

The jury after a quarter of an hour found a verdict for Monson with damages of one farthing. The question of the injunction and the knickerbocker suit was then considered. After some discussion Tussauds undertook to remove from their exhibition the figure of Monson together with the gun and any thing which connected Monson with Ardlamont. "Then," said the Lord Chief Justice, "I don't think that the 'Scene of the Tragedy' need be removed." Tussauds also undertook to return the suit, and the Lord Chief Justice awarded Monson 1s. damages for its detention. But no order was made as to the costs of the action, and each side was left to pay its own.

Very different was the trial in 1929 of the action which Mr. Cyril Tolley, the amateur golf champion of England, brought

against Messrs. J. S. Fry & Sons Limited, the chocolate manu-
facturers. The subject-matter of this action was an advertisement,
published in the Press without Tolley's knowledge or consent,
which contained a caricature of him in the act of playing a stroke,
with a packet of Fry's chocolate sticking prominently out of his
pocket, while a comic caddy danced about with another packet
in his hand and compared the excellence of the champion's drive
with the excellence of the chocolate in the following doggerel
limerick:

> "The caddy to Tolley said, 'Oh, sir!
> Good shot, sir, that ball, see it go, sir!
> My word how it flies,
> Like a Cartet of Fry's,
> They're handy, they're good and priced low, sir!'"

Was this advertisement a libel or not? The trial of this question
lasted a day before Mr. Justice Acton and a common jury, with
Rayner Goddard, K.C. (now Lord Goddard) appearing for Mr.
Tolley and Norman Birkett, K.C. (now Lord Justice Birkett)
representing Frys.

Mr. Tolley, a stockbroker "in private life", gave evidence and
said that he did not object to the caricature or the limerick in
themselves, though he made the comment that it was not "a
particularly good swing" and not a very good limerick. And he
added that the presence of a packet of chocolate in his pocket
implied that he chewed chocolate while he played golf, which he
never did. But that, of course, was hardly libellous. His objection
to the advertisement was the insinuation that he had consented
to its publication either for money or to advertise himself, or for
both purposes, and had therefore "prostituted his reputation as an
amateur golfer" and "been guilty of conduct unworthy of his
status as an amateur golfer". Or, as counsel for Frys put it later,
the only suggestion of a libellous meaning was that some people,
on seeing the advertisement, might say, "I wonder what Mr.
Tolley got for that." But as an amateur Mr. Tolley was not
allowed to advertise, whether for reward or not. The tradition of
English sport had drawn a clear and important distinction be-

tween the amateur and the professional, the Gentleman and the Player, and the law was now called upon to recognise it. This advertisement was one of a series which included a Countess, a cricketer and several prominent politicians. But when it was pointed out to Mr. Tolley that he was in company with the Lord Privy Seal and the late Home Secretary, he replied, "Those Cabinet Ministers are professionals."

Two witnesses were called in support of Mr. Tolley's case. The first was an eminent golfer, who declared that if an amateur lent himself to an advertisement scheme many people would think he was betraying his amateur status. The other witness, the secretary of two well-known golf clubs, said that unless a golfer proved he had nothing to do with his appearance in such an advertisement, he would probably be asked to resign from any reputable club. But Mr. Tolley's case was assisted more than anything else by the correspondence which had taken place between Frys and their advertising agents. Frys from the very start had feared that these advertisements might lead to libel actions, and they asked their agents for an indemnity. This the agents refused to give, but they took Counsel's Opinion instead. "Tolley and the Caddy" apparently survived this "screening", and thereafter it was printed in no less than sixty-four newspapers! But there was on the file a letter from the agents rejecting a suggestion by Frys that in another advertisement Suzanne Lenglen be replaced by Helen Wills and Betty Nuthall. The reason given was that "both Betty Nuthall and Helen Wills are amateurs, and in tennis circles, even more than in golf circles, the amateur status must be carefully guarded; hence, if Cyril Tolley has any quarrel with us, it is more than likely that both Helen Wills and Betty Nuthall would be upset at our caricaturing them for advertising purposes." The inference drawn from this correspondence by Tolley's counsel was that a risk of legal liability had been knowingly run at the expense of a man's feelings. It is probable that these letters had some influence on the jury's findings.

No witnesses were called by counsel for Frys, who relied mainly upon arguments of law. He pointed out that there was nothing in the advertisement, and no evidence had been given, to show that anybody would or should assume that Tolley had given his consent, still less that he had given it for payment. The advertisement contained, not a photograph, which a person may well be taken to have supplied himself, but a caricature. Therefore the whole basis of the innuendo raised by Mr. Tolley was gone. Moreover, even if the public were for any reason led to believe that Tolley had consented, there was still nothing libellous in the advertisement—what Tolley was really complaining of was the unauthorised use of his name, an occurrence which English law, though it frowns at it, does not in ordinary circumstances regard as an actionable wrong. And so, submitted counsel, the advertisement was incapable of a defamatory meaning. But the Judge overruled this submission, and left it for the jury to decide. The jury decided in favour of Tolley and awarded him £1,000 damages.

Frys appealed. As Lord Justice Scrutton said in his judgment: they "took two points: (1) the cartoon with the evidence was not capable of a defamatory meaning; (2) damages excessive. Then there was also a third point, which Mr. Norman Birkett said was difficult to express in words, but which, as he never made me understand what it was, I cannot deal with." But Mr. Norman Birkett won this appeal, though Lord Justice Scrutton's judgment went against him. The chief reason of the other two judges for allowing the appeal was Birkett's first argument: the advertisement gave rise to no presumption that Tolley had agreed to its publication. Lord Justice Scrutton, however, was not impressed with this point. He preferred to accept it as common knowledge that people are in fact paid for allowing their names and portraits to appear in advertisements. "I do not know," he said, "if a judge is allowed to know of the Duchess who made an income by vowing that

> 'her complexion
> derived its perfection
> from somebody's soap,
> which it doesn't,'

or to know that Gilbert would not have written those lines if less exalted though more prominent people than Duchesses did not

receive payment for allowing their names to be used as advertisements of goods. It is difficult to know what judges are allowed to
know, though they are ridiculed if they pretend not to know. A
jury is certainly allowed to know something not in the evidence
when they are constantly told to use their knowledge 'as men of
the world' in interpreting the evidence."

The three judges of the Court of Appeal were unanimously of
opinion that in any event the damages were excessive, and Tolley
accepted their judgment on this aspect of the matter, but appealed
to the House of Lords on the question of liability. And so for the
third time the same arguments were ventilated by the same
counsel before different Judges. The House of Lords decided, as
Mr. Justice Acton had decided in the first place, that the advertisement was capable of a defamatory meaning. The order of the
Court of Appeal was reversed and Mr. Justice Acton's judgment
restored, except that a new trial was ordered on the amount of
damages. Frys were ordered to pay all the costs, except Tolley's
costs in the Court of Appeal, where they had succeeded on the
question of damages. Four Law Lords agreed with this judgment.
But there was one dissenting voice. Lord Blanesburgh thought
that the caricature was so vulgar, while the consequences of his
conniving at it would have been so prejudicial to his amateur
status, that no one knowing anything of Mr. Tolley could for a
moment have supposed or even suspected that he had had anything whatever to do with it.

Experience of the law shows that there is almost nothing of
which it can be said that there are not at least two ways of looking
at it.

XII

A ROSE BY ANY OTHER NAME

Marlborough v. *Gorringe's*
Travel & News Agency Ltd. and others (1935)

SOME years before the War an American magazine with the apt name of *Hooey* published a scurrilous lampoon which so enraged the then Duchess of Marlborough that she brought an action against five newsagents for importing the thing into England. The lampoon was a drawing of two standard rose trees closely intertwined in a garden bed and each bearing a single rose. The two roses bent towards and touched each other as though they were kissing. In the background was a gardener talking to a stout lady in front of a stately mansion, and the caption under the drawing read:

"I guess we shouldn't have planted the Duchess of Marlborough and the Rev. H. Robertson Page in the same bed."

The five newsagents pleaded "innocent dissemination" of this foul libel, that is, they claimed to have distributed the paper without knowing or having any reason to know of its existence. They were represented at the trial by a variety of counsel, for whom Lord Chief Justice Hewart, true to form, provided a tempestuous passage.

Maurice Alexander, opening the case on behalf of the Duchess, disclosed the full implications of the matter. "The libel is a very serious one," he said, "for, in addition to the wording which appears, there is the objectionable drawing itself, which can be seen by people who cannot read." Counsel went on to describe the distinguished American ancestry of the Duchess as well as her own high reputation, none of which was, of course, disputed. Unfortunately before the publication of the libel there had been some differences of opinion between the Duke and the Duchess. Publicity had been given to them, and later it was announced that they had been settled. But it was a sensitive time for the Duchess.

Counsel had not spoken for very long before the Lord Chief Justice began to interrupt. "This is a lamentable action. Ought it to go on?" he asked. Then, to strike terror into the defendants, he asked counsel for the plaintiff: "Have you considered the wisdom of prosecuting in this case?"

Counsel: "I am obliged."

Lord Hewart: "Well, do consider it."

Counsel: "I will give full attention to it."

The Duchess of Marlborough gave evidence. The cartoon, she said, had started people talking. "What did you think about it?" her counsel asked. "It is obvious," she replied.

"I cannot," said the Judge, "understand what other meaning there could be to it. It would be simply fatuous if it were not indecent."

"Have you throughout your life," counsel continued, "ever met a man named the Rev. H. Robertson Page?"

The Lord Chief Justice again intervened: "Does it matter whether she has or not?"

Counsel: "I think it is right that she should be given the opportunity of saying she has never heard of such a man."

Lord Hewart: "I should have thought the question was quite immaterial."

Counsel: "Then I will not press it."

(The Register of the National Rose Society contains the names of two roses—the Duchess of Marlborough, which is a brilliant lilac, and the Rev. F. Page Roberts, which is yellow with red shading and was first bred by that clerical rosarian from Queen Mary and an unnamed seedling.)

In cross-examination the Duchess was asked about a letter written by her Solicitors, but she knew nothing about it. "Do you agree," she was asked, "that you have no desire to make money, but merely to clear your reputation?"—"I have come here," answered the Duchess, "to ask for justice."

The Lord Chief Justice was impatient for her to have it. He consulted with counsel in his private room, and as a result two of the defendants withdrew from the action. Then the Lord Chief Justice declared in open Court:

"I take a very serious view of this case—very. I will adjourn it until to-morrow and let the other defendants think over their position."

When the morrow came, there were prolonged consultations between the Judge, the Duchess and counsel, and eventually a settlement was announced. Each of the remaining defendants were to offer an unqualified apology and contribute a fixed sum towards damages and costs. "I would like to express to your Lordship," said counsel for the Duchess, "my personal gratitude for your help and intervention in this case." Counsel for each of the defendants then apologised in turn. "I should like," said one of them, "to express regret for any pain that may have been caused to the Duchess."

"I do not know why you say 'for any pain'," came a growl from the Bench. "It is perfectly obvious that pain has been caused to the Duchess."

The Lord Chief Justice then consented to the withdrawal of the record on the terms endorsed on counsel's briefs, and closed the proceedings with these remarks:

"In my opinion this plaintiff, in circumstances of great provocation, has acted with magnanimity towards the defendants. They were at her mercy.

The documents in this case, including the foul emanation from the printing press which published this libel, will remain in the custody of this Court.

Not the least mischief which is done by a publication of this kind is that it may tend to cast some discredit even upon journalism itself, a profession which, as everyone knows, contains a great number of able and conscientious gentlemen."

XIII

RASPUTIN

Youssoupoff v. *Metro-Goldwyn-Mayer Pictures Ltd.* (1934)
Chegodieff v. *Metro-Goldwyn-Mayer Pictures Ltd.* (1937)

RASPUTIN was murdered in December, 1916. Ten years later Prince Youssoupoff published an account of how, and why, he planned and carried out the assassination. The Prince had been the head of perhaps the oldest and richest family in Imperial Russia. In 1914, after coming down from Oxford the previous year and attending the 300th anniversary celebrations of the Romanoff dynasty, he married the Princess Irina Alexandrovna, a niece of the Tsar, and took up residence in the Moika Palace in St. Petersburg.

He gives a vivid description of Rasputin, the corrupt mystic who dominated St. Petersburg society and the Imperial Court at Tsarkoe Selo. Rasputin was a man of incredible physical strength and hypnotic power of will. At the time when the young Tsarevitch was dying of hæmophilia—the hereditary disease of the dynasty—and the unhappy, religious parents were distraught, Rasputin, a Siberian peasant who was never a monk, though he had passed some time in a distant monastery, had been introduced to the royal palace as a wandering man of God, and, whether by hypnotism or herbal medicines, had succeeded in halting the advance of the disease. He seemed to have the power of life and death over the boy, and from that time he became, not only the indispensable counsellor of the Tsarina, but the most influential man in Russia, with the patronage of positions in the Government and imperial appointments.

It was natural that the Russian aristocracy should resent the insolence of this spiritual *arriviste*, whose asceticism alternated with bouts of debauchery. But as the war unrolled its disasters and the leadership required of the Imperial Crown was lost behind the occult manœuvres at the Palace, Prince Youssoupoff, like many other Russians, became convinced that Russia could only be saved by the removal of Rasputin from public life. For this purpose he won Rasputin's friendship and confidence. When Rasputin told him in as many words that he was in communication with German Agents, and was drugging the Tsar with Tibetan herbs, the Prince resolved as a patriotic duty to destroy him. He made his plans with four friends—the Grand Duke Dmitri, Purishkevitch, Sukhotin and Dr. Lazovert. Rasputin was invited one night to the Moika Palace. There in an underground room, while his friends played "Yankee-Doodle" on a gramophone above, the Prince offered him cakes and wine— cakes filled with powdered cyanide and wine from glasses smeared with the same poison. Rasputin ate the cakes and drank from the poisoned glasses. But the only ill effect he suffered was an irritation of the throat and stomach and a heavy sleepiness—he had always boasted immunity to poison.

Rasputin made the Prince sing to him on his guitar, and then suggested a visit to the gipsies, his favourite nocturnal expedition. But the Prince shot him with a revolver, the bullet passing through the region of the heart, and all five friends agreed he was dead. Later the Prince returned to the basement room, and Rasputin came to life again! Foaming at the mouth, with eyes crossed and knotted fingers, he tried to strangle the Prince. The Prince escaped from his demoniac clutch, and Rasputin, "bellowing and snorting like a wounded animal," found his way out into the courtyard. Four more shots were fired at him, one penetrating his neck, and he fell on a pile of snow. When he was carried in again, it seemed that he was still alive, and the Prince in an insane rage battered him to death with a loaded stick. The Prince then collapsed in a dead faint and Rasputin's body was thrown into the river Neva, where it was found a week later.

But the death of Rasputin did not save Russia. Within a year the first Bolshevik Government was in power, the Tsar and all his family had been slaughtered, Russia had withdrawn from the war, and Prince Youssoupoff, who had been exiled by the Tsar to Kursk, was in Paris with his Princess, permanently exiled

from Russia, with many of his friends and relatives dead and
all his inheritance lost.

In the early 'thirties the Metro-Goldwyn-Mayer film company
made a film called *Rasputin—The Mad Monk*, which told the
story of Rasputin's life from the time of the Romanoff celebrations to his death.   Neither Prince nor Princess Youssoupoff
appeared as characters in the film.   But there was a Prince Chegodieff who lived in a Moika Palace and played Prince Youssoupoff's part in the destruction of Rasputin.   Until the very end of
the film, when he married her, Prince Chegodieff was engaged to
a Princess Natasha.   This Princess Natasha was shown as an
admirer of Rasputin, and the film contained a scene of the familiar kind which clearly implied that the Princess was either raped
or seduced by Rasputin.   At the end of the film she said to Prince
Chegodieff: "I thought he came from God, but he is only a man,
and I am not fit to be your wife."   Thus to any patriotic motives
which Prince Chegodieff may have entertained in his design to
kill Rasputin the film script added a very natural desire for
revenge.

Princess Youssoupoff, who was in the Crimea in 1916 and had
never met Rasputin (it was ostensibly to meet her that her husband had invited Rasputin to the Moika Palace) brought actions
for libel against Metro-Goldwyn-Mayer throughout the world
and did all she could to have Princess Natasha cut out of the film.
The English action came on for trial in February, 1934, before
Mr. Justice Avory and a special jury, with Sir Patrick Hastings,
K.C., as leading counsel for the Princess and Sir William Jowitt,
K.C. (now Lord Jowitt) for the defendants.

The defendants contended that Princess Natasha was a wholly
imaginary character and there was nothing to link her with
Princess Youssoupoff.   Sir Patrick Hastings, with his eye for the
essential point in any case, realised that the chief link, and indeed
the only one of importance, was that in real life she was the wife
of the man who killed Rasputin, or at any rate of the man who
was popularly supposed to have killed Rasputin.   Thus it would be
necessary for the Prince to tell the dreadful story of Rasputin's
death in the witness-box, unless the other side were willing to
admit that the Prince had killed him—an unusual requirement

for the winning of a libel action. But, of course, the other side was not willing.

At the end of Sir Patrick's opening address, the jury were taken to see the film, and both the Prince and Princess gave evidence—with great dignity and candour. They sought to extenuate nothing. The Princess was cross-examined by Sir William Jowitt to show that no one who knew her could have thought that she was Princess Natasha, and that her only purpose was to extort damages. Here are some of the questions and answers:

"Do you think that anybody who knew the real circumstances could suppose for one moment that you were portrayed by Natasha?"—"Yes, they might."

"But they would know that you had never met Rasputin?"—"I never met him."

"In every book that has been written about this tragedy is it not made plain that you had never met him?"—"I never met him."

"After the film had been shown in London in June, 1933, was there one single soul among your friends in England who wrote to you about the film?"—"No."

"If your friends had really thought that the film was in the smallest degree a reflection on you, you would surely have heard from someone, and you did not?"—"I did not."

"Are you bringing proceedings in respect of the film in Austria, Germany, Italy, France, United States and England?"—"Yes."

"Have you also threatened proceedings against some 288 Picture Houses up and down the country?"—"Yes."

"If it is a matter of money I can well understand it, but if your object is to remove a slur on your name the present proceedings would remove it?"—"Yes."

"Then what is your object in taking proceedings against more than 200 Picture Houses?"—"I want to stop the film."

Sir William Jowitt pointed out many differences between the

Princess and Natasha and many historical inaccuracies in the film—especially in the scenes enacting Rasputin's death.

"The Producer was obviously playing fast and loose with history?"—"They always do."

"If they do, don't you think it rather ridiculous to try to assign a historical counterpart to every character in the film?"—"They are historical characters in the film."

Finally, Sir William suggested that Prince Chegodieff, if he was like anyone, was more like the Grand Duke Dmitri, who had assisted in the assassination. The Grand Duke Dmitri was a strong, soldierly figure. Prince Youssoupoff was a man of culture.

"Would it be fair to describe him as frail and effeminate?"—"He did not appear like that to me."

"He was intelligent and had æsthetic tastes, but was a dilettante?"—"Yes."

Even, said Sir William, if Prince Chegodieff was supposed to be Prince Youssoupoff, there was no more reason for associating Natasha with the Princess than with any of the other ladies of high position, such as Vyrubova or Munia Golovina, who had in fact, as in the film, venerated Rasputin as a man of God.

Neither the Prince nor the Princess denied that the appearance and character given to Chegodieff and Natasha were quite unlike theirs, but one cardinal fact predominated, and Sir Patrick Hastings put it as a question to every witness for the plaintiff and the defendants alike: "Who is the person popularly supposed to have killed Rasputin?" The answer always was "Prince Youssoupoff", and this answer did much to negative the evidence of the many witnesses for the defence who had been in Russia during the Great War, and who had not thought that Princess Natasha was a caricature of Princess Youssoupoff. One of these witnesses, Commander Locker-Lampson, M.P., who had commanded a British armoured car unit in action with the Russians, said that he had himself been invited by Purishkevitch to murder Rasputin.

Sir Patrick Hastings: "You will be in the papers even more than as an M.P. if you go on like that."

The Honourable Member was unabashed by this threat, and went on to say that Natasha did not look a bit like the Princess Youssoupoff, but "It would not be difficult to make up like the Princess, despite her beauty." "You will be in the headlines again, if you are not careful," said Sir Patrick.

No witnesses were called from America—to speak of the intentions of the author of the script and the makers of the film. Sir Patrick made the most of this fact in his final speech in reply. He poured scorn on the defence. If the defendants succeeded, he argued, film companies would be given appalling license to take the true story of real men and women, make a man wear different clothes and get the character acted by an actor who did not look like the original. But in a film dealing with the murder of Belle Elmore, Crippen could not be made less Crippen because the producers made him wear plus-fours on Saturday, which Crippen never did. The story of Rasputin's death, which Prince Youssoupoff had told in the witness-box, was cruelly true, but other men and women had done the same. A woman killed Marat because she thought it was her duty. Joan of Arc killed because she thought it her duty to do so. When Prince Youssoupoff told his story there was not a person in the Court who was not thrilled to the marrow, and that was the effect which the defendants wanted to secure for their film. Chegodieff was Prince Youssoupoff thinly disguised.

Sir William Jowitt was a little technical with the jury. He argued that there was nothing in the acting of the film, even assuming that Princess Youssoupoff was Natasha, which cast any imputation against her chastity. If there was anything of that kind, it was in the words spoken and they were slander and not libel, and no action could be brought for slander without proof of damage, unless a woman had been charged with unchastity. To say she had been ravished was not such a charge—indeed it was not defamatory at all, since it was not her fault, and he quoted a verse from Shakespeare's *Rape of Lucrece*. But this, said Mr. Justice Avory in his summing-up, was an unfortunate reference, as he had re-read the poem since the beginning of the case,

and found another verse which was a direct authority for saying
that a woman who had been ravished had lost her chastity.

> But she hath lost a dearer thing than life,
>   And he hath won what he would lose again:
> This forcèd league doth force a further strife;
>   This momentary joy breeds months of pain,
>   This hot desire converts to cold disdain,
> Pure chastity is rifled of her store,
> And Lust, the thief, far poorer than before.

The Judge summed up in favour of the plaintiff. After two
hours the jury, who had seen the film for a second time, returned
a verdict in favour of the Princess for £25,000 damages. The
defendants took the case to the Court of Appeal, and the legal
arguments which Sir William Jowitt ventilated there still provoke enthusiastic discord among professors of jurisprudence. But
the Court dismissed the appeal and refused to reduce the damages,
holding that there was ample evidence for the jury to arrive both
at their verdict itself and the huge sum they had awarded.

More than three years later it was announced in the legal
columns of *The Times* that an action against Metro-Goldwyn-
Mayer by a Prince and Princess Chegodieff for both libel and
slander in *Rasputin—The Mad Monk* had been settled. The
amount of the damages was not disclosed, as judgment was given
in the terms endorsed on counsel's briefs. It might have been
interesting to argue for the defence in that case that Prince Chegodieff and Princess Natasha in the film were really Prince and
Princess Youssoupoff, and that no reasonable person—especially
if he knew the history of Russia or the history of the case of
Youssoupoff against Metro-Goldwyn-Mayer—could ever have
thought otherwise.

XIV

A POLICEMAN'S FEET

Plumb v. *Jeyes Sanitary Compounds Co. Ltd.* (1937)
Honeysett & Wife v. *News Chronicle Ltd. & another* (1935)

ON a hot summer's day in 1929 Police Constable Plumb, while on point duty, removed his helmet and wiped his brow. A newspaper cameraman, who happened to be passing, snapped the Constable unawares. That evening a very good picture of the incident appeared in the papers over the caption, "A warm arm of the law wipes the sweat from his brow." Constable Plumb had no complaint to make about that. Mrs. Plumb thought it was rather good of Dad, and so did every one else. In any case, before the year was out, Constable Plumb had retired from the Force and entered the service of the Post Office, where the memory of those hot afternoons at the crossroads grew pleasantly cool and remote.

To take a photograph and publish it can hardly of itself be libellous, but libel very often lies in the context or circumstances in which something otherwise quite innocent is reproduced.

Imagine Civil Servant Plumb's surprise when five or six years later the old photograph appeared in an advertisement over the words: "Phew! I am going to get my feet into a Jeyes' Fluid foot-bath." It was Plumb's uncle—"a keen student of contemporaneous literature"—who noticed the photograph and sent it to his nephew, and other relatives and friends all over the country spoke or wrote to him about it. As a public servant, Plumb felt that he might have suffered an injury, for anyone "dealing in publicity" was looked on with grave disfavour in the Post Office. The public too would naturally assume that he had given permission for this use of his photograph, and the more commercially-minded reader would not doubt that he had been paid for it. It is not only mannequins who appear professionally in advertisements. But most of all Plumb resented the suggestion that his feet were smelly—almost something his best friends might never have told him. So the old Constable went to law and sued the makers of Jeyes' Fluid for libel.

In due course a Statement of Claim drawn up by counsel was delivered. It contained the innuendo on which the plaintiff relied: that the publication meant that by reason of slovenly and un-uncleanly habits or otherwise, the exudation and/or general condition of his feet was so unpleasant and noisome, that a bath or wash would be inadequate and a solution of Jeyes' Sanitary Compound would be necessary to deodorise or disinfect his feet.

The defendants answered that there was nothing defamatory in implying that a man needed, or wanted, to use Jeyes' Fluid on his feet. But counsel for Mr. Plumb refused to admit that personal remarks could be made about policemen's feet except, perhaps, their size.

At the trial Mr. Plumb was cross-examined by Norman Birkett, K.C. (now Lord Justice Birkett), whose experience in taking evidence was only matched by Plumb's in giving it.

"Do you entertain some dim recollections of your days as a
    policeman?"—"Yes."

"Happy days?"—"Some were."

"Do you seriously suggest that anybody looking at this ad-
    vertisement would say that you had got bad feet?"—"Yes:
    The advertisement for Jeyes' says it is good for feet or smel-
    ling feet."

"Do you agree that a policeman, standing on a beat in all sorts
    of weather, is the kind of man who would benefit by a foot-
    bath?"—"He would."

"Is anybody going to think a penny the worse of you because
    you have a foot-bath?"—"No, but this is associated with a
    disinfectant. I would use a foot-bath because my feet ached
    and not because they were smelly."

"Supposing they did smell, do you think you would be unique
    in the world, or that ordinary people's feet smell as a com-

mon thing?"—"They do. But it is possible to use bath salts—
quite different from Jeyes' Fluid."

"Do you think that your reputation would be enhanced if
you washed your feet in scented salts?"—"Oh! no." Nevertheless, said Mr. Plumb, anybody reading the advertisement
would think he had feet smelling so highly that he needed
Jeyes' Fluid, and in fact, the advertisement had led to jokes
against him.

"It is a good joke and there it ends?"—"No. It has caused bad
feeling in the family. I have lost my temper at times over the
continual joking about it. We have arguments about it."

Norman Birkett spoke strongly to the jury. "I have heard of
families being broken up in the Divorce Courts," he said, "but
I have never heard about families being broken up by Jeyes'
Fluid."

But "the warm arm of the law" protected the feet of its old
servant. The jury awarded Mr. Plumb £100 damages, and
judgment was entered for him for that amount with his costs.

Mr. Plumb has not been the only sufferer from an inconsiderate
use of his photograph. There was the case of Mr. and Mrs.
Honeysett. Mrs. Honeysett, before she married, had been a keen
member of a cycling club, and while out one day on a tour with a
girl friend she had the good fortune to be photographed. The
photograph appeared at the time in several newspapers. Mrs.
Honeysett thought no more about it and in the following year
she married Mr. Honeysett and went to live with him in New
Guinea. Several summers later, when Mr. and Mrs. Honeysett
were living once more in England, the *News Chronicle* ran a
series of articles under the title "Unchaperoned Holidays". One
of these articles commented on the freedom with which young
people of the same or opposite sex went off together on holidays
without their families. It was illustrated with the old photograph
of Mrs. Honeysett on her bicycle before her marriage, but in the
place of her girl friend there appeared riding along with her a
young man whom Mrs. Honeysett had never seen and who was

"leering at her over the handlebars of his bicycle". The photograph of this young man had in fact been extracted from an all-male cycling group. It was plain that he and Mrs. Honeysett were supposed to be setting off on an unchaperoned holiday together. This inference was confirmed by the words of the article which appeared immediately below:

"For some time past girls have been spending their holidays with other girls without a chaperon. Once a girl has left school and gone to college or begun to earn her own living she no longer plans her holiday in terms of 'where is the family going this summer?' Instead, she finds out where she wants to go herself, and then looks round to see which of her friends she would like to go with. If the friend she chooses happens to be a man, she is not very much perturbed."

Mrs. Honeysett had never in her life taken an unchaperoned holiday, and had not even bicycled for some years, as she was now the mother of a young child. She and her husband brought an action against the *News Chronicle*. The libel on Mrs. Honeysett, albeit accidental, was grave and glaring, but Mr. Honeysett complained that the photograph also libelled him, because it meant he had no control over his wife and was a complacent husband who deserved neither respect nor sympathy, being one who through weakness failed to uphold the dignity of married life. Mr. Justice Hawke, however, was not prepared to take the authority of a husband to these extremes, and he refused to allow the jury an opportunity of placating Mr. Honeysett with damages. But Mrs. Honeysett received £100 damages for her unchaperoned holiday.

XV

A DRAMATIC DANCE

Regina v. *Ledger* (1880)

In the days when Society was a Republic of its own within the Kingdom, impregnable behind a social "iron curtain", the Theatrical Profession was, or thought itself to be, no less circumscribed and exclusive. It had its own leaders, its own high etiquette and its own unwritten list of members. Its *bon ton* was guarded and sustained by a journal called *The Era*. *The Era* has passed away, but in those days it was read by every respectable actor over his porridge. Nothing more clearly shows how libel is the servant of the sacred conventions of each generation than the prosecution of the Editor of *The Era* for criminal libel in January, 1880.

A Mr. Hodson Stanley, who was an actor and theatrical manager of experience but obviously not of the highest standing in the Green Room, arranged to give a ball at the Cannon Street Hotel. The printed invitations bore the following legend:

"Great Hall, Cannon Street Hotel.
Mr. Hodson Stanley, at the request of numerous friends of the Theatrical Profession, has arranged to give a grand dramatic full and fancy dress ball at the above hall on Tuesday the 28th of October. Full quadrille band of the Orleans Club, under the direction of Mr. Sibold.
Gentlemen's tickets, 10s. 6d.
Dancing at 11 o'clock."

Mr. Hodson Stanley called at the editorial offices of *The Era* and invited the Editor to attend, asking at the same time for a good write-up. The Editor, Mr. Edward Ledger, replied that he could not go alone and asked for another ticket, which was

duly supplied to him. When the time came, Mr. Ledger went to
the ball with Mr. Clement Scott, the dramatic critic, and according to Mr. Stanley they congratulated him on the success of the
evening. But in its next number *The Era* published a letter containing a vitriolic description of "A Dramatic Dance". "What,"
it was asked, "would be said if an ungenerous person determined
to go back to the seamy side of the profession and to thrust it
under the very nose of the public, who, in order to show the
preposterous fallacy of any social advance, made the drama look
as contemptible as it could, dragged out its dirty linen to wash it
in public, exhibited the love and hunger for all this booth and
parade life, magnified the importance of certain very insignificant
people, and used the name of the drama and the popularity of the
Theatrical Profession in order to degrade the one and vulgarise the
other? I hold that this was done on Tuesday evening, not in an
insignificant hole-and-corner way, but openly and publicly . . ."
Nothing, continued the writer, could have been seedier than the
fancy dresses. There might have been one or two corsair-like
Albanian costumes fairly provided with spangles, but the representatives of artless childhood, with skipping-ropes and short
frocks, seemed to forget that innocence might be assumed, but
age could not be conveniently concealed under the glaring light
of a ballroom. He did not suppose, wrote the author of the letter
with spite, that half-a-dozen ladies in the room had ever been
honoured with a speaking part, but, though mute on the boards,
they had evidently great powers of persuasion and were apparently well known and popular with that curious and miscel-
laneous entertainment. The letter concluded with the pious hope
that the punctiliousness which the public had displayed towards
photographs of Zulus would not be withheld from the dramatic
ball. The letter was signed "Cannon Ball", but was written by
Mr. Clement Scott.

But the ball was not without its friends, and a letter of protest
arrived from "D" of the Junior United Service Club, which *The
Era* printed, and added its own comment:

"The first question that will suggest itself to the reader of this
letter is, 'What was the inducement which took a member of the
Junior United Service Club, and presumably an officer and a

gentleman, to a ball arranged, according to his theory, for the enjoyment of 'hard-working actresses and chorus singers'? Was he in search of a wife, or are hard-working actresses and chorus singers supposed to be under the special protection of the distinguished club alluded to? If 'D' really is of opinion that dramatic talent was well represented, and that some among the numerous painted harlots in attendance at the ball in question will some day rise to eminence in the dramatic profession, perhaps he will furnish us with the names of the promising ones and will back his opinion by his own signature. Then our readers will be able to put an estimate upon his judgment, and the Junior United Service Club may congratulate a member on the philanthropic spirit which moves him on behalf of 'actresses and chorus singers'. Let us tell our correspondent that no actress or chorus singer worthy of the name would degrade herself by appearing at such a despicable gathering as that in question; we repeat that the 'dramatic dance' was a deliberate attempt to drag the drama through the mud and it proved neither more nor less than a disreputable orgy, and the announcement of its origin in 'the request of numerous friends in the theatrical profession' was an excuse for sullying the fair name of the stage and for holding up its art exponents to derision and contempt."

The result of all this was the prosecution of Mr. Ledger for criminal libel at the instance of Mr. Hodson Stanley. The trial took place at the Old Bailey, with Serjeant Ballantine, Q.C. and Henry Kisch for the prosecution, Charles Russell, Q.C. (later Lord Russell of Killowen), and Montague Williams for the defence.

What had been wrong with the ball? There were really two issues in the case. The first was the charge of impropriety. Representatives of that seductive Victorian underworld, described as "ladies of the *demi-monde*", had been present in force. A few had their hair down their backs, a few wore fancy dresses with short (but probably not so very short) frocks, two were dressed up as sailors and quite a lot bought their tickets at the door. Even so, there were some 250 gentlemen to 100 ladies present. Nevertheless, it was a very shocking thing. "For the defence," wrote Montague Williams ten years later, "a number of ladies

who actually attended the ball were called; and a more extraordinary group of persons I never saw. A great many of them
gave addresses in Pimlico and St. John's Wood, and some of them
admitted that they had paid for their tickets at the door."

But there was no evidence of any indecency or drunkenness.
The "orgy" turned out to have been a very ordinary dance.
Charles Russell accordingly concentrated on the other issue in
the case—that it was only called a "dramatic ball" for the purpose
of attracting young gentlemen with the prospect of meeting
young actresses. If this was so, it was an insult and an injury to the
fair reputation of the Theatrical Profession and a proper subject
of harsh comment in *The Era*.

Charles Russell's cross-examinations were largely devoted to
developing this side of his defence. The main target of his attack
was Mr. Hodson Stanley himself, who was the first witness for
the prosecution. It soon came out that Mr. Stanley had hawked
his tickets round the town. Some he had tried to sell in an
establishment called "Evans's". Some he had left with the hall
porter of the Naval and Military Club, and doubtless also at the
Junior United Service Club. "To prevent questionable characters
being admitted," he added, "I placed a retired police officer at
the door." He invited certain Leading Ladies, but none came.
But those who did come were not, he assured the Court, in any
way "loose". Mr. Stanley, however, was obliged to disclose
that he had been expelled from the Junior Garrick Club (an event
in Victorian life which was almost equivalent to a criminal conviction) and that all the profits of the ball, which were "good",
went into his own pocket. Mr. Hodson Stanley's reputation in
the Court had fallen very low by the time he stepped out of the
witness-box.

Only Robert Villiers, the manager of the London Pavilion,
came forward to testify to the seemliness of the entertainment.
Though he saw no "painted harlots", however, he did catch
sight of several members of the *"demi-monde"*.

The star witness for the defence, apart from the "extraordinary
persons", was Mr. Henry Irving. Irving was aloof and majestic
in the witness-box. He represented the Dignity of the Stage. "I
have known Mr. Ledger," he remarked, "for fifteen or sixteen

years, and his paper, *The Era*, is the recognised organ of the dramatic profession, while his character as a literary man is strictly honourable." Serjeant Ballantine cross-examined. "I know," said Irving, "of no respectable person in the profession who was in any way connected with this ball." "If I were asked," he continued in answer to the questions, "whether a vast number of other balls were respectable, I don't know that I should say they were not. It would depend upon where they were. I know nothing of this ball. There are thousands of balls I know nothing about. All I know about this ball is what I read in *The Era*. All I know is that it was not at all connected with the Theatrical Profession. No one I know in the Profession was connected with it. They wouldn't be. What I thought on reading the article was that it was not severe enough, because I think it was infamous to connect such a calling as ours with anything so disgraceful. A great many of the public, who know no better, believe what they read." And then with a forbidding finality: "I should not call young ladies of the ballet members of the Theatrical Profession."

Other celebrated figures of the Theatrical Profession followed Irving into the witness-box, and all of them agreed with the evidence of their most eminent member. The ball was not a dramatic ball after all, but a dance of the *"demi-monde"*. When the last witness had departed, counsel on both sides made long and powerful speeches. The Recorder of London summed up in favour of the defendant, and after three-quarters of an hour the jury returned a verdict of "not guilty", but added that in their opinion the comments made by *The Era* were severe. "I presume," said the Recorder, "that you mean severe, but honest?" To which the foreman replied, "Yes," and the Editor of *The Era* walked out of Court a free man.

XVI

BOTTOMLEY'S LAST CASE

Bottomley v. F. W. Woolworth & Co. Ltd. (1932)

MARCH, 1932. The amazing old rogue was now seventy-two. It was five years since he came out of prison, and in that time, though two books and a paper had been failures and he was bankrupt once again, he had earned about £12,000 by journalism and £5,000 by way of damages in libel actions. Bottomley "earned" his damages, if ever a man did. In forty years to and fro the Courts he had been his own advocate every time, and no less successful in the Courts than on the public platform.

It was almost exactly forty years since that first prosecution at the Old Bailey over the failure of the Hansard Union. Ironical to reflect now that the most discredited man in the country had been the co-founder of the *Financial Times*! Bottomley had sold out his share to his partner in return for some paper mills. Then he bought out Hansard, the family firm which had published the debates of Parliament for nearly a century, and floated an enormous public company, which, once the public's money had been invested, collapsed, and charges of fraud followed. That was Bottomley's first acquittal. The Judge was so impressed by his defence that he said in his summing-up that "nobody could doubt the honesty of his motives", and after the trial he sent for him and recommended him to go to the Bar.

But none of the Inns of Court would accept him, and Bottomley turned to the City, which proved more amenable than the Temple. Then came the boom years of the Joint Stock Institute—racing stables, a Riviera villa, a country mansion, a seat in Parliament—the Liberal Member for Hackney. After a decade of prosperity, there was another prosecution and another acquittal, and then bankruptcy. He rose again with the tide of war, the most popular orator, journalist and financier in the country, and he was sent back to his old seat in the House with a huge majority—the Independent Member for Hackney. It was not until 1922 that the third prosecution succeeded and he went down for seven years for the Victory Bond swindle.

During all those years of personal boom and slump Bottomley, who began life as a Solicitor's clerk, had established himself as the most brilliant lay lawyer who frequented the Courts. Who has counted the number of his libel actions? No man's reputation had tottered for so long without falling or see-sawed so high in the vacuum of optimism. Once, when the see-saw was down, Bottomley tipped it up again with a libel action. He arranged with a confederate for the publication of the libels which were already circulating as rumours: Bottomley sued, the defendant was forced to admit that the libels were untrue. Bottomley was awarded £500 damages and costs, but in fact the defendant received £100 for his assistance. No one could say that Bottomley was afraid of the exposures of a libel suit! Yet a libel case had been his undoing. Years later the same confederate was stricken with conscience and made it his one object in life to bring Bottomley into the witness-box. Bottomley always accepted a challenge, and brought proceedings for criminal libel. But when the case was called on, his courage failed and he offered no evidence. Bottomley also prosecuted him for blackmail, but though his old conspirator made the most damning charges against him, Bottomley refused to go into the witness-box to contradict them, and the man was acquitted. Bottomley then challenged the Director of Public Prosecutions to prosecute him—his one deadly mistake.

Now the old man had overreached himself again. He sued Woolworths. Woolworths did an enormous trade in out-of-date American magazines, which they bought by the ton from the American Magazine Remainder Company. From their 458 shops they sold two-and-a-half millions of these magazines in a year. There were sixty to seventy different publications, and they were sent direct to the different shops, the managers of which merely specified whether they wanted love, adventure or crime. Apart from that, Woolworths took no interest in and had no knowledge of what the magazines contained.

One of the remainders was a five-year-old number of the *Detective Story Magazine* which contained an article called "Swindlers and Scoundrels. Horatio Bottomley, Editor and Embezzler", with contents to match.

Now a man may have swindled and embezzled, but, once he has been convicted and served his sentence, he is presumed to have expiated his offence and to have regained the right to a good reputation. The man who walks out of prison at the end of a long sentence for theft is not a thief. And so, said Bottomley in opening his case, "by putting this magazine on the English market at a time when I am endeavouring to lead a clean and honest life, Woolworths have done me a great wrong, and they are in a position to pay. In my fifty years' experience of these Courts I have never known a libel case in any way akin to the present one with regard to the cruelty and cowardice of the libellers."

Bottomley then spoke feelingly of his downfall and his sufferings in prison. He poured scorn on the apology which Woolworths had inserted at the end of their written defence; it was hypocritical and humbugging, he said, since they had given him notice that in mitigation of damages they intended to call evidence that he was a person of no credit or reputation. But when it came to the point, they did not do so. After calling two witnesses who had bought copies of the magazine in question, one in the Strand and the other in Great Yarmouth—thus proving, as he must, that Woolworths had in fact been selling it—Bottomley entered the witness-box himself. "Do you tender yourself for cross-examination, Mr. Bottomley?" asked Mr. Justice Horridge. "No," he answered, "what I propose to do is to say: 'I am the plaintiff in this case,' and leave it there." As he had given no evidence, he could be asked no questions. But it was surely a sad moment. Questions were unnecessary, as everybody knew the answers already.

The actual writer of a libel is not the only person who may be penalised for "publishing" it. Anyone who prints it or distributes it or authorises it to be circulated may equally be liable. This is why in an action for a libel in a book the author, the publisher and the printer are usually sued together as joint defendants.

Generally the law allows no excuse to any of the parties concerned. But anyone who may have technically "published" a
libel is not liable if he can prove that, when, as in the case of a
bookseller, he sold a particular book, he did not know and had
no reason to know there was anything libellous in it. In other
words, he has to prove that he acted without negligence. This
was the defence which Woolworths pleaded in this case.

In order to decide whether Woolworths had been negligent
it was possible to approach the matter in two different ways.
On the one hand there had been nothing to put them on their
guard. Their buyer gave evidence that the *Detective Story Magazine* had always been devoted only to the detective stories of
fiction and there was nothing to lead him to suppose that it might
contain the life story of a British subject. (Bottomley said he
wanted to know why they should have altered that rule for his
particular benefit, and the foreman of the jury remarked that it
was extraordinary to find an article like this among detective
stories.) This evidence was supported by Woolworths' Secretary,
who added that this was the first complaint of libel ever to be
received in connection with these magazines. On the other hand,
Woolworths had taken no steps whatever to look at any of these
magazines. They employed no examiners to inspect them. They
said it would be impossible to have them all read for libel. And
so they read none of them.

After some legal discussion the case was adjourned to the
following day, when Malcolm Hilbery, K.C. (now Mr. Justice
Hilbery) for the defendants and Bottomley himself addressed the
jury, and Horridge summed up. The Judge said that Bottomley
had conducted his case with his usual ability and discretion, and
one could not help feeling sympathy with him in the unwar-
ranted attack on him in that American magazine, but that was
quite a different matter from making a person who distributed it
responsible for damages, and on the point at issue he summed up
heavily in favour of Woolworths. There were fifty or sixty
magazines of different titles and each weekly, fortnightly or
monthly edition would be different from the last: was it reasonable
to suppose that in dealing with books of that kind there should be
an examiner to read every word of the magazines before they

were despatched to the shops? A periodic scrutiny would probably not have discovered the libel on Bottomley. In these circumstances his Lordship doubted whether there was any evidence
of negligence to go before the jury. However, he put the following questions, which are given with the jury's answers:

1. Were the defendants innocent of any knowledge of the libel
   contained in the magazine disseminated by them?—Yes.
2. Was there anything (*a*) in the magazine, or (*b*) the circumstances in which it came to them or was disseminated by
   them, which ought to have led them to suppose that it contained a libel?—(*a*) Yes. (*b*) No.
3. When the magazine was disseminated by them, was it by
   any and what negligence on their part that they did not
   know that it contained a libel?—We find that there was
   negligence owing to the absence of periodical examination
   of specimen magazines.
4. Damages?—£250.

Bottomley asked for judgment. Hilbery argued, and Mr.
Justice Horridge held, that there was no evidence to support the
jury's findings on the two points in favour of Bottomley, and
judgment was entered for Woolworths with costs. Was this
quite fair? The Court of Appeal agreed with it, and perhaps it
was not for Bottomley to complain: no man had done better by
the law. But, as *The Times* obituary said a year later, "after this
he fell on evil days, and it was said that he had been obliged to
apply for an old-age pension."

XVII

BLACKMAIL

Hobbs v. *Tinling* (*C.T.*) *& Co. Ltd.* ⎫
Hobbs v. *Nottingham Journal Ltd.* ⎬ (1928–9)

DAMAGES in libel actions are intended to compensate an injured reputation. It follows that no one is entitled to complain of injury to a reputation he does not possess. But reputation is a thing of many aspects, and may be lost and won again. The law is anxious that a man with one vice shall not be accused of another, or that a man with a past shall not be made a cockshy for every sort of false rumour in the present. It is libel to call a drunkard a thief. It is libel to call a man a thief, merely on the ground that he has served a sentence or half a dozen sentences for theft. To refuse protection to all except those with an unblemished record would be tantamount to a sentence of outlawry on tens of thousands of citizens. On the other hand it would be wrong for a man of little merit to be awarded the price of virtue. How are the scales of justice to be balanced?

In their efforts—not always successful—to see fair play between the citizens and the world, the Judges have worked out rules. If a man proceeds against you for a libel, you may try to prove the libel, or if you do not choose that course, you may call witnesses to say, in mitigation of damages, that he is a man of bad reputation. But you may not make random charges against him, for you cannot defend one libel by uttering another. If your opponent gives evidence, you may question him about other incidents in his life with a view to showing him up as a liar and thus destroying his evidence. This is known as cross-examination 'to credit', which means to credibility, your object being to discredit. But you are not allowed in cross-examination to accuse the witness of every crime under the sun, in the hope that the jury will give no more than a farthing damages to a man who is accused of so much! The rules of what you may and may not do have been developed by generations of precedents, and the Judge is there to explain them and see them obeyed. If the Judge fails in his duty, a clever litigant may be able to tip the scales unfairly in his favour.

In 1925 William Cooper Hobbs was sentenced to two years' imprisonment for his part in the extortion by blackmail of £150,000 from the Indian prince whose identity was at one time thinly veiled as "Mr. A." Hobbs was a solicitor's clerk, and, though he had never been caught out before, his hand was suspected in fraudulent dealings over the past quarter century. His conviction was accordingly greeted by the Press throughout the country with the most lurid accounts of his life and crimes. Some of the charges were true, while others probably were not, but most of them could not be proved.

When Hobbs came out of prison, with no reputation to lose, he determined, as Bottomley and others have done, to turn the law of libel to his own pecuniary advantage and blackmail the Press. He issued between twenty and thirty writs against different newspapers, and waited for results. Some of the newspapers paid up, to save the trouble and expense of an action. But others decided to fight, and the first case came before the High Court in December, 1928. It was a claim against the *Liverpool Evening Express*, and it was tried by Lord Chief Justice Hewart and a special jury. Serjeant Sullivan, K.C. led for Hobbs, Norman Birkett, K.C. (later Lord Justice Birkett) for the defendants. The article which was the subject of complaint accused Hobbs of financing burglaries, running "a passport office for criminals", ruining rich young men and many another foul practice. The article, said Serjeant Sullivan, contained twenty-four distinct defamatory allegations, charging Hobbs with thirteen or fourteen different crimes. The defendants admitted that the article was defamatory, but made no attempt to justify its contents. They contented themselves with the payment of 20s. into Court.

Serjeant Sullivan put Hobbs into the witness-box, where he denied the charges, and then faced Birkett. The object of the cross-examination was to ensure that the jury would not award the plaintiff more than the 20s. which the defendants had paid into Court. This object might have been achieved quite early, without the assistance of the Lord Chief Justice. The result of that assistance was its ultimate frustration.

"Why," asked Birkett, "have you brought this action?"— "To show the world and my children that the stories which have been told about me are absolute concoctions, and to get damages."

"I am glad that you added the last words. Have you brought twenty-three actions before this against newspapers?"— "Yes."

"Is this the first one that has been fought?"—"Yes."

"Did you issue the writ in this action after you had settled with other newspapers?"—"I could not issue them all at once."

"Have you more on your waiting list?"—"I think that there are one or two."

A man who has been involved in blackmail must expect a difficult passage. "Do you agree," Birkett asked, "that blackmail is the most horrible crime that a man can commit?" —"I think that it is a wicked thing."

"Do you agree that a blackmailer is a villain of the deepest dye?"—"I am not in a position to answer that." There was laughter in Court at this answer, and Hobbs protested. "They are only paid *claqueurs*," he said. "It is desirable that there should be silence," rejoined the Lord Chief Justice, "but you have no business to say that."

Birkett went remorselessly on. "Do you agree that a man who attempts to blackmail another is a man who has no character?" The question was slightly altered, and so was the reply. "I am not in a condition to answer that," said Hobbs.

"Physically or mentally?"—"Both."

"Do you mean," asked the Lord Chief Justice, "that your physical and mental condition is such that you cannot express your opinion of a blackmailer?"—"I think he ought to be shunned."

"Have you heard judges say that morally blackmail is often worse than murder? Do you agree with that?"—"I do."

These were some of the opening questions. The whole of the next day was devoted to questioning Hobbs about a number of incidents calculated to expose his unpalatable way of life. But he denied the blunt suggestions of dishonesty and no evidence had been called to prove them, when on the third day of the trial the case came to a sudden and tempestuous end. From the opening of the trial the Lord Chief Justice's attitude had been plain and it now was to become still plainer.

"Do you intend," he asked Serjeant Sullivan, "to offer evidence other than that of Mr. Hobbs himself?"—"I was proposing," replied the Serjeant, "to consider that matter at the end of the cross-examination."

"I am asking you to consider it now. I have received an intimation from the members of the jury in which they say that they are unanimously agreed that they have heard sufficient evidence in this case." His Lordship then turned to the jury, and asked: "Do you mean by that intimation that, on the plaintiff's own evidence, you are prepared to find a verdict for the defendants?"

The Foreman: "Yes, my Lord."

"May I take it as a consequence that if, as a matter of law on these pleadings, it is necessary that there should be a verdict for the plaintiff for some amount of damages, your verdict would be for the smallest possible amount?"

The Foreman: "Yes, my Lord."

"In other words, for a farthing?"

The Foreman: "Yes, my Lord."

Serjeant Sullivan sprang to his feet. "Before that result is arrived at," he declared, "I should insist on addressing the jury."

"You would insist? That is a strange phrase to use."—"I conceive that I am entitled to address the jury."

"Please do not use the word 'insist'."—"Of course, I did not do so as against your Lordship."

"Are you entitled to address the jury when they have said that, on the evidence of the plaintiff himself, they are satisfied that he ought not to recover?"—"I respectfully submit that I am entitled to point out that on the evidence of the plaintiff there is nothing to disentitle him from recovering substantial damages."

Serjeant Sullivan was therefore permitted to address the jury, but not without constant interruption from the Bench. He told them they had come to an unjust decision, based merely on allegations put to Hobbs in cross-examination and denied by him. His denials should be accepted. "Are you addressing the jury as counsel," snapped the Lord Chief Justice, "or are you summing-up to them as Judge?" Serjeant Sullivan fought on to the end of his speech, and when he had finished it, the Judge, without any summing up, said to the jury: "At ten-thirty you intimated that you were prepared to find a verdict for the defendants, but that, if it were legally necessary that there should be a verdict for the plaintiff for some amount, it should be for a farthing. It is now nearly eleven-thirty. Are you still of the same opinion?"

The Foreman: "Yes, my Lord."

The point about the farthing was this: the article in the newspaper was admittedly defamatory and contained charges which could not be proved. It followed that the plaintiff was entitled to damages as a matter of law, since damage is always presumed and does not have to be proved in a libel action. The jury could only reduce the damages to the smallest coin of the realm. But this did not satisfy the Lord Chief Justice. "No doubt," he said, "the law presumes some damage, but can that presumption not be rebutted? May a plaintiff not obviously be so worthless that it is impossible for him to suffer damage from any libel?"

Birkett, for the defendants, did not want the Judge to go too far. "I can conceive the possibility of such a case," he assured his

Lordship, "but as the present defendants have paid twenty shillings into Court—19s. 11¾d. too much—a verdict and judgment for the plaintiff for a farthing would, from the practical point of view, be a judgment for the defendants. I know of no case where a plaintiff who has been entitled to damages has failed to get a farthing." The jury thereupon returned a formal verdict for the plaintiff for one farthing, but because of the twenty shillings in Court judgment was entered for the defendants with their costs from the date when they paid in the 20s.

But this was by no means the end of the story. The next case in the list was Hobbs' action for a similar libel against the *Nottingham Journal*. When the case was called on, Serjeant Sullivan rose and applied for an adjournment, to consider his position. "I object most firmly," said Birkett, and the Lord Chief Justice agreed with him. "Certainly," he said, "you need not say a word. I never heard of such an application. If the case is to be gone on with, it must be gone on with now." Serjeant Sullivan then asked for another jury. "There is," replied the Judge, "no other special jury present." "Mr. Hobbs says that he is not content to have this case tried by the same jury." The Lord Chief Justice relented with an ill grace. "In view of that objection—I say nothing about its merits—and as there is no other special jury present, it seems to me that the better course would be for this case to go over till to-morrow morning." But he added menacingly that he would impound the documents in the first case and send them to the Director of Public Prosecutions.

That evening and the following morning the Press was filled with reports of the first case, and big headlines were given to the partisan observations of the Lord Chief Justice. When the Court sat again, Serjeant Sullivan asked for the second case to be adjourned until the next sittings. He read an affidavit sworn by Hobbs that it would be impossible to find jurors whose minds were not influenced and prejudiced by the newspaper reports. Birkett in reply read an affidavit of the defendants' solicitors attacking Hobbs' *bona fides*. There was an argument between counsel, settled by the Lord Chief Justice in these words: "In my opinion there is no reason for an adjournment, and the application is refused." "May I apply for liberty to appeal?" asked Serjeant

Sullivan. There is always an appeal from the refusal of any application to the High Court, with the consent of the Judge, or, if he refuses his consent, with the leave of the Court of Appeal. But the Lord Chief Justice said: "I do not think that you want liberty to appeal. If you do, I do not give it to you."

Serjeant Sullivan was prepared for this, and he marched out of Court, followed a few seconds later by Martin O'Connor, his junior counsel. The case of Hobbs against the *Nottingham Journal* was then called on, and the following uneasy colloquy took place between the Lord Chief Justice and counsel for the defendants:

Lord Hewart: "The usual document is handed to me which purports to show the names of learned counsel who appear for the plaintiff. Two of them who were in Court a moment ago appear to be in Court no longer."

Birkett: "I am not certain whether they left the Court to consult with their client or whether it was part of a fixed procedure. If the latter, it is interesting to remember that when this case was fixed in your Lordship's list the ground of the application by the plaintiff's counsel was that Mr. Hobbs should meet with speedy justice. It seems a strange way of obtaining it, to leave the Court when the case is called on. I must assume that they have left the Court of set purpose."

Lord Hewart: "It looks like part of a transparent manœuvre."

Birkett: "I ask for judgment for the defendants with costs."

Lord Hewart: "I have made inquiries and I find that no intimation was received by the Officers of the Court of any such intended course of conduct. I can, therefore, only put my own construction on what we have seen and heard. . . ."

And the jury were then asked to return a formal verdict for the defendants, and judgment was entered accordingly. Birkett applied for the return of 20s. paid into Court.

Lord Hewart: "Are you entitled to 20s. or 19s. 11¾d.?"

Birkett: "To 20s. to-day. To 19s. 11¾d. yesterday."

The Court then rose.

That afternoon Serjeant Sullivan presented himself before the Court of Appeal. The eventual result was that a new trial of both the actions was ordered. The Court of Appeal was unanimously of opinion that there had been a miscarriage of justice, although it was likely, perhaps more than likely, that no jury properly directed in a properly conducted trial could ever have awarded Hobbs more than a farthing damages. "It is not admissible," said Lord Justice Sankey, "to do a great right by doing a little wrong. The inequalities of life are not so dangerous in a State whose subjects know that in a Court of Law at any rate they are sure to get justice, and it is not sufficient to do justice by obtaining a proper result by irregular or improper means. . . . In a strong desire to do justice a Judge may make mistakes. So may counsel. So may a jury. It is easy to criticise, but no system can ensure infallibility; the best it can do is to provide for finality. In attaining finality, open Courts and a vigilant Bar will reduce the margin of error to a minimum."

The new trials never took place. All Hobbs' libel actions were settled for a total of £17,000 damages, a high price to pay for too strong a judicial desire to do justice.

XVIII

BLACK MAGIC

Crowley v. Constable & Co. Ltd. and others (1934)

THE law may concede a farthing to a blackmailer. It has refused even that contemptuous trifle to a black magician.

No other man in the prime of his life has ever enjoyed, or enjoyed so greatly, the dark, satanic notoriety which attached to the name of Aleister Crowley, mountaineer, poet, sex-maniac, drug-fiend and, above all, magician. As a mountaineer Crowley took part in the first expeditions to Chogo Ri (K2) and Kanchenjunga, the highest mountains in the world after Everest and both of them still unclimbed. As a poet he wrote powerful, if glutinous, songs of love and hate. But his upbringing in a family of fanatical Plymouth Brethren left him with a correspondingly fanatical hatred of all organised religious and social conventions, and from before the turn of this century, when he came down from Cambridge, he found release for his developing egotism in sex, drugs and magic. From these three unstable elements he compounded a system intended—under his own quasi-divine inspiration—to rejuvenate the world. Each year he advanced in the knowledge of magic and the grandeur of self-worship, until at last with an appropriate ritual he promoted himself to the highest grade of magician—Ipsissimus, the Utmost Self.

Crowley was christened Edward Alexander, but besides substituting Aleister for these somewhat ordinary names he invented for himself a succession of grotesque titles. His mother in a moment of resentment asking if he was "The Beast" mentioned in the Apocalypse, Crowley at once seized upon the name, adding the mystic letters "666", and kept it till the end of his life. At other times he passed himself off as Lord Boleskine, Frater Perdurabo, Prince Chioa Khan, The Master Therion, and many another figment of his twisted imagination. He even assumed

the role of Baphomet, the idol said to have been worshipped by
the mediavel Knights Templar, to a new mockery of whose Order
he belonged. Such was his love of names that he called his first
daughter Nuit Ma Ahathoor Hecate Sappho Jezebel Lilith—a child
said to have died of Acute Nomenclature.

For each different title Crowley appeared in a different costume, and even a distinct *coiffure*. Stripped of its hocus-pocus,
however, his new system of magic was nothing more nor less
than a revival of the pagan sex-cults associated with Pan, Diony-
sus and other gods of the ancient world. Nevertheless, it attracted
a few disciples, whom Crowley treated with unfailing callousness.
Before his life was over he had driven his two wives into lunatic
asylums and abandoned all his mistresses, each of whom was
known in her turn as "The Scarlet Woman". Crowley was in
every sense the *bête noire* of the Edwardian *demi-monde*.

After the Great War (which he spent writing anti-British
articles in New York) he moved his abode of magic, with two
Scarlet Women and a number of children, to a farmhouse at
Cefalu in Sicily. This he called the Abbey of Thelema, which
was the name chosen by Rabelais for his Abbey on the Loire. But
it was given to Crowley in a vision by his Holy Guardian Angel,
a spirit who rejoiced in the name of Aiwass. Visitors went out
to the Abbey of Thelema, and returned with strange tales of the
rites performed there.

When in 1922 Crowley published a novel called *The Diary of a
Drug Fiend* it was hardly surprising that the London Press took the
opportunity of debunking the sinister English magician. *John Bull*
and the *Sunday Express* attacked him violently, and the attacks
were renewed the following winter when Raoul Loveday, a
young disciple of Crowley's from Oxford, died of dysentery in
the Abbey of Thelema, and it was hinted that his death was not
wholly due to natural causes. Information was given to the Press
by Loveday's wife, an artists' model well-known in London as
Betty May. But although he was dubbed "The Wickedest Man
in the World" and "The King of Depravity" and accused of all
manner of orgies and profligacy, Crowley remained silent.

The Italian Government, however, took note of the charges
and expelled Crowley from Sicily. Some years later his permit

to stay in France was withdrawn, and after wanderings in Germany and North Africa this disagreeable product of the occult renaissance returned to England.

But the time for Crowley's brand of magic had passed, and England no longer gave him the attention which his megalomania and extravagant habits required. There came a moment when these needs—his need for publicity and his need for money—could only be satisfied by success in litigation, and Crowley entered his name in the lists of seekers after public consolation, computed in £. s. d. When the Courts of Love had failed him, he betook himself to the Courts of Law.

He began in a small way. Walking one day down Praed Street, Paddington, he saw in the window of a bookshop a copy of a novel which he had written called *Moonchild*. Attached to the book was an announcement that "Aleister Crowley's first novel, *The Diary of a Drug Fiend*, was withdrawn from circulation after an attack in the sensational Press." This was untrue, and in the resulting action Mr. Justice Bennett, deciding that the bookseller wanted the public to believe that *Moonchild* was indecent, awarded Crowley £50 damages and costs. "There is not," he declared, "the smallest ground for suggesting that any book Mr. Crowley has written is indecent or improper."

That was doubtless true of the facts disclosed by such investigation into the plaintiff's publications as had been made at that trial. But emboldened by this success Crowley now challenged a more powerful protagonist. He brought an action for libel against Constable & Company and Nina Hamnett, the publishers and authoress of a book of reminiscences entitled *Laughing Torso*. The words of which he complained were these:

> "Crowley had a temple in Cefalu in Sicily. He was supposed to practise Black Magic there, and one day a baby was said to have disappeared mysteriously. There was also a goat there. This all pointed to Black Magic, so people said, and the inhabitants of the village were frightened of him."

The trial about these words took place in 1934 and lasted for four days before Mr. Justice Swift and a special jury. Crowley was represented by J. P. Eddy (now Q.C. and a stipendiary magistrate), while Malcolm Hilbery, K.C. (now Mr. Justice Hilbery) appeared for Constable & Company and Martin O'Connor for Nina Hamnett.

Crowley set himself up as a white magician, an altruist whose life had been a crusade against Black Magic. "There is," said his counsel in opening, "White Magic, which is on the side of the angels, and rests on faith in the order and uniformity of Nature. Black Magic is a degrading thing, associated with the degradation of religion, the invocation of devils, evil in its blackest forms, and even the sacrifices of children." Eddy then gave a sympathetic account of Crowley's system. The initiates at Cefalu had greeted each other with the catch-phrase: "Do what thou wilt shall be the whole of the law," to which the response was given, "Love is the law, love under will." But these principles were designed, not for the indulgence of desires, but to enable men and women to find their true "will", or purpose, in life.

Crowley went into the witness-box and confirmed the story which he had given to his solicitors and his solicitors had passed on to his counsel. Of the difference between Black and White Magic he said, "In boxing you can fight according to the Queensberry rules or you can do the other thing." "Does that mean," Hilbery interposed, "that his definition of Black Magic is the same as all-in wrestling?"

Hilbery's cross-examination quickly destroyed the picture of Crowley as a harmless eccentric. The fact was that most of his writings had been privately printed at his own expense, but the defendants had acquired a representative selection. The most dreadful blasphemies and indecencies were presently brought to light from his books, while Crowley displayed a ludicrous flippancy.

"Did you take to yourself the designation of 'The Beast 666'?" —"Yes."

"Do you call yourself 'The Master Therion'?"—"Yes."

"What does 'Therion' mean?"—"Great wild beast."

"Do these titles convey a fair impression of your practice and outlook on life?"—"'The Beast 666'," replied Crowley, "only means 'sunlight'. You can call me 'Little Sunshine'."

Hilbery read some of Crowley's lascivious verses, and asked: "Have you not built a reputation on books which are indecent?"—"It has long been laid down that art has nothing to do with morals."

"We may assume that you have followed that in your practice of writing?"—"I have always endeavoured to use the gift of writing which has been vouchsafed to me for the benefit of my readers."

"Decency and indecency have nothing to do with it?"—"I do not think they have. You can find indecency in Shakespeare, Sterne, Swift, and every other English writer if you try."

From this position there could be no withdrawal. Crowley did complain of the tone in which Hilbery read some of his lines, but declined, when invited, to read them himself. So Hilbery continued, and Crowley said, "You have read it as if it were magnificent poetry; I congratulate you." But he refused to admit that he was "known" as the author of these poems, which had had a very small circulation. "I regret," he said, "that my reputation is not much wider than it is."

"You would like to be still more widely known as the author of these, would you?"—"I should like to be universally hailed as the greatest living poet. Truth will out."

When the Judge said he had heard enough of this poetry, Hilbery turned his attention to magic, quoting from "The Confessions of Aleister Crowley":

"The forces of good were those which had constantly oppressed me. I saw them daily destroying the happiness of my fellow men. Since, therefore, it was my business to explore the spiritual world, my first step must be to get into personal communication with the Devil. I had heard a good deal about this operation in a vague way;

but what I wanted was a manual of technical instruction.
I devoted myself to Black Magic."

"Does that truly represent," asked Hilbery, "the spirit in
which you approached magic?"

Many passages from Crowley's writings were read to him. His
magical experiments began, of all unlikely places, in a flat
in Chancery Lane, where " 'I had two temples: one white,
the walls being lined with six huge mirrors, each six feet
in height; the other black, a mere cupboard, in which stood
an altar, supported by the figure of a negro standing on his
hands. The presiding genius of this place was a human
skeleton' . . ."

"Yes," said Crowley, interrupting Hilbery's reading, "Millikin
and Lawley, £5."

". . . 'Which I fed from time to time with blood, small birds,
and the like' . . ."

"Was that true?"—"Yes."

"That was White Magic, was it?"—"It was a very scientific
experiment."

". . . 'The idea was to give it life, but I never got further than
causing the bones to become covered with a viscous
slime' . . ."

"I expect," said Crowley, "that was the soot of London."

And so the dreadful story was unfolded. Demons appeared in
Chancery Lane, and in the house which Crowley then took in
the Highlands. Workmen and neighbours were mysteriously injured. In Mexico he carried out experiments in invisibility. "By
invoking the God of Silence, Harpocrates, by the proper ritual
in front of a mirror, I gradually got to the stage where my reflection began to flicker like the images of one of the old-fashioned
cinemas . . . I was able to walk out in a scarlet and gold robe
with a jewelled crown on my head without attracting any attention. They could not see me."

He had written that in India he sacrificed a goat and on another occasion crucified a toad. His "magical writings" spoke much of "the bloody sacrifice" to be made "within the Circle or the Triangle". "Those magicians who object to the use of blood have endeavoured to replace it with incense. For such a purpose the incense of Abramelin may be burnt in large quantities. Dittany of Crete is also a valuable medium. . . . But the bloody sacrifice, though more dangerous, is more efficacious; and for nearly all purposes human sacrifice is the best." Even in his treatises on magic Crowley could not refrain from absurd bombast. "For the highest spiritual working one must accordingly choose that victim which contains the greatest and purest force. A male child of perfect innocence and high intelligence is the most satisfactory and suitable victim," and he added in a footnote: "It appears from the Magical Records of Frater Perdurabo that he made this particular sacrifice on an average about 150 times every year between 1912 and 1928." This, said Crowley, showed that these passages were not to be taken seriously—they were only a historical account of ancient practices.

Even after his issue of the writ in this action Crowley had boasted of his notoriety in a series of articles in the *Sunday Dispatch*. "They have called me the worst man in the world," he wrote. "They have accused me of doing everything from murdering women and throwing their bodies into the Seine to drug peddling." Hilbery enquired if that was his general reputation. "Any man of any distinction has rumours about him," Crowley observed.

> "Does any man of any distinction necessarily have it said about him that he is 'the worst man in the world' by way of rumour?"—"No, not necessarily: he has to be very distinguished for that."
>
> Hilbery continued to quote from the article: "James Douglas described me as 'a monster of wickedness' . . . Horatio Bottomley branded me as 'a dirty degenerate cannibal' . . ."
>
> "You never took any action against any of the persons who wrote and published those things about you, did you?"— "No."

"And then comes this silly little paragraph in this book and you run to your lawyer with it, according to you, to bring an action for injury to this reputation, the reputation of being 'the worst man in the world'. Is that the case?"—"I also have the reputation of being the best man in the world."

Hilbery had exposed Crowley as the blackest of Black Magicians and a pathological liar. It was left to Martin O'Connor, cross-examining on behalf of Nina Hamnett, to show him in the character of a fraud and impostor.

"I understand you to say that you are a gentleman who sees visions; is that right?"—"Sees visions, yes." Crowley was asked about a bill from Mrs. Rosa Lewis for his stay at the Cavendish Hotel in Jermyn Street.

"Were you summoned for the amount of your bill by Mrs. Lewis in the Westminster County Court in April, 1933?"— "I have no information on the subject."

"What?"—"I do not know. People do all sorts of things like that, and I never hear of them."

"That is peculiar, and I will tell you why. County Court Summonses have to be served personally."—"Yes, but I do not know. Some one gives me a paper, and I put it in my pocket. I think no more about it. A fellow gave me a Judgment Summons only yesterday. I have never seen one before. It was a very nice shade of yellow."

But the Judgment Summons was not to be found, and so O'Connor proposed a test: "You say that you have visions. Conjure up a vision of when you are going to pay Mrs. Lewis the £24 for which she had judgment against you last April. Now throw a vision. Tell my Lord and the Jury when the vision tells you that you are going to pay Mrs. Rosa Lewis the amount for which she has judgment for your board and residence?"—"If I am bound to pay her I shall pay her."

"When?"—"When I can. . . ."

O'Connor now conceived the idea that Crowley's magic should be demonstrated in Court, where so many arts, crafts and sciences have been exhibited to a select and critical audience.

"You said yesterday that as a result of early experiments you invoked certain forces with the result that some people were attacked by unseen assailants. That is right, is it not?"—"Yes."

"Will you try your magic now on Mr. Hilbery?"—"I would not attack anybody."

"Is that because you are too considerate or because you are an impostor pretending to do things which you cannot do?"—"I have never done wilful harm to any human being."

"My friend, I am sure, will consent to your harming him. Try it on."

But the magician was reluctant, and the Judge objected.

"Mr. Martin O'Connor," he said, "we cannot turn this Court into a temple."

"There is one other question," O'Connor resumed. "You said, 'On a later occasion I succeeded in rendering myself invisible.' Would you like to try that on? You appreciate that if you do I shall not denounce you as an impostor?"—"You can denounce me as anything you like. It will not alter the truth."

Crowley remained visible, and Martin O'Connor resumed his seat. The Judge asked Crowley for a definition of magic.

"Magic," came the answer, "is the science and art of causing change to occur in conformation with the will. It is White Magic if the will is righteous and Black Magic if the will is perverse."

"Does magic involve the invocation of spirits?"—"It may do so. It involves the invocation of the Holy Guardian Angel, who is appointed by Almighty God to watch over us."

"Is magic the art of controlling spirits to affect the course of events?"—"That is one small branch of magic."

"If the object of the control is good, then it is White Magic;
but if the object of the control is bad, it is Black Magic?"—
"Yes."

"When the object of the control is bad, what spirits do you
invoke?"—"You cannot invoke, or bring down, evil spirits.
You must evoke them, or bring them up."

"When the object is bad, you evoke evil spirits?"—"You put
yourself in their power, but it is possible to control evil
spirits for a good purpose."

That was the end of Crowley's evidence.   Out of all his
acquaintances in the literary and artistic worlds only one man, a
German merchant, then came forward to testify to his good
character.

The defence called "Betty May", who had been Raoul Loveday's wife. She described life at the Abbey of Thelema in Sicily.
Each evening there was a magic ritual known as "Pentagram"
which lasted for about two hours and longer on Fridays. Crowley
and his Scarlet Woman appeared in robes. Crowley gave long
readings, interspersed with incantations such as "Artay I was
Malcooth—Vegabular, Vegadura, ee-ar-la, ah moon." The walls
of the *Chambre de Cauchemar* ("Room of Nightmares"—Crowley's bedroom) were decorated with terrible and indecent paintings, and there was a bureau full of bottles of drugs, all labelled.
Finally Betty May described the sacrifice of a cat called "Mis-
chette". Raoul had drunk its blood.

Eddy attacked Betty May's evidence. She was the authoress of
a highly-spiced autobiography called *Tiger Woman*, which contained a sadistic account of her adventures with an Apache gang in
Paris. These, she now said, were a complete fabrication. In another chapter she wrote that at one stage of her life she "took to
doping and drugging", which she admitted to be true. Moreover,
the account of her visit to the Abbey of Thelema, which she gave
in her book, differed somewhat from that which she gave to the
Sunday Express, and neither was precisely identical with the
account she now gave in evidence. Finally, Eddy suggested that
her whole interest in the case was to make still more money out

of the matter, and he produced copies of two of her letters, one written to the solicitors asking for a further remittance to cover "expenses", and the other, discussing the trial and addressed by "Poddlediff" to "Bombletoff" (nicknames which she shared with a friend).

Betty May swore that these letters had been stolen from her, and the Judge thereupon ordered them to be impounded. Three months later Crowley was tried and convicted at the Old Bailey for "feloniously receiving" these letters (valued at 7½d.) and sentenced to be bound over for two years and to pay fifty guineas towards the costs of the prosecution.

But to return to the libel trial. No other witnesses were called on behalf of Constable's, the first defendants, and Martin O'Connor then made his opening speech on behalf of Miss Nina Hamnett, the second defendant. Towards the end he invited the jury to intervene, and Mr. Justice Swift observed: "Members of the jury, I thought that you were speaking to each other."

"My lord," the foreman replied, "I was whispering to my fellow juror."

Mr. Justice Swift: "There is no reason why you should not whisper to him."

The Foreman: "May I be given an opportunity to do so?"

Mr. Justice Swift: "I have stopped learned counsel so that you might speak to each other, if you want to do so."

The Foreman (after conferring): "I think that it is unanimous amongst the jury to know whether it is a correct time for us to intervene?"

But as the trial had begun and evidence been given, it could not be ended in this way before counsel for the plaintiff had once more addressed the jury. Eddy did what he could. He pointed out that no evidence had been brought to support the allegation that a baby had disappeared mysteriously from the Abbey or that the local peasants were afraid. He suggested that Betty May's evidence was wholly unreliable. But the jury and the Judge were still remembering Crowley's admissions in cross-examination.

"I have been over forty years engaged in the administration of the law in one capacity or another," Mr. Justice Swift declared in his summing-up, "I thought that everything which was vicious and bad had been produced at one time or another before me. I have learnt in this case that we can always learn something if we live long enough. I have never heard such dreadful, horrible, blasphemous, and abominable stuff as that which has been produced by the man who describes himself to you as the greatest living poet. Are you still of the same mind or do you want the case to go on?" The jury thereupon returned a verdict against Crowley, and judgment was entered for the defendants with costs.

But Crowley appealed. For three days in November Eddy argued before the three Lords Justices of the Court of Appeal that a man is entitled to damages, even if they are only nominal, once he has proved that a libel has been published about him. However bad his reputation, he cannot be deprived of his farthing, until the specific libel has been proved. The Court conceded this point. But, they held, no jury could ever have decided the case in any other way, and no miscarriage of justice had occurred. Accordingly they refused to order a new trial, and the appeal was dismissed, like the claim, with costs. But while the plaintiff got no damages, the defendants got no costs, since the plaintiff went bankrupt.

Crowley had revelled in the publicity of the trial. But thereafter he passed out of the lurid limelight which had been his special attribute for so long, and in 1947 the only man ever to have staged a performance of the Eleusinian Mysteries in the Caxton Hall, Westminster, died in a Hastings boarding house. At his funeral in Brighton Crematorium his Hymn to Pan and part of his Gnostic Mass were recited, a magical performance which provoked the wrath of the Town Council.

> "Rose of the World!" Crowley once apostrophised
>   his wife,
> "If so, then what a world!
>   What worm at its red heart lay curled
>   From the beginning?"

XIX

THE WESTMINSTER LIBEL SHOP

Stockdale v. *Hansard* (1836–40)
The Sheriff of Middlesex (1840)

THE Inspectors of the Prisons of Great Britain did not disclose the means by which the book had found its way into Newgate Gaol. They probably did not know, and in any case it is not an important part of the story. The Inspectors were only concerned in their Report to point out that they had seen the book in Newgate Gaol and most strongly objected to its being there. They gave what particulars of it they could. It was called, they reported, *The Generative System*, and had been published by Stockdale in 1827. They described it as "a book of the most disgusting nature, and the plates are obscene and indecent in the extreme".

These observations were contained in the Report which the Inspectors presented, under Act of Parliament, to the House of Commons in 1836. The House of Commons, conceiving the Report might be of interest to the general public, ordered it to be printed and put on sale. The Report was thereupon printed by the family firm of Hansard, who had been the official printers to the House of Commons for more than half a century and were also the editors of the series of reports of parliamentary debates to which their name still clings.

A copy of the Report fell into the hands of Stockdale. Stockdale was London's most aggressive publisher. Prominent in the movement for the Suppression of Vice, he had made and lost more than one fortune out of the proceeds of vicious publications. *The Memoirs of Harriette Wilson* had been his outstanding best seller, but the libel damages exceeded the profits and he was thrown into prison for debt. By 1836 he was an old and a poor man. He remembered, however, that many years earlier his father had been prosecuted for libelling the House of Commons and acquitted after a famous defence by Erskine. Stockdale now decided to have his revenge and restore his fortunes at the same time. The comments made by the Prison Inspectors constituted a gross libel on his honour and repute as a publisher, and, though he could not sue the Inspectors or the House of Commons, he saw no reason why he should not sue the printers. He accordingly made James Hansard, Luke Graves Hansard, Luke James Hansard and Luke Henry Hansard joint defendants on a writ for damages.

The Hansard family were dismayed at being thus called to account for doing only what their great masters, the House of Commons, had commanded them, and they sought the advice and protection of the House. The House, equally shocked by the impertinence of the proceedings, nevertheless instructed the Attorney-General, Sir John Campbell, to defend them.

These were the first moves in a preposterous conflict between the House of Commons and the Common Law Courts. The trial of the Seven Bishops, a slander action, had deposed the last Stuart King. A libel case now bid fair to divide the constitution against itself. The House and the Court, sitting under adjoining roofs in the Palace of Westminster, hurled declarations of defiance at each other.

The Attorney-General entered two pleas to Stockdale's claim. He alleged in the first place that the comments made by the Prison Inspectors about the book were true. When the case was tried in the Court of Queen's Bench before Lord Denman, the Lord Chief Justice, and a jury, the jury decided, in spite of a long and impassioned speech from Stockdale, that this defence had been made out, and accordingly Stockdale lost the action.

But it was upon the other defence that future events were to turn. This was a plea that the words were published by order of the House of Commons and that therefore no action could be brought upon them. The House claimed (as it still claims to-day) to be immune in some matters from the ordinary law, and in particular it claimed the right to decide what its own privileges were. The right to absolute freedom of speech in debate had long been recognised. It was now argued that this right extended to any written matter which was published by order of the House. The argument was roundly condemned by Lord Denman. "I am not aware," he said, "of the existence in this country of any body of men whatever who can privilege any servant of theirs to publish a libel on an individual."

Both sides seized upon this hint. The House appointed a Select Committee to consider the matter, while Stockdale looked round for an opportunity to drive the point home. It was not long in coming. The Home Secretary had been conducting a correspondence about the offending book. The Court of Aldermen of the City of London wrote: "It appears on a careful examination to be a scientific book; the plates to be purely anatomical, and calculated only to attract the attention of those connected with surgical science." But the Prison Inspectors stuck to their guns and even fired a further salvo: "We also applied," they wrote, "to several medical booksellers, who all gave it the same character. They described it as 'one of Stockdale's obscene books'. . . ." As Stockdale was unpopular with his fellow publishers, this was scarcely the most impartial of sources. Nevertheless the House ordered these letters to be printed also, and Stockdale at once issued another writ for this repetition and aggravation of the libel. He claimed £5,000 damages.

The House now decided to lay its cards upon the table. It passed a string of bellicose resolutions. It had power, it declared, to publish such of its reports as it wished. It had exclusive jurisdiction to determine its own privileges. The bringing of any legal proceedings for the purpose of discussing or deciding its privileges was itself a high breach of those privileges and rendered all the parties concerned amenable to punishment. For any Court to assume to decide contrary to the House's own determination on any question of privilege was likewise a breach and contempt of the privileges of Parliament.

This was a shameless attempt to intimidate the Lord Chief Justice and set his Court at naught. Anger flared up throughout the country. People talked bitterly about the new Libel Shop in Westminster. The unrestrained destruction of private reputations by irresponsible politicians presented hideous possibilities to a still proud and aristocratic public opinion.

But the House had no intention at this stage of endeavouring to enforce its resolutions. On the contrary it was determined to

ensure that the Court gave a decision in its favour. If Lord Denman chose to neglect the warning, other steps might be taken.
When therefore the Hansards were served with the second writ
and once more put themselves in the hands of the House, the
House once more ordered the Attorney-General to defend the
action. This time no plea of justification was put in, and the sole
defence, set out at great length, was the plea of parliamentary
privilege. The issue was fairly and squarely set before the Court.

Stockdale replied with a demurrer. A demurrer was a formal
objection under the old rules of legal pleading, that the claim or
defence put in by the other party to a lawsuit was bad in law. In
this case the demurrer stated "that the known and established laws
of the land cannot be superseded, suspended or altered by any
resolution or order of the House of Commons: and that the
House of Commons, in Parliament assembled, cannot, by any
resolution or order of themselves, create any new privilege to
themselves inconsistent with the known laws of the land: and
that, if such power be assumed by them, there can be no reasonable security for the life, liberty, property or character of the
subjects of this realm."

The question raised by this demurrer was tried in April, 1839,
before the Court of Queen's Bench, presided over as before by
the Lord Chief Justice. It was unlike any other libel trial. There
were no witnesses, no cross-examinations, no conflict of human
character—nothing but a legal argument. Indeed the libel was
quite forgotten, like a frontier incident which has provoked a
war. Principles took the place of personalities and, though
arrayed in the austere rhetoric of the Courts, proved no less fascinating to the public attention.

Six counsel—the Attorney-General, the Solicitor-General (Sir
Thomas Wilde, afterward Lord Truro), Follett, Pollock (afterwards Baron), Maule (afterwards Mr. Justice Maule) and Wight-
man appeared for Hansards, the defendants. Stockdale was now
suing as a poor person, and the Court requested Curwood, an
elderly junior of good repute, to represent him. Curwood was
so blind that he could not himself see to read the legal authorities
upon which he relied. But his opening address to the Court was
no less effective for that. In the last two centuries the House of

Commons had claimed ridiculous, illegal and tyrannical privileges, he said in his quavering, courageous voice. It had declared it a breach of privilege to poach a Member's rabbit, or to fish in his pond, or to serve a notice to quit on his tenant. A solicitor had been sent to prison for sending in an exorbitant bill of costs which "highly reflected upon the honour of the House". If such privileges could be created by a mere resolution, and the House was the sole judge of them, there was no rule of law. "My Lords," the old man ended, "I have had a task imposed upon me which I dared not shrink from, though I have come to it with much weakness, I have come to it with a mind distressed and distracted by domestic affliction: my sight is nearly gone: and when I retire from your Lordships' Court I shall undergo an operation, by means of which I hope to have my sight restored; if I should not, and the issue is in other hands, not mine, be my days of darkness and misery few or many, it will be a consolation to me that one of the latest efforts of my professional life has been to defend the laws and liberties of my country."

When the old man had sat down, Sir John Campbell began his speech. It lasted for three days, and in the course of it he referred to nearly 150 previous cases. Towards the end of the second day it is recorded that he "complained of indisposition and said it would be a great accommodation to him to be allowed to proceed disencumbered by a part of his professional costume". Lord Denman replied, "I should be delighted to see you without it;" whereupon the Attorney-General "having retired, returned in a short time without his wig, and addressed the Court so disencumbered, this and the following day".

The argument was long. It was, however, simple, and amounted to this: The House of Commons was the sole judge of its own privileges, and its resolution on the subject was equivalent to the judgment of a Court, a Court superior to the Courts of the country. Therefore, in any case where a question of privilege arose, the Courts had no jurisdiction. The House of Commons was above the law.

The Attorney-General was filled with that passion for absolute supremacy which the Palace of Westminster seems always to nourish in its members. "I represent here the House of Com-

mons of the United Kingdom," he cried, "who are called before
an inferior tribunal for doing that which they thought essential
to the discharge of their legislative functions—for exercising a
privilege which they have enjoyed from ancient times—long
before the Revolution—a privilege which is required in the Bill
of Rights, and which, since the Revolution has never been questioned by anyone except Mr. Stockdale. . . . The representatives of the people are called upon to repel an alleged presumption of malice, and to show that in communicating with their
constituents they are not liable to be treated as libellers and
slanderers. The House of Commons, representing the third
estate in the realm, having, with the Lords and Queen, supreme
legislative authority—having by their own peculiar powers a
right to enquire into the administration of justice and to anim-
advert upon the conduct of judges—are called upon before a
tribunal subject to their superintendence and control to discuss
the extent and limits of their power—and to answer as criminals at
your bar."

Was this a threat? There were precedents for the imprisonment of High Court judges for offending the House. Yes, the
Attorney-General did not try to conceal it. The House wanted
their Lordships' decision, but would not be bound by it. "My
desire is—as long as possible—to allow justice to proceed in its
usual course." But "no judgment of a Court of Law can be
effectual to deprive the House of Commons of the privilege it
now claims. There are ways known to the constitution of nulli-
fying the erroneous decisions of law against privilege; but I own
that I, a lover of concord and tranquillity, cannot look forward
without dismay to the scenes through which we might have to
pass in the conflict. My Lords, why should this be necessary?
Why should not things be allowed to remain as they have been
for at least a period of two centuries, a period of unexampled
liberty and prosperity?" The Court heard the Attorney-General
out in silence.

Curwood replied. His short address was brought to a close
with another valedictory peroration, brave but touched with
sadness, a noble apologia spoken by a barrister unblessed by
fortune:

"My Lords, I claim to stand here as an advocate charged with the rights of a poor man. I will not shelter myself behind the resolution of the House of Commons, which gives me permission to be heard here; I stand here in bold defiance of their resolution. . . . My Lords, I have never been thought worthy to change the texture of my gown; but whether I wear stuff, or whether I wear silk, whether in office or out of office, I would not surrender the right of my brethren at the Bar, I would not surrender the rights of my profession, no, not for personal emolument, for family aggrandisement; no, not for personal safety. I have spoken in the spirit of honest independence, which I hope may cleave to me to the last, and if I transmit an unsullied character and that spirit to my children, I hold it a fairer inheritance than wealth or title basely and sordidly acquired. My Lords, I have done."

The following month the three members of the Court delivered fearless judgments in favour of Stockdale, Lord Denman turning the Attorney-General's argument against his own case. "This," he said, "is a claim for an arbitrary power to authorise the commission of any act whatever on behalf of a body which in the same argument is admitted not to be the supreme power in the State. The supremacy of Parliament, the foundation on which the claim is made to rest, appears to me completely to overturn it, because the House of Commons is not the Parliament but only a co-ordinate and component part of Parliament. . . . In truth, no practical difference can be drawn between the right to sanction all things under the name of privilege, and the right to sanction all things whatever, by merely ordering them to be done . . . the power claimed is arbitrary and irresponsible, in itself the most monstrous and intolerable of all abuses."

So judgment was given for Stockdale on his demurrer, and the case was at an end, except for the question of damages. These were assessed by a jury at £100 with twenty shillings costs. The House appeared to accept its defeat, and resolved to take no steps to prevent the judgment from being carried out. But Stockdale did not rest content with his £101. In August he issued a further writ for a further publication of the same libel.

The House of Commons now hardened its heart, and devised a malevolent scheme to frustrate this vexatious litigant. For cen-

turies it had been the duty of the Sheriffs of each County to
execute the judgments of English Courts, and in the case of the
Courts at Westminster Hall this duty fell on the Sheriff of Middlesex. The House of Commons was reluctant, in the middle of the
nineteenth century, to cast the Lord Chief Justice into irons, but
the same high constitutional sanctity did not attach to the person
of the Sheriff of Middlesex. The Court had given judgment
against a servant of the House for acting under the House's orders:
let the House now avenge itself on the servant of the Court—if he
tried to enforce a judgment against the wishes of the House!
The House accordingly allowed judgment in the latest of Stockdale's actions to be signed in default, and waited to see what the
Sheriff of Middlesex would do.

The Sheriff was in a position of impossible delicacy. If he
executed the judgment, he would be committing a contempt of
the House. If he declined to execute the judgment, he would be
in contempt of the Court. He found himself mercilessly ground
between the upper and nether millstones of Westminster. He
tried tactics of delay. He tried to enlist the sympathy of the
Court. But the Court was adamant. Stockdale's damages were
assessed by a jury at £600, and the Sheriff received a prompt and
peremptory command to levy execution. And so he was obliged
to send his men into the Hansards' premises and sell sufficient of
the firm's goods and chattels to raise the sum of £600. Even then
he refused to pay it to Stockdale.

The House of Commons now intervened. It ordered the
Sheriff to refund the £600 to Hansards, and at the same time it
committed him to the custody of the Serjeant-at-Arms. Nevertheless on the following morning the Court made an order for
the Sheriff to pay the money to Stockdale. "I infer," said Lord
Denman, "from the resolutions brought before us, that the House
of Commons disapprove of our judgment in the former case
between these parties, and I deeply lament it; but the opinion of
that House on a legal point, in whatever manner communicated,
is no ground for arresting the course of law or preventing the
operation of the Queen's Writ on behalf of every one of her
subjects who sues in her Courts." Mr. Justice Coleridge was still
more laconic: "It appears only," he observed, "that by reason of

what may be termed *vis major*, the Sheriff is in a situation of difficulty."

The Court proceeded to make that situation one of impossibility. The Sheriff applied for a writ of *Habeas Corpus* against the Serjeant-at-Arms, but the Court refused to question the lawfulness of his arrest. The reason for this decision was historical. The power of the House of Commons to commit an outsider for contempt had been recognised on previous occasions, and there was one case in which it was said that if the committal warrant signed by the Speaker did not specify the nature of the contempt, the Court could enquire no further into it. Such was the Speaker's warrant in this case, and although the Court knew and disapproved of the reasons for the Sheriff's arrest, it felt itself bound by the authority of the earlier case. It was a lamentable decision. For the result was that, although Stockdale could lawfully bring his actions, the House could with equal lawfulness imprison him for doing so, and any one else who took any part in them, perhaps even the judges themselves. This was indeed an achievement of legal ratiocination.

Three days later the same Judges made an order for the arrest of the Sheriff—for contempt of Court in refusing to pay Stockdale his £600. But since the Sheriff was already in prison for contempt of the House in refusing to repay the money to Hansards, and the Court had refused to order his release, no further hardship was inflicted on that unfortunate officer. Stalemate had been reached.

The only thing to do was to alter the law. So Parliament lowered its pride and took steps to rush through both Houses a Bill which became the Parliamentary Papers Act, 1840. The game now was to stop any further judgments being given against Hansards before the Bill was passed. For, unscrupulous though the House of Commons may have shown itself, it was not yet unscrupulous enough to pass retrospective legislation. It achieved its object by other means. Stockdale went on issuing writs, but he and his solicitor and his solicitor's clerks were thrown into prison by the House, as each took a hand in serving documents on Hansards. There they were kept until the Bill had received the Royal Assent and thereby become an Act of Parliament. The new Act decreed that no action could be brought for any libel in any "reports, papers, votes and proceedings published by or under the authority of either House of Parliament". It also provided that an action already begun should go no further. Stockdale's two outstanding actions were thus brought to an everlasting halt.

The publisher had followed his book into the dark cells of Newgate Gaol—perhaps a piece of deliberate irony. But he had little reason to grumble. The judgment of the Court was carried out, and he received the total of £701 damages and costs awarded him in his two successful actions. He was profitably avenged on the House of Commons, though in fact the money came from the taxpayer, as Hansards were reimbursed by the Treasury. Stockdale lived for another seven years on his lawfully gotten gains.

The Sheriff of Middlesex did not fare so well. Although he has been referred to in the singular, in fact that office was held by two respectable old gentlemen. One of them became extremely ill in prison, and was presently released. But the House ventilated its spite against its other innocent victim, and refused to let him go, even on the petition of the City Corporation that he might be able to "assist in presenting an address of congratulation to Her Majesty upon her marriage". It was not until he also became gravely sick that his liberty was restored to him.

So ended the least dignified episode in the annals of the British Constitution. The immediate crisis, after the manner of that amorphous and adaptable institution, was settled by Act of Parliament, while the unsolved conflict of jurisdiction was permitted to fall into the oblivion of legal history, and England returned to the proper pursuits of the nineteenth century.

XX

SURGERY IN 1828

Cooper v. Wakley (1828)

SURGERY in 1828 was scarcely a fine art. There were no anæs-
thetics, and the patient was bound to the operating table while
the surgeon worked with septic instruments and unsterilised
hands. But it was an art as old as civilisation itself, and though
the methods at their best were primitive, there was still room for
a wide variation in skill. Speed was naturally the essence of success. When Mr. Bransby Cooper, assistant surgeon at Guy's
Hospital, took fifty-five minutes to perform an operation for the
removal of stone and the patient, after being bled by leeches,
died on the following day, *The Lancet* published a gruesome
account of the operation and-accused Mr. Cooper of being an
incompetent surgeon and losing his nerve. Mr. Cooper sued
Mr. Thomas Wakley, the founder and editor of *The Lancet*, for
libel, and the result was a surgical *cause célèbre*.

Behind the immediate issue of Mr. Cooper's competence lay
a deeper discord. The conservative and the radical impulses
within the world of medicine were in collision. Mr. Cooper was
a nephew of Sir Astley Cooper, the President of Guy's and the
most celebrated surgeon of the day. "A nephew and surgeon,"
wrote *The Lancet*, "and surgeon because he is nephew." The
Treasurer of Guy's Hospital, sub-pœnaed at the trial to produce the
hospital records, revealed that Mr. Cooper had been elected
surgeon on the day that his uncle had vacated that office and
become consulting surgeon to the hospital. He also disclosed that
Sir Astley had another nephew on the surgical staff, and that all the
surgeons at Guy's had been his apprentices. Yet Sir Astley had no
hand in any of these appointments. It was an unquestioned
system. The venerable Treasurer might also have recalled, if he
had been asked, that Sir Astley himself in years gone by had been

made a surgeon at Guy's on the retirement of his uncle. Mr. Bransby Cooper, therefore, was a symbol of the *ancien régime*, the aristocratic, dynastic tradition of surgery, aloof and discreetly veiled.

The Lancet, on the other hand, stood for the advance of scientific enlightenment. It campaigned against nepotism in hospital appointments. It made a name for itself by publishing the lectures delivered to the students by the teaching staff of the big London hospitals, a practice which led to some trouble over copyright. It also paid young doctors for clinical reports of new cases and accounts of the treatment given, and was thus enabled to appraise the comparative qualities of the different hospitals and the physicians and surgeons at work in them. Such constant and unaccustomed public scrutiny was unpopular with the medical men concerned, but *The Lancet* gained a large circulation among the younger generation of doctors. If Mr. Cooper represented the surgical oligarchy of the day, *The Lancet* was the voice of the new democracy associated with outspoken journalism, public examinations and popular knowledge.

In these circumstances it was not surprising that when in December, 1828, the trial of the case of *Cooper v. Wakley* opened in the Court of King's Bench before Lord Chief Justice Tenterden and a special jury, "the different avenues leading into the Court were so crowded that there was scarcely any possibility of forcing a passage. It was with the utmost difficulty, with the most active assistance of constables and the officers of the Court, that counsel, jury and witnesses could obtain an entrance. When they reached their seats, many of them presented a most ludicrous appearance; some of the wigs of the barristers were off, others half off; some gentlemen had parts of their coats torn entirely away, and large rents were made in those of others. Almost every hospital surgeon and eminent practitioner in London was present, besides an immense number of students."

Mr. Cooper was represented by Sir James Scarlett (later Lord Abinger), who was as pre-eminent in advocacy as was Sir Astley in surgery. Mr. Wakley, though he had briefed Brougham and Kelly, elected, like many another intrepid editor before and after, to conduct his own defence.

The trial lasted for two days. The proceedings opened with a legal argument. Mr. Wakley had admitted the publication of the libel in *The Lancet*, but pleaded that it was true. Since, therefore, he had to prove the only issue in dispute, he claimed and obtained the right to open the case and call his witnesses first, a right which includes the right to make the last speech to the jury after the witnesses for the other party have given their evidence.

Mr. Wakley's chief witness was the surgeon who had written the report of Mr. Cooper's operation and was in fact paid eight guineas a month for a weekly contribution to *The Lancet*. Was this an unbiassed report? Sir James Scarlett's cross-examination of this witness on this question shows that in some respects at any rate the methods of English advocacy have not changed in a hundred years. "Now, sir," he snapped, "attend to this question. Did Mr. Bransby Cooper ever threaten to turn you out of a room on one occasion?"—"I never recollect that."

"Well, I will give you a little time to recollect it: did he never threaten to turn you out of a room? (a pause) eh? (still pausing) what do you say?"—"Yes: I remember, at the occasion of Guy's dinner, on which Mr. Bransby Cooper addressed me angrily, but I cannot say whether he said that or not: there was a great noise."

"Well, now come, my question is not to a particular time or place; did he never threaten to turn you out of a room?"— "I cannot say that: there was some angry altercation."

"What was it about?"—"I objected to a toast that was given, and he came from the chair, with others, and addressed me, thinking that I had disturbed the harmony of the meeting, and I left the room."

"Oh! You left the room: he did not turn you out?"—"No."

"Why did you leave it?"—"Because I saw there was evidently very strong feeling against the measure I had adopted."

"Well, now you have mentioned that circumstance, I will

come to another: had you never had any difference with
Mr. Bransby Cooper before or after that—I shall give you
time to recollect it?"—"I don't remember any quarrel."

"Oh, no, but quarrel, quarrel! I don't mean that you came
to blows: do you never remember Mr. Bransby Cooper
saying, 'Sir, you must leave the room, or I must leave the
room, unless you make me an apology'?"—"No, sir."

"I believe the popular name by which you call the hospital
surgeons in *The Lancet* is Bats, is it?"—"The word is used."

"Now attend to me, I have brought that word to your recollection: do you never remember any angry words with
Mr. Bransby Cooper respecting that word as applied to him
or hospital surgeons?"—"I do not recollect it."

"Was it not on that occasion, sir, that he said, 'You must
make me an apology, or you or I must leave the room'?—
"I distinctly swear I do not remember his saying it."

"Do you remember ever making him an apology?"—"I
remember using the word 'Bat' in speaking of a trial, and I
had no hesitation in saying I did not mean it to apply to him,
and had no personal intention in using it."

"Did you make him an apology?"—"I did say I did not intend
it to be personal."

"Did you not say afterwards that you would watch your
opportunity and make him repent it?"—"I don't remember
ever saying so."

"Will you swear you did not say so?"—"I will swear, to the
best of my recollection, I never did."

"Might you not have said it, and forgot it?"—"I may: I am a
man of warm feelings, and I may have said many things in
the course of my life which I do not remember, but I do not
know that I ever said so."

"How many bets have you laid on this trial?"—"None."

"Have you never offered any?"—"I may have said something
about it."

"Have you offered any bets?"—"No, sir; I may have said that the odds were so and so, but I never made any bets."

"You may have said the odds were so and so?"—"Yes."

"Then you mean to say you have said so?"—"Yes."

"Then you knew what the odds were?"—"I knew we had a great number of good witnesses."

"You say *we* had a great number of good witnesses, and you thought *we* would win?"—"I thought the cause would go for us."

"How many were the odds, for I should like to know?"—"I really don't recollect."

"Whether it was two to one, or three to one?"—"No, I cannot swear that even I made the remark: I may have said—I might have said so."

"Have you any doubts about it?"—"Yes, I have some doubts about it."

"Well, but as you treated the cause something like a horse, you know that when you want a horse to win, you take pains to bring him up—did you not do that here; have you not taken pains to get this cause up?"—"I have taken pains to collect evidence."

"You have examined a great many witnesses?"—"I have examined several."

"Have you had them at your house?"—"Two or three have called at my house."

"Only two or three?"—"I don't remember more than three of the witnesses having called at my house."

"Pray, at what other place have you seen them?"—"At the anatomical theatre."

"How many at a time have been there when you have been discussing the subject, or training the horses, in other words?"—"Several of our witnesses."

"A dozen?"—"No, sir."

"Was Mr. Wakley there?"—"He has been there."

"Had you a model there?"—"Yes."

"Was a lecture given upon it?"—"No, sir."

"Now attend to me, sir: has no lecture, or anything in the shape of a lecture, been given upon the model of this specific operation, for the purpose of proving Mr. Bransby Cooper's want of skill?"—"I don't know that there has been, nor had I ever seen the model."

"Was the model not there?"—"It was taken one day, I believe, and the next it was removed to Mr. Wakley's house."

"Now, whether it was or was not, were you not there when a lecture was given?"—"I have been present at a demonstration."

"With a view to this cause?"—"I don't know." (Several questions later the witness answered 'Yes' to the same question.)

"Have you done it yourself?"—"I have shown it."

"Have you demonstrated it to those around you with a view to this cause?"—"I have shown it to those in the room."

"Have you not demonstrated the parts to the person in the room with a view to this cause?"—"No, I have gone down to that room and examined the parts repeatedly."

"With what view was it then?"—"I have gone down there, and I may have made observations."

"With the witnesses present?"—"Some on both sides present."

"Did you not explain to them the parts with a view to this cause?"—"I explained those parts to them, but not with a view to this cause."

"Why did you go there yourself?"—"I went with a view to refresh my own memory."

"Was Mr. Wakley present?"—"I have met him there on two occasions."

"Did you ever hear him explaining them?"—"Yes."

"To the pupils?"—"To the pupils."

"Were there any present that were to be witnesses?"—"Some of them were to be so, I believe, on both sides."

"I think, then, that for the purpose of justice you have displayed a good deal of zeal in this cause——"

But the Lord Chief Justice would allow Sir James no sarcasm, "No, no;" he interrupted, "why not ask your questions?"

Thus was a bad witness neatly discredited in cross-examination, and Mr. Wakley was so impressed by it that he began his re-examination by saying to his witness: "I am sorry that you should have shown any hesitation in giving your answers, for there is nothing in Sir James to be afraid of, and there is nothing to conceal: therefore don't be afraid, speak out and answer everything."

But Mr. Wakley had other witnesses—several visiting surgeons and a number of medical students at Guy's. About 200 people had attended the operation. It is impossible to complete the reading of this evidence without coming to the conclusion that Mr. Bransby Cooper by his handling of the instruments had displayed an inexcusable absence of surgeon-like skill.

Only one eye-witness to the operation was called on behalf of Mr. Cooper—the other surgeon who assisted at it. But a host of established surgeons, including Mr. Cooper's uncle, supported him by testifying to his known skill—one of those rare occasions when doctors have agreed. But if the reader perseveres through the thundering speech delivered by Sir James Scarlett (and here the change in the fashion of advocacy is marked), he finds, at the end of it, that he is almost as incensed against *The Lancet* as was Sir James himself. When Sir James, asking for heavy damages, exclaimed, "Away, then, in a case like this, with any notion of temperance!" the reader is persuaded that £2,000, even in 1828, was scarcely enough to ask for. The modern lawyer, however, may perhaps read one passage with a somewhat uneasy pride: "In the ordinary traffic of life, called commerce, there is a course of plain-dealing, of simple integrity, that marks the line between honesty and the want of it, and which every man can understand; but in the practice of a liberal profession, there is a certain feeling of honour, which becomes a gentleman, and which a gentleman can only feel, which renders it not sordid, but gives to it a character which belongs to such a profession—a certain dignity, a certain pride which makes the man feel that profit is a secondary object to him—that fame, that reputation, and the means of utility, are his true rewards, and that everything else is only secondary. If once the Press gets power either in the profession of the law, or the profession equally honourable, and perhaps equally useful, or more useful, of surgery, that principle is debased, that principle is destroyed, if a man finds that his fame depends upon whether he makes concessions to the Editor of *The Lancet. . . .*"

But Sir James had lost the right of reply, and at the end of the day Mr. Wakley himself made a speech, less sonorous, but full of a sharp, vulgar wit that the jury may have found no less appealing. Defending *The Lancet's* nickname for hospital surgeons, he said: "If we have Whigs in the political state, why should we not have Bats in the surgical? I am sure that hospital surgeons are just as much, or more, like Bats, than Sir James Scarlett is like sour milk— and yet that is the meaning of Whig. The conduct of hospital surgeons warrants the application of the name. Bats belong to the class mammalia: they move in the dark, they suckle their young, they live in the creaks and crevices of old walls, hospitals and dungeons, they thrive and fatten on the destruction of their prey, and I fear it is too frequently the case, that hospital surgeons thrive and fatten in nearly a similar manner on the miseries of their fellow-creatures. . . . John Hunter used to say that bad surgeons were like bad carpenters—they made work for one another—and that good surgeons would starve if it were not for the unskilful ones. It seems that John Hunter's axiom found its way into Guy's Hospital, for presuming on what the operations of Bransby Cooper would be, it was thought necessary to elect a consulting surgeon and an assistant surgeon at the same time, to accomplish the additional work. . . . Well, we have heard much of the reputation of Mr. Bransby Cooper, but I think the learned counsel must have forgotten the satire of Iago, 'reputation is oft got without merit.' There are some additional words to be sure—'and lost without deserving'—but in this case there was none to lose."

Wakley notes that "at the conclusion of this address there was loud applause from various parts of the Court". But when the reader has come to the end of the Lord Chief Justice's impartial charge to the jury (emphasising only the admitted facts that the operation was one of great difficulty and that no one could judge of its difficulties so well as the operator himself) he finds himself in agreement with the result.

There was a long, strained wait for the jury's verdict. "The Bats," wrote Wakley spitefully, "appeared as though they had taken their last flight to Westminster Hall; they were confused, feeble and only a few inches above the mire. Sir James Scarlett left the Court soon after the learned Judge had concluded his charge, with an expression of countenance by no means indicative of that delightful feeling of self-satisfaction and self-esteem for which the learned gentleman has so long been celebrated. Some wag remarked that the worthy knight, owing to the extreme heat of the court, had taken an unusual quantity of sour milk, a favourite beverage, for a time, with Bats, Rats and Barristers."

Nevertheless, when the jury filed back into Court at eleven o'clock that Saturday night, long after the Judge had (with the consent of both sides) gone home, they brought with them a verdict for Mr. Bransby Cooper for damages of £100.

XXI

REVOLUTION BY VIOLENCE

Laski v. Newark Advertiser Co. Ltd. and another (1946)

AT the time of the General Election in 1945 Professor Harold Laski was the Chairman of the National Executive Committee of the Labour Party. He had already been for twenty-five years Professor of Political Science at the London School of Economics, a point of intellectual vantage from which he indoctrinated the English-speaking world with Socialism. Everywhere his books were read by the young and rebellious, and his students from the countries of the British Empire were prominent in their national anti-British movements. In those twenty-five years the world and England changed rapidly, but Laski continued to see all things through the unnatural focus of the Marxist dialectic.

He was not a Communist. He was too genuine an internationalist, too independent by temperament to take the Moscow whip. A Polish Jew by origin, his first affection was neither for Russia nor for England, but for the abstractions of his political philosophy. He accepted and preached the academic theory of revolution, believing that every Capitalist Society worked itself up sooner or later into a revolutionary situation—a process which nevertheless required years of active fomentation—and it was then the business of the workers by hand and brain to establish the Socialist State. To this orthodox dogma Laski added a single variant: he desired and hoped, and to some extent believed in the possibility—the slight possibility—that in England the revolution might be brought off without violence. At the same time he was always careful to stress that never in the whole of history had a ruling class been known to surrender its privileges in a peaceful and constitutional manner.

As Chairman of the Party and pre-eminent among its workers by brain, Laski took a vigorous part in the Election campaign.

When Mr. Churchill invited Mr. Attlee to accompany him to the Potsdam Conference, so that in the event of a Labour victory at the polls some unity of foreign policy might be preserved, Laski issued a pompous pronouncement to the effect that Mr. Attlee must attend "in the role of an observer only". As Mr. Attlee was a member of the Cabinet and Laski had no official position, this intervention caused general anger in the country, and Laski became the target for attack in a section of the Press. The attack was intensified after a meeting which Laski had addressed in Newark Market Place in support of the local Labour candidate. The meeting had been calm, but at the end of it Laski was provocatively heckled by a political opponent, and the incident was reported as follows in the *Newark Advertiser and South Notts Gazette*:

"REVOLUTION BY VIOLENCE"
PROFESSOR LASKI QUESTIONED

There were some lively exchanges between Mr. Wentworth Day and Professor Laski following the latter's speech in Newark Market Place on Saturday night.

Mr. Day asked the Professor why he had openly advocated "revolution by violence" in speaking at Bishop's Stortford and Bournemouth during the war, "whilst most Englishmen were either fighting or being bombed at home," and why he (Professor Laski) had spent the whole of the last war lecturing in America. If he were unfit, why did he not join the Red Cross?

REJECTED

Professor Laski replied that he was twice rejected in this country during the 1914—18 war and had medical certificates to prove it. He also attempted to enlist in Canada, and then he went to Harvard University, and he had a certificate from the Medical Officer of the British Army in New York of his inability to be accepted on medical grounds. He also said concerning the other part of the question: "That was said about me in the House of Commons . . . and if you look at Hansard for 29th November, 1944, you will see an ample and generous apology made to me for being as insolent as you are in suggesting it now."

REFERENCE TO VIOLENCE

As for violence, he continued, if Labour could not obtain what it needed by general consent, "We shall have to use violence even if it means revolution." When people felt it was the moment for great experiment, for innovation, because when war is over people so easily forgot—especially those who had the power in their hands—that was the time for experiment. Great changes were so urgent in this country, and if they were not made by consent they would be made by violence, and judging by the temper his questioner had displayed he would be perfectly naturally one of the objects of violence when it came.

Mr. Day submitted to the Professor that when general consent was against him he substituted revolution.

Professor Laski said it did not lie in the mouth of any member of the Tory Party, who helped to organise mutiny in the British Army over Home Rule in 1914, to discuss the question of violence. When a situation in any society became intolerable—and when twenty-five per cent of the people had inadequate nutrition it did become intolerable—it did not become possible to prevent what was not given by generosity being taken by the organised will of the people.

NOT AN ASSET

Mr. Day: "You are precisely the sort of bloodthirsty little man, full of words, who has never smelt a bullet, but is always the first to stir up violence in peace.

"We expect serious constructive thought from the Chairman of the Labour Party, but since you have consistently attacked everyone and everything from Mr. Churchill to the leaders of your own party and the constitution of this country, and have been disowned by Mr. Attlee only this morning, how can anyone take you seriously? I suggest that you are not an asset to the Labour Party but a liability."

The Daily Express came out on the same day with the head-line: "LASKI UNLEASHES ANOTHER GENERAL ELECTION BROADSIDE: SOCIALISM EVEN IF IT MEANS VIOLENCE." Other references to the meeting appeared, and Professor Laski at once issued writs for libel against the *Newark Advertiser*, *Nottingham Guardian*, *Daily Express* and *Evening Standard*. Further public discussion was thereby arrested until the pending actions had been either tried or settled. The country went to the polls and a Labour Government was returned with an overwhelming majority of seats. But Laski, as always, carried on regardless of events, and by the time that his actions were ready for trial in late November, 1946, the first instalments of the Socialist revolution had been introduced by Act of Parliament, without even the fall of a policeman's helmet.

The first of the four actions in the list was against the *Newark Advertiser*, who agreed to leave the conduct of their case in the hands of the *Daily Express*. The trial lasted for five days before Lord Goddard, the Lord Chief Justice, and a special jury (numbering seven only, under the war-time regulations). G. O. Slade, K.C., (now Mr. Justice Slade), Sir Valentine Holmes, K.C., and Peter Bristow appeared for Professor Laski. Sir Patrick Hastings, K.C., Holroyd Pearce, K.C. (now Mr. Justice Pearce), Arthian Davies (now Mr. Justice Davies) and Anthony Gordon represented the *Newark Advertiser*. Professor Laski's Statement of Claim alleged that the words of the report in the *Newark Advertiser* meant, by innuendo, that Laski had declared his intention to commit and to conspire with others to commit the crimes of treason, treason felony, sedition, riot and breach of the peace, if the policy of the Labour Party should not be put into operation by constitutional means, and that Laski was guilty of treason felony (a form of treason which carries a maximum sentence of life imprisonment). The Defence pleaded that the words were a fair and accurate report of a public meeting, that they were fair comment, and that they were true in substance and in fact.

It was admitted on Professor Laski's behalf that the report in the *Newark Advertiser* was fair and accurate, except for the sentence, "As for violence, if Labour could not obtain what it needed by general consent, 'We shall have to use violence even if it means revolution'." Two issues were therefore raised by the pleadings:

(1) Did Laski speak these words in Newark Market Place that evening?

(2) Had he spoken these or similar words on other occasions? If the defendants could establish an affirmative answer to either of these questions, they had won the case.

The answer to be given by the jury to the last of these two questions depended entirely upon whether Laski's theory of Socialism could stand up to cross-examination by Sir Patrick Hastings. What does the word "revolution" mean? Like all words, it has more than one connotation. Laski claimed that when he advocated revolution, he meant nothing more than a constitutional social transformation, while the violent revolution, which he dreaded, would be engineered by the enemies of Socialism. But was this borne out by his writings? Many passages were read to him. They were necessarily torn from their context—a fact of which Laski complained—but if the passage was clear, could the context make any difference to its meaning?

"Mr. Laski, do you believe," began Sir Patrick Hastings, "that the use of violence to achieve your political ends is practically inevitable?"—"No."

"Have you ever believed that which I have put to you?"— "No."

". . . Supposing a person for years were preaching this doctrine to a dissatisfied proletariat, 'The use of violence to achieve your political aims is practically inevitable,' do not you think such a person would be a public danger?"—"That would depend upon the degree of his power to persuade those to whom he spoke."

"You mean to say he might be useless and therefore not a danger or powerful and then a danger?"—"Yes."

Laski denied that he was sufficiently powerful to be a danger, and Hastings continued:

"Do you believe that if achievement of political aims cannot be arrived at without the use of violence, then violence is justifiable?"—"Not in all circumstances. In circumstances where a burden is intolerable, violence may be inevitable because the burden is intolerable, but not otherwise."

"In the circumstances which existed on the 16th June, 1945, the date you made this speech, did you then believe that if the aims of the proletariat could not be achieved without the use of violence, then violence was justifiable?"—"No."

"Do you agree that anyone who preached that doctrine would be a public danger?"—"Yes."

"And have you preached it for twenty years?"—"No."

"We shall have to see. If you have preached it for twenty years, you agree you would be a public danger?"—"If I had preached to the proletariat the inevitability of violence for twenty years, I should certainly be a public danger."

Hastings then disconcertingly quoted from one of Laski's books: "A London jury is fairly certain to award damages for libel to a Tory Member of Parliament, but it is also fairly certain to assume that a Labour sympathiser cannot be libelled."

"Would you agree with me," asked Hastings, "that that is unfair, stupid and offensive?"—"No, I think it is an accurate summary of the history of political libel actions in London from some such period as the treason trials of 1794 down to some such period as 1924."

After this diversion Hastings returned to his muttons.

"You have written many books in which the word revolution is contained, and you define it in your books. Have you preached the doctrine that this revolution may be brought about in one of two ways, either by consent—you call it a revolution by consent—or else a revolution by violence?"—"That is so."

"And by a revolution by consent do you mean this—because the enemy are always Capitalists, are they not?"—"Broadly."

"Do you mean that the enemy, if there is to be a consent, must in the very nature of things consent to their own elimination—that is to say, they have to consent to go?"—"They have to consent to great changes."

Hastings took exception to this answer, and substituted Laski's own word "erosion". "Erosion," explained Laski, "means rubbing away."

"How do you consent to rub yourself away?"—"By fading out of the picture in which you have been previously the most prominent part."

"By disappearing?"—"Yes."

"Consent to their own disappearance?"—"To their loss of power."

"And have you pointed out that that is unlikely if not impossible?"—"No, not impossible; I have said that it is historically unlikely."

Hastings then read this passage from *Democracy in Crisis*, published by Laski in 1933:

"To transform the system of valuation in any society involves either a fairly universal admission of its necessity or else the frank abandonment of consent as the basis of change. The implications of that alternative are important. If the change is to be built upon consent, it assumes the possibility of co-operation by capitalists in their own erosion. That is an immense hypothesis of which, for the moment, it is only necessary to say that it envisages something entirely new in historic experience. It may be right, but there is little in the past to justify the expectation that it is right. If the change is to be built upon force, then, clearly enough, for any period in which force is the technique upon which the governors mainly rely the ideal of democracy is abandoned."

"Do you agree with me that if somebody advocated openly a revolution by violence he would probably be locked up?"—"I think he probably would, yes."

"And have you been very careful in your books, while advocating it in the sense of saying it is quite inevitable and justifiable to avoid any definite sentence saying 'I advocate it'?"—"No, because I have not advocated violence—on the contrary."

But a few questions later Hastings asked:

"Do you go on to agree that the conditions which it (capitalism) creates are such that they make use of force to destroy those conditions practically inevitable?"—"There is great danger of their making it practically inevitable."

"Do you understand the meaning of the word 'practically'?"—"I do."

"Do you understand the meaning of the word 'inevitable'?"—"I do."

"I will ask you the question again: Is it your argument in chapter three (of *Democracy in Crisis*) that the conditions created make the use of force to destroy those conditions practically inevitable?"—"Yes."

Did this imply the advocacy of violence? The Professor drew a distinction between diagnosis and exhortation. "I take the view," he said, "that the maintenance of social peace and the avoidance of violence is one of the most vital things at which our society can aim. That is why I am a member of the Labour Party and not a member of the Communist Party. Every part of the material that you have quoted is careful, and I hope accurate, diagnosis; and I think that you put me in an unfair and unjustifiable position by asking me to accept diagnosis as exhortation."

Sir Patrick Hastings was an aggressive and relentless cross-examiner. When Laski mentioned the struggle between the "privileged" and the "unprivileged", Hastings enquired, "Are there any privileged in the Socialist Party?" And Laski was stung to reply, "Why, indeed, Sir Patrick, when you were a member——"

But answering back is not allowed, and the Lord Chief Justice said, "No, Mr. Laski." Hastings seized this chance. "It may be difficult for you to be courteous," he said, "but do not be rude. . . . You are rude to everybody, are you not?"—"I do not think so."

"I will just ask you a question which I was not proposing to ask you. You know that some people in this country possess religious beliefs, do you not?"—"Yes."

"I want to read one short sentence which I suggest is the most offensive thing you have ever said . . . 'Nor was it an accident that no influence was more persuasive than that of Wesley in inducing the masses in England to accept the grim discipline of the new factories in return for the dubious consolation of an unproved and unproveable eternal bliss!' By that passage, addressed to people who had some religious beliefs, you meant that it was rubbish, and that Wesley blackmailed the workers to accept conditions in the old factories by promising eternal life?"

Laski sought to justify his remark as a historical judgment, but Sir Patrick Hastings said: "Of course, when you are rude to other people, Mr. Laski, you think that is argument; when people say something about you, you bring actions for libel. That is your view of fairness, is it not?"

In *The State in Theory and Practice* published in 1934 Laski wrote: "The view here taken is one that naturally disturbs many generous minds. It postulates the inevitability of revolution as the midwife of social change, and it admits that there are phases of human evolution in which men cease to settle their differences in terms of reason, and resort to force as the ultimate arbiter of destiny." Hastings read another sentence from this book: "I have therefore urged that, at this stage of economic development, the difference between classes can only be settled by force."

"Let us face it," said Sir Patrick. "Does that mean what it

says?"—"Yes, certainly, at the time at which it was written."

". . . Inevitable revolution by violence?"—"Yes."

Laski now said that he had changed his mind when conditions changed at the beginning of the war. He had, indeed, looked upon the war solely as a revolutionary opportunity. "The possibility of revolution by consent," he wrote in 1943 in his *Reflections on the Revolution of Our Time*, "will last only as long as the drama of war makes the common interest more compelling than any private interest; it will not survive the natural urge that peace will bring to recover our wonted routines." In the same year he attacked Churchill in an article in the *Chicago Sun* for refusing to nationalise the coal mines in the middle of the war. "Nothing, in my view," he wrote, "shows more decisively that Churchill is fundamentally the aristocratic Tory to his finger tips than his refusal to utilise the dynamic of democracy to begin the process of social change which, whether by consent or coercion, must come rapidly if we are to win the peace as well as the war." It was sentiments of this kind which Laski expressed in his wartime speeches at Bournemouth and Bishop's Stortford.

Sir Patrick Hastings moved on to his second point, that in Laski's view violent revolution was as justifiable as it was inevitable. As Laski was a proud adherent to the teachings of Hobbes' *Leviathan*, he did not believe that there was any moral duty to obey the law. But Hastings, like Laski himself a little while before, overstepped the bounds in his eagerness. "In your view, if the Socialist Party think the State are not doing what is right for them, they are entitled to resist by violence?"—"Where they come to the conclusion that there is no other way, certainly."

"You do not think that is a terrifying theory, do you?"—"It is a theory that Mr. Abraham Lincoln——"

"Never mind about him. He is not in Court. Let us keep to ourselves."

"I think," said Lord Goddard, "the witness is entitled to answer in that way."

"I am sorry," said Sir Patrick at once, "I apologise to Mr. Laski."

"May I, my Lord," Laski asked, "explain that when Abraham Lincoln said——"

"I do not think you need go into it in full," Lord Goddard rejoined. "What you mean is that great people in the past have led revolutions?"—"Yes, and have been held by posterity to be justified."

Laski's cross-examination lasted for the best part of two days. As the Professor had written the same thing again and again, a good deal of it involved repetition. But in the end Hastings obtained an admission that the violence which Laski had foreseen was the violence of Socialists, and not the violence of Conservatives or Capitalists resisting Socialism.

"This is what you are saying and what you admit you are saying: If these socialistic changes are not made by consent they will be made by the violence of those who believe in Socialism?"—"Yes."

"But where in the world does that differ from what you say in the passage of which you complain? I cannot follow it. Is it not exactly the same?"—"No."

"Is there some dialectic difference between the two? Let me read it to you again. I will read you the two passages side by side. This is what you admit you said: 'Great changes were so urgent in this country, and if they were not made by consent they would be made by violence'—by the violence of those who believed in Socialism. That is what you said. Now this is what you complain of: 'If Labour could not obtain what is needed by general consent'—'Labour' I will take as meaning those who advocate Socialist principles—

'we'—that means 'they'—'will make them by the use of violence.' Why is that not exactly the same thing?"

The exhausted Professor could give no clear answer to this question and took refuge in circumlocution. Hastings then obliged him to admit that the violence with which he had threatened Mr. Wentworth Day and the violence of which he had said it did not lie in the mouth of the Tory Party to complain would be—must be—the violence of Socialist revolutionaries, not Conservative reactionaries. The cross-examination had achieved its purpose, and was over.

The rest of the trial was devoted to an enquiry into the first question in the case—what were the actual words used during that fatal "exchange of incivilities" at Newark? For Professor Laski ten witnesses who had been present at the meeting—either on the open speakers' truck or among the crowd—came forward to say they had not heard the sentence threatening violence. As most of them did not recollect hearing some of the other remarks which Laski admitted to be accurately reported, Sir Patrick Hastings was able to dispose of their evidence in a series of short but devastating cross-examinations. Here, for instance, is the whole cross-examination of the Secretary of the Newark Labour Party:

"Did you make any note at all of what was said?"—"No."

"You did not pay much attention to it, did you?"—"Of course I did."

"Why?"—"Well, sir, as Secretary of the Party and it being a man like Mr. Laski."

"Why did you pay attention to it? There was no importance in it."—"I paid attention to all the meetings."

"You mean you listened to what he said?"—"Of course."

"What did he say about violence?"—"I have just told you what he said." (In answer to Mr. Slade the witness had said that if reforms could not be made by constitutional means there was always a danger of a drift towards revolution.)

"Did he say anything at all like this: 'Great changes were so
urgent if they were not made by consent they would be
made by violence' ?"—"No."

"Nothing of that sort at all?"—"No."

"You see, Mr. Laski has told us that he did, but you say he did
not?"—"It is quite possible I did not hear it."

"Quite possible you did not hear a great deal of what he said?"
—"I definitely did not hear that."

That was all. One of these witnesses was even more helpful.
When asked by his own counsel if he had heard Laski make the
crucial remark—"As for violence, if Labour could not obtain
what it needed by general consent we shall have to use violence
even if it means revolution"—or anything like that, he replied,
"Similar, but the words 'Labour Party' were never used in it at
all."

The shorthand reporter of the *Newark Advertiser* had not himself heard the remark, and it was incorporated in the final report
from copy supplied by Mr. Wentworth Day, Laski's challenging
questioner, who was acting as "publicity adviser" to the Conservative candidate at the Election. But two or three independent
witnesses also swore on behalf of the defendants that they had
heard Laski say something in identical or very similar words.

There is all the difference in the world between advocating an
event and pointing out the likelihood that it will happen, if a
certain course is not pursued. There is a difference, in other
words, between an incitement to violent revolution and a warning to the country to avert the danger before it is too late. But if a
political preacher, who desires the revolution, but not the violence,
incessantly tells the multitude that if their just grievances are not
remedied there will be violence—what then? Lord Goddard,
after argument by counsel in the absence of the jury, ruled that
the libel could not reasonably be construed as accusing Laski of
treason felony, but that it might well amount to a charge of sedition, and he quoted in his summing-up part of the judgment of
Mr. Justice Coleridge in a trial for sedition in 1909: "A man . . .
may seek to show that rebellions, insurrections, outrages, assassi-

nations, and such-like, are the natural, the deplorable, the inevitable outcome of the policy which he is combating. All that is allowed, because all that is innocuous; but, on the other hand, if he makes use of language calculated to advocate or to incite others to public disorders, to wit, rebellions, insurrections, assassinations, outrages, or any physical force or violence of any kind, then, whatever his motives, whatever his intentions, there would be evidence on which a jury might, on which I should think a jury ought, and on which a jury would decide that he was guilty of a seditious publication."

But the jury in this case did not find it necessary to decide whether Professor Laski had been accused, and whether rightly or wrongly, of being a seditious libeller. After an absence of forty minutes they returned with the verdict that the report in the *Newark Advertiser* was a fair and accurate report of a public meeting, dealing with a matter of public concern and published for the public benefit. It was therefore a privileged publication, and judgment was entered for the *Newark Advertiser* with costs. A few days later Laski discontinued his actions against the other newspapers. His costs, amounting in all to £13,000, were paid by public subscription. Laski himself continued to be on the National Executive Committee of the Labour Party. But he disagreed with the policy of the first all-powerful Labour Government. He resigned in 1949 and died the following year.

XXII

THE LAST TRIAL IN WESTMINSTER HALL

Belt v. Lawes (1882–4)

FOR more than five hundred years every English trial of importance had taken place in Westminster Hall. Beneath that vast roof, carved with oaken angels, Saint Thomas More, Anne Boleyn, Guy Fawkes, Charles the First and a thousand others had been condemned to death. There since their origins in the Middle Ages had sat the Court of Chancery and the Courts of Common Law—known as Queen's Bench, Common Pleas and Exchequer. Though all the Courts have gone, the Hall still stands. Looking now down the length of that great empty space, it is hard to imagine the scene which it presented for so long. The Courts sat behind screens in the corners of the Hall, the rest of which was given over to stallkeepers and the general public. At the beginning of the last century the hucksters were driven out and new Courts were built alongside the Hall, where the statue of Cromwell now stands. Judges, counsel, witnesses and the public at large continued to pass along the Hall through the narrow doorways that led into the small, stuffy, candle-lit Courts.

Yet despite all the murders, conspiracies and political trials—to say nothing of the countless money or property claims—which marked the course of our history or the development of our law, the last trial ever to be held here was a libel action between two sculptors. This little matter lasted for forty-three days—not counting the time taken by the various appeals. It took place in 1882, and with the exception of the Tichborne case it was up to that time the longest trial ever held in an English Court. The London worlds of art and fashion were bitterly divided on the issue, and many leaders of each gave evidence. Eighty-two witnesses took the oath for the plaintiff, sixty-one for the defendant. Fashion was for the plaintiff, art for the defendant, and salons, clubs and studios buzzed with furious dissension.

The plaintiff was Richard Belt, a self-made man and almost a self-taught artist, who had suddenly, within two or three years, become the fashionable sculptor of the day. The Church, the Peerage and the Queen had commissioned him. It was only a short time since his statue of Byron had been ceremonially unveiled. This huge bronze which sits to this day upon a slab of pink marble not far from Hyde Park Corner, was the subject of much dispute in the case, and almost the only example of Belt's work which was not produced in the Court. A modern critic has called it "one of the worst statues—if not the very worst—in London, showing Byron hunched up in a would-be poetic pose, half-toppling over sideways, with an apology for a dog (poor old Bo'sun) at his side." But in 1882 both sides were proud to claim the credit for it.

How had Belt, a rank outsider, achieved this sudden success? The defendant, Charles Lawes, a famous Cambridge athlete and oarsman as well as a sculptor, who had at one time employed Belt in his studio, meditated upon this problem with his friends, especially one Verhyden, who in turn had worked for Belt. Belt's success, they decided, was the result of an outrageous fraud. This conviction they proceeded to proclaim to the public. In August, 1881, the Editor of *Vanity Fair* agreed, after suitable indemnities had been signed, to publish the following broadside, entitled "Mr. Belt":

"After leaving Mr. Lawes' studio in 1875, Mr. Belt began to do business on his own account. He published as his own work a statuette of Dean Stanley, of which a good deal has been lately heard. This statuette, however, was worked up for him by Mr. Brock, as Mr. Brock himself declares. In like manner the memorial busts of Charles Kingsley and Canon Conway, which also passed as the work of Mr. Belt, were, in fact, invested by Mr. Brock—as Mr. Brock himself declares— with whatever artistic merit they possess. Mr. Brock, equally with Mr. Lawes, declares that Mr. Belt himself was incapable of doing anything in the shape of artistic work. In 1876 Mr.

Belt took in partnership Mr. Verhyden. Mr. Verhyden states that the drawings that procured for Mr. Belt the Conway Monument (the bust of which was, as already stated, worked up by Mr. Brock) were his, not Mr. Belt's at all.

"Mr. Verhyden further declares that he and not Mr. Belt entirely modelled the sketch which enabled Mr. Belt to gain the victory over all the Artists of the day in the Byron competition; and that he also entirely modelled the Byron statue itself.

"In short, we are assured that all Mr. Belt's works from the year 1876 when he began on his own account up to the year 1881 were executed by Mr. Brock and Mr. Verhyden.

"Mr. Verhyden states equally with Mr. Lawes and Mr. Brock, that Mr. Belt was quite incapable of doing any artistic work whatever.

"The names we have cited are those of only some among a number of men of the highest position in the artistic world among whom our enquiries have been made, and we feel bound to say that, in the face of the detailed statements made to us, the bare outlines of which we have here set down, we find it difficult to believe that Mr. Belt has any good claim to the authorship given to the public as his or to any other title than that of a purveyor of other men's work, the editor of other men's designs, a broker of other men's sculpture. If he declared himself to be this, there would be no harm in it. But the point is that, if our information is correct, he has systematically and falsely claimed to be the author of the works for which he was only the broker, that he presents himself as a sculptor and an artist, when in reality he is but a statue jobber and a tradesman. If then the statements made to us are true—and we frankly avow that at present we fully believe them to be perfectly true—Mr. Belt has been guilty of a very scandalous imposture, and those who have admired and praised him as a genius are the victims of a monstrous deception.

"Why this deception if it be one should have been allowed to exist so long is a matter which does not concern us, though we must say that it does very greatly concern those artists who were aware of it.

"But we, having got a hint of it, and having upon this hint made very full investigations, should not be doing our duty were we to withhold from the public the result of that investigation.

"Accordingly we have set down the information we have obtained and with it the conviction which that information has produced upon us, that Mr. Belt is not the author of the works that have made him to be believed to be a sculptor of genius. Every paper in London announced on Thursday morning the fact that Mr. Belt had received from the Queen a commission to execute another statuette of Lord Beaconsfield. We shall be glad to know that Her Majesty's choice of an artist is really warranted."

The next month Lawes sent this article to the Lord Mayor of London with the following letter:

Dear My Lord:

As the newspapers state that there is a probability of the Corporation commissioning certain works of sculpture before long, I beg to submit to your Lordship's attention the enclosed paragraph from Vanity Fair.

As this notice appeared some time ago, and as there has been no denial or refutation of the charges therein contained, though such denials have been repeatedly challenged by the Editors and others in the public press, and as also I must add that I am aware that no such denial, were it made, could possibly be substantiated, I consider it my duty to my profession to lay the matter before your Lordship.

I am, your Lordship's obedient servant,

CHARLES LAWES.

(Sculptor)."

Hence the case of *Belt* versus *Lawes*. Ruskin's famous attack on Whistler a few years before seems but the palest water-colour in comparison with the ruthlessness with which Lawes was determined to destroy his upstart rival. Belt was obliged to prove his art and skill, or withdraw into the obscurity out of which he had thrust himself. The public subscribed an enormous sum of money to pay for his legal costs. His counsel was Sir Hardinge Giffard, Q.C., later Lord Halsbury, supported by Messrs. Pollard, Montague Williams and Cavendish-Bentinck, while Lawes was represented by Charles Russell, Q.C., later Lord Russell of Killowen, Richard Webster, Q.C., and Lewis Coward. Throughout the trial the Court was littered everywhere with works of sculpture. Marble busts stood upon every bench, counsel studied their briefs amid rows of plaster casts, and bronzes circulated freely between the Judge and the jury. The Judge was Baron Huddleston, who had tried Whistler's action against Ruskin. (The Judges of the Court of Exchequer, which no longer exists, were styled Barons.)

It is impossible to give a day by day account of the trial. It began on the 21st June, but on the 29th it was adjourned until November. In those days the Long Vacation of the Courts lasted for four months, and during that time the Judges went on assize. Baron Huddleston offered to give up his circuit in order to finish the case, but he was not allowed to do so. When, therefore, on the 28th December, the jury returned their verdict, exactly six months had elapsed since they had heard the plaintiff in the witness-box. But as counsel took four days in making their final speeches, and the Judge took another four days over his summing-up, even the most distant incidents of this Marathon of trials were recalled to the jury's memory.

Belt told the Court the story of his life. While employed as a "machine boy" for Mr. Nicholls, the Engineer of the House of Commons, he took to sketching the eminent Victorians who frequented the Lobbies. Fired with enthusiasm, he joined an art class at a Working Men's Club and began to toy with mallet and chisel. His first head, he said, he did with a nail and hand-brush out of a piece of the Clock Tower. Then for the first time he worked for a sculptor, one Plows, and was engaged on the head of the elephant over the Elephant House in the Zoo. Five years later he became a pupil and assistant to Foley, a Royal Academician, at a salary of £1 per week. Foley, he added, was reluctant to take him, because Lawes (the defendant) had been his first pupil and had turned out to be unsatisfactory. Foley was the sculptor of the figure of Prince Albert on the Albert Memorial, a work at which Belt assisted him. At this time Belt made his "probation work" for the Royal Academy—a clay copy of the Farnese Hercules—and was successful first time, while Lawes, he observed, was twice "plucked". He also made a statuette of Lord Beaconsfield from observations and photographs. He had done Gladstone too, but only the remnants of him were left. This remark caused the first outburst of laughter in the case.

It was when Foley fell ill that Belt went for three or four years to Lawes' studio. Here he received his first commission—from his old employer, Mr. Nicholls. He did heads of Mr. and Mrs. Nicholls, which were shown in the Royal Academy. Then came a head of Dean Stanley, which was unfortunately destroyed by the firm who were casting it. When Belt sued them for negligence, and was given £50 damages, Lawes, Brock and Birch all gave evidence for him without claiming any part in the work, but soon afterwards Belt and Lawes fell out over an account.

Belt now took his own studio, and had an immediate success. Dean Stanley recommended him to Charles Kingsley, and he went down to Eversley Rectory, returning with two heads, one of which, when shown in the Academy, appealed so much to the Queen that she commanded a copy.

The unknown doodler in clay now had the best professional connections in town. As Belt told the story of each of his commissions, the work in question was carried into Court. Canon Conway—the only assistance he had from Brock was some suggestions about the hair—Lord Stanhope, Lady Castlebury, Lord Shrewsbury, Miss Nellie Plimsoll, and others were called for. The Usher brought in the head of Miss Nellie Plimsoll covered with a dust sheet. When the sheet was removed it turned out to be "a melancholy bronze bust of Lord Beaconsfield". Then there was the Prince Imperial (Napoleon III) of whom he did a bust after his death. This was shown to the Queen and the Royal Family at Windsor; they made suggestions, which Belt followed. These took some days to complete, and Her Majesty, said Belt, was present on each occasion. When Her Majesty was satisfied, Belt took the cast to the Empress at Chislehurst, where he stayed with it for over a fortnight, carrying out further alterations at the Empress' wish. A copy of the work was eventually sent to the Queen at Windsor, and a smaller version, specially adapted to give it an appearance of greater youthfulness, to Paris.

By the time Belt had finished his story, there were forty or more sculptures in the Court. The defendant's case was that most, though not all, of these busts were the work of a "sculptor's ghost"—Verhyden. Charles Russell recalled the plot of a French comedy about American artists in Rome. "As soon as the sitter arrived," he said, "a ghost was installed in a convenient hiding place, and the artist proceeded to go through the accustomed forms of his profession and to show off what little he knew about modelling, accompanied by a large amount of tall and appropriate conversation. The sitting concluded and the patron departed, the ghost comes from his hiding place, and with the aid of photographs and peeps taken during the sitting he puts the bust into artistic trim. This manner of carrying on business, so amusingly illustrated on the French stage, is evidently unknown to the English public, but to the sculptors it is a very old story." Verhyden entered Belt's studio in Hugh Street, he continued, by climbing up a ladder from an alley-way and passing through a trap door—so that he was invisible not only to the sitters but also to the other men working there!

The studio to which Belt moved in Wilton Place had similar possibilities. At the far end there was a "curious small apartment closed off by a door which was partly a folding door and partly a sliding door. Supposing that anyone had been invited to retire beyond that sliding door he could have passed out, for there was another door closed simply by a cross-bar, which gave egress into a Mews."

These preposterous allegations met with a warm reception from Belt in cross-examination. "I can refer you to artists of celebrity who have seen me execute works of merit," he cried, pouring out a dozen names or so. "Those and many others have seen me work and stood by my side while I manipulated the clay, thousands of others have seen me, and you can all see me do it here now, if you like." "If such a test should appear desirable in the course of this case," said the Judge blandly, "I shall certainly permit it." Loud applause broke out in Court at this remark, and was, as usual, promptly suppressed.

Charles Russell then asked Belt how much should be done by an assistant on a competition work, to which he answered, "As much as the competing master thinks fit, provided the assistant does it under his direction and is competent. The assistant may have as much or more ability than the competitor—it will be the difference between execution and mind. The assistant might do the whole under direction; it is usual and justifiable. Many people employ persons superior in art."

Russell: "I quite agree with you."

This offensive comment from counsel infuriated the witness. "In the case of Mr. Birch, R.A.," he shouted, "there is not a piece of work leaves his studio that is not touched by a dozen." "I do not desire to stop you," put in Russell, effectively doing so. "I will say no more," said Belt, but went on after a pause: "Many of my busts are posthumous from masks or from photographs. The master should not adopt the pupil's design; that is dishonourable. With a mask and a 'squeeze' we produce animation. I do not take measurements from living persons and give them to my assistant. I would not permit it."

Russell: "Do not be angry, Mr. Belt. You seem to resent it as something wrong or immoral."—"No hand but mine touches these heads from skull to finish. No one has ever put animation or expression into any head for me."

Russell: "Take Admiral Rous, one of the best."—"I am very glad to hear you say so."

Baron Huddleston: "It must have struck everyone who knew the original that it is a remarkable likeness. I remember the singular brevity of one of the Admiral's decisions when I practised before him as counsel." (The learned admiral had been a judge of the Admiralty Court.)

Russell: "Perhaps he gave no reasons, my Lord."

Baron Huddleston: "He did not."

Belt now burst out: "No finger but mine touched that bust."—"Do not shake your finger at me please, Mr. Belt," said Russell. "I beg your pardon, Mr. Russell. I was pointing at that bust. This bust would take some time, some weeks,

to do it properly—give me one to do and you will see. I
cannot say exactly. I work on four or five at a time."

Early the next day Baron Huddleston made up his mind that
the only way of finding out the truth was by the practical experiment which the plaintiff had suggested. "After Mr. Belt
has finished his evidence," he announced, "I propose that a stage
be fitted up and some clay given to the plaintiff on which he may
work before the jury. I think it is a fair test, but I will not suggest
either Mr. Russell or Sir Hardinge Giffard." "I hope," said
Russell, "Mr. Belt will spare both me and my learned friend."
Belt was equal to the situation. "I hope your Lordship will allow
me to model you." His Lordship did not dissent from this invitation. "You have this advantage," he said, "that I shall be here
the whole time." Meanwhile the questioning of the plaintiff continued.

The *Times Law Report* for the following day became unusually
descriptive. "Every available space in Court," it confided, "which
was not occupied by Mr. Belt's busts, bronzes, etc., was filled
with Members of the Bar and the general public," and it added
a list of distinguished persons who "were accommodated with
seats upon the bench". Again an endless series of questions were
put, all suggesting that Belt had paid large sums of money to
Verhyden in order that Verhyden's work might be passed off as
Belt's. From time to time Belt's indignation soared. When he
struck the desk with his fingers, Charles Russell said, "Do not
hurt your knuckles, Mr. Belt." When he raised his voice,
Russell said, "Do not please shout." At last the Judge felt bound
to intervene. "We are going at inordinate length into this. The
witness has answered that question over and over again."

"I really must discharge my duties and put these questions,"
replied Russell. "I would very much rather be elsewhere, but if
your Lordship thinks so, I will sit down." But it was his Lordship
who subsided. "Very well," he sighed, "we are very much in
your hands," and the cross-examination continued.

The Byron memorial statue could not be brought from Hyde
Park. But it was in a sense the *pièce de résistance* of the case. Not
only was it Belt's largest and most remunerative commission—the

prize money was £3,500—but his victory in the competition had established his status as a leading sculptor. Verhyden claimed to have made the original model and drawings at Belt's invitation. As he knew nothing of Byron, Belt had lent him a copy of *Childe Harold*, from which he conceived the idea of the poet sitting alone on a rock on the seashore with his favourite dog looking up at him. (One wonders which verse suggested this image.) Belt promised him ten per cent of the prize money if his design was successful. In the same month in which the result was announced Belt paid him £300, and further amounts later on, and he, Verhyden, then executed the work itself. Belt denied the whole of this story, except the payment of £300, which he explained as compensation for his accidental loss of Verhyden's cartoons for a stained glass window in memory of Izaak Walton. According to Belt, Verhyden had nothing to do with the Byron except that, like others employed in his studio at the time, he helped to build up the full-size figure on its iron-frame foundation.

Belt's evidence was corroborated, not only by all his studio assistants, except Verhyden, but also by his distinguished clients, who saw, or thought they saw, their features being modelled before their eyes. As each one appeared in the witness-box, his bust was put up next to him, so that the jury might compare the original with the portrait. It must have been a bizarre spectacle! There was Mr. Webb of Newstead Abbey, where Belt had gone to inspect the collar of Byron's dog, and other relics, but stopped to do a head of Mr. Webb. There was the Honourable Alexander Yorke, who had seen Belt at Her Majesty's request altering the expression of Napoleon the Third's eyes. There was Lord Clarence Paget who had watched Belt at work on Byron's feet and Earl Russell's head, and added modestly, "I dabble a little in sculpture myself, having done a colossal study of Nelson on the Menai Straits, as a landmark for the Survey Department, and I once exhibited at the Royal Academy." There was Mr. Samuel Plimsoll, "beside whom was placed, amid some merriment, a statuette in a declamatory attitude with outstretched arms." There was a witness who had watched Belt putting the sight into Lord Beaconsfield's eye, and another who had noticed how Belt built up his face-bones and skull anatomically, according to measurements taken with callipers, gradually adding muscles and tissues—"I watched him add small pieces of clay about the size of a pea, saw it grow into a likeness. There was no way into the studio from which anyone else could have watched him and taken my bust." There was Sir Richard Wallace, owner of the Wallace Collection and Trustee of the National Portrait Gallery, who had seen many sculptors at work and had no doubt of Belt's qualities. There was a Mrs. Bishoppsheim, who described her experience: "We had twelve or fifteen sittings on the ground floor—my face to the window—Mr. Belt was standing there. I was on a raised platform on a wooden box. He stood on nothing." "Was that the 'sculptor's ghost'—'he stood on nothing'—my Lord?" asked a fearless juror.

These and many others came and went before the end of June. In modern litigation there is a strong inclination to settle actions out of Court, in the hope of avoiding further costs. In the light of the evidence which had already been given in this case, it is almost inconceivable that the action, if it had been fought in the present day, would not have been settled before the end of the Long Vacation—indeed a compromise would probably have been reached within half an hour of the rising of the Court. But the Victorians were made of sterner stuff. Only eight days of the trial had gone—too short a time to decide so grave an issue of artistic honour—and thirty-five more days were to follow. When the same Judge and counsel, the same twelve special jurymen, and the same fifty-odd sculptors had been reassembled on the 3rd November, the plaintiff continued to call his witnesses.

The jury were already wondering how long it would all last. One of their number asked the Judge whether any arrangements had been made as to their remuneration. His Lordship replied that, much as he wished to fall in with the jury's wishes, knowing the great inconvenience which a case of this magnitude occasioned them, he feared the Statute did not permit him to award to each juryman for the whole case more than the munificent sum of one guinea, except with the consent of counsel on both sides. If any such intimation were made to him, he would take care to let the jury know. But it does not appear from the record that it ever was made. (Jurymen now receive, under the

Juries Act, 1949, up to 20s. a day compensation for loss of earnings as well as travelling and subsistence allowances.) One morning, on his Lordship taking his seat, a juror said he was very loath to intrude personal matters, but some months earlier he had made an engagement to go to Yorkshire on the following Monday—it would be a great convenience to him if the Court would adjourn over that day. This request the Judge was happy to grant.

Every witness was interesting, since each revealed either his opinion on some particular point of art or his personal memory of an artist at work—and of whatever kind or quality Belt must certainly have been an artist. George Augustus Sala, the illustrious art critic of the *Daily Telegraph*, for instance, had been much struck by Belt's skill in putting on Lord Beaconsfield's hair—not, he explained meticulously, the forelock which Lord Beaconsfield cherished, but the hair on the side. As an amateur modeller himself he had paid many visits to the studio and observed that "Belt worked accurately, turning rough clay into smooth modelling material in the manner of other sculptors". Still closer testimony came from Belt's studio assistants. One of them, Schotz by name, had "obtained all the high honours at Louvain and the Gold Medal of the Royal Academy of Antwerp". It turned out, however, that "there were only two students of any consequence at Louvain"—he and Verhyden. The school had gone down, as "the director's brain was weak". Schotz declared that, although he knew Belt and Verhyden had fallen out in 1880, he had never in his life had a quarrel with Belt, who was "too much of a gentleman for that".

"The gallery of fine arts in the body of the Court," wrote *The Times*, "was further enriched to-day by a large life-size plaster-cast of 'Hypatia', one of Mr. Belt's later works. This greatly impeded the witnesses in giving their evidence and caused them to remove to the other side of the Court." But then Mr. Russell complained, and the monstrous beauty was placed next to the jury-box. And still the stream of witnesses flowed in and out. The Dowager Duchess of Cleveland (who had Belt down at Osterley Park, where no sculptor's ghost could have walked unseen), Dean Stanley's footman (now a verger in the Abbey, who recalled that Lady Augusta had thought the Dean too tall, and so he was cut through the body and the drapery re-modelled), even Baron Lionel de Rothschild's hairdresser (whom Belt had sent for to find out the proper arrangement of the Baron's hair on a posthumous bust), and a professional gentleman who had sat, or stood, for Belt for both Mr. Gladstone and Mr. Disraeli!

"The collection of busts, bronzes, statuettes, medallions, etc., in the body of the Court was further enriched"—some days later —"by a dazzling plaster cast of the Lord Mayor in his robes of office, lately done by Belt. To compensate for this, a striking bust of Edgar Vincent received so rude a shock from a barrister extricating a book from a shelf, that he completely lost his head. This is as yet the only casualty among a vast collection of all sizes and shapes exposed to the dangers of handling by different people, and being jostled by those passing in a densely crowded Court." The Lord Mayor gave evidence in support of his statue from the Bench. He had a polite passage of arms with Charles Russell.

"Are not your eyebrows more arched?" asked Russell. "You remember what the scripture said?"

" 'A man beholds his natural face in the glass,' " replied the Lord Mayor, " 'and goes and straightway forgets what manner of man he is.' It is far better looking than I think I am." "It is," Russell conceded, "a fair presentable Lord Mayorish sort of person."

How did Russell hope to refute this accumulation of testimony from men and women in every walk of life? He had two cards up his sleeve. The first was Verhyden's diary. This was a large volume written in French, recording the dates on which Verhyden worked on the different sculptures, the hours he put in, and the amount which Belt paid him on each occasion. But a number of entries in the diary had been altered. After his quarrel with Belt, Verhyden had shown this diary to Monsignor Capel, the Headmaster of the Catholic Public School in Kensington, where Verhyden had been art master for three years. "I attributed such mistakes," said the priest, "to the fact of the diary being made by a person half-educated, if I may be excused for saying so." But he readily agreed with the Judge that "such mistakes might also happen if a person were too well educated". Moreover, after cross-examining Verhyden for five days, Sir Hardinge

Giffard proved that the diary contained certain definite in-accuracies. There was evidence on which the jury could decide that it had been, as Sir Hardinge put it, "falsely manufactured".

Russell's other card was the Royal Academy. There was no dignity in this case, he said, if it was the outcome of narrow and petty jealousies within the noble profession to which Belt said he belonged—in consequence of the rapid and mighty success he had achieved. If that was so, it was a scandal and a disgrace that it should have occupied so much of the public time. But that was not a correct view of the matter. Rightly or wrongly, he said, there had existed in the artistic world the impression that Belt's work was not his own genuine production, but that he traded on other men's genuineness, decorating himself with plumes and feathers stolen from others. This raised an issue of importance between the parties, but a still graver question as regards the public. Pointing out that no sculptor known to fame had given evidence for Belt, he said: "The merits of the professional man are best known to his professional brethren. Speaking of the profession to which I belong, the most severely competitive of all, much as I value the opinion of the public and of the Judges, above and beyond that undoubtedly I value the estimation of the brethren of my own profession. If it appears that Mr. Belt stands alone and is not supported by any body of artists, it does suggest grave consideration of how this has come out, if Mr. Belt is the man he represents himself to be." (The only artist of the first rank who gave evidence for Belt was William Morris.) Russell relied on the massed judgment of the experts against the opinions of amateurs or mere spectators with untrained eyes. Before the trial was over it was being said with truth that Belt was suing the Royal Academy, and when the case was taken to appeal there was disagreement among the Judges on the weight which should be attached to this expert evidence, a disagreement which raised the old philosophical question of the objective nature of artistic criticism.

Sir Frederick Leighton, President of the Royal Academy, led the way. "I am the author," he said by way of introduction, "of the 'Python' in the South Kensington Museum, which has been purchased by the Nation." On two occasions he had examined the statues in Court. (Viewing days had been arranged.) He stated boldly that they had not been executed by the same hand. In the Kingsley, Stanley and Plimsoll busts he recognised the work of Brock, even in the Conway he recognised Brock's treatment of an eye. The Admiral Rous was different again. "No artist," he asserted, "could assimilate thoroughly the manner of another, still less the manner of two others." The artist who produced the Kingsley could not have produced the Rous, and, had that been possible for any hand, it would have been impossible for the same hand or hands to have done the Duchess of Cleveland or the Lord Mayor. "In these last two," he said, "there is an extreme artistic inferiority. But Rous is a work of art, while Kingsley is a very fine bust." The President fixed his critical scrutiny upon all the busts in the Court. He remarked that the earlier works were very much better than the later ones (they had been arranged in chronological order) and he did not think a young artist could have deteriorated so quickly. He praised the Cardinal Newman— a statue which Verhyden had made and brought in as an exhibit— and found a strong similarity of treatment between it and some of Belt's efforts. On the subject of authorship he described the assistance he had received from Brock in completing the "Python". "I made a highly finished sketch in clay. I put it into the hands of Mr. Brock, who caused it to be set up and descended to various operations for which so skilled a sculptor is not required, but in all cases performing myself such offices as left the artistic individuality of the work wholly mine." (Applause in Court—immediately suppressed.)

The President was supported by Hamo Thornycroft, R.A., who was years afterwards to carve the statue of Oliver Cromwell for the site on which the Court then stood; by Laurence Alma Tadema, R.A., who had studied the Byron in Hyde Park—the feeling of the composition, the rendering of the subject and the position of the limbs had struck him strongly as being the work of a Belgian sculptor; and also by William Calder Marshall, R.A., who made some scathing comments on Belt's sculptural method. This was to take a skull, and then add flesh, muscles and tissues. Such a practice, he declared, was wholly unnecessary and served no useful purpose.

But this was by no means the last appearance of the Royal Academy. Belt's offer to prove his skill by modelling the Judge had been forgotten, until Russell observed in his opening speech that it had not been repeated at the close of the plaintiff's case. Whereupon Giffard leapt up and repeated it there and then. After some discussion Baron Huddleston decided against a demonstration in open Court, and a room was set apart to which no one would be admitted except Belt himself, his sitter and two representatives of each side. The jury were to be allowed to visit the room, whenever the Court had adjourned, and watch Mr. Belt at work, his Lordship warning them not to make any remarks or suggestions. It was also agreed that Belt's subject for this trial should be one of his studio assistants called Pagliati. An earlier head of Pagliati was among Belt's works exhibited in the Court.

And so, while the trial went on and on, the plaintiff was hard at work behind closed doors. The case of Van Meegeren presents a modern parallel; this Dutch artist executed a large oil painting under observation in prison, in order to prove his claim to be the author of Vermeer's Walk to Emmaus! At long last, after the passage of many days, it was announced that the new bust of Pagliati would be produced at three o'clock that afternoon. When the time came, the new exhibit was carried in like the boar's head at a Christmas banquet. *The Times* described the dramatic moment in these words: "The bust here made its appearance, preceded by Mr. Belt, and behind it Mr. Pagliati. It was received by a round of applause from the back of the Court, but it was instantly suppressed."

Mr. Belt came back into the witness-box to make his comments. "The light," he said, "in making the Pagliati bust was not such as I should have in an ordinary studio. There is a great disadvantage in this respect where I have been working. After casting the work will not appear as it is now. There are a great many points in the bust that would be destroyed if it were cast. I should like the jury to see it by daylight. (It was late in the afternoon of a December day.) After that I have no objection to having persons watch it being cast."

On the following morning the new and the old Pagliati were

exhibited side by side. Then a remarkable thing happened. Until that moment no one had suggested that the old Pagliati was not Belt's work. Now the President and no less than eighteen Royal Academicians (including such well-known painters as Frith and Millais) came forward and swore that Belt could not have made it. "They are not done by the same hand," declared Sir Frederick Leighton, "The earlier one is the best." But Sir Frederick had created an impression of partisanship. "Were you not underneath my learned friend," Giffard asked him, "while the last witness was being cross-examined, making suggestions?" Sir Frederick denied it: "I made an observation on something that had been said—that is not a suggestion." To this Giffard said, "I only wish to draw attention to the attitude taken up by the President of the Royal Academy with reference to this case." "I have given quite my disinterested opinion in this matter," the President retorted. "The differences between the two busts are twofold—first the personality and execution of the details: the red one is a work showing knowledge, dignity, refinement and true picturesqueness. In the other later one I see an absence of knowledge; I see an absence of dignity, for it is grimacing; an absence of refinement—it is coarse and puffy. As to minor details, the indication of the bones and sinewy formations varies in every way. The outline of the shoulder shows in the red one greater knowledge of anatomy than in the second. The treatment of hair and beard is different in both works. In the clay one, in the deep furrows that divide the separate portions of the beard and hair, there is a peculiar touch of the tool, a series of punctured touches, through the whole length of the line, which constitute a distinct peculiarity of handling not present in the red one. The whole front of the last bust is different from the first." Nevertheless he admitted that, "it is not wholly wanting in spirit and life by any means," adding, "I have not compared the busts with the original Pagliati." "See," said one of the jury, "whether the character of the model approaches 'dignity' or 'grimacing'." Mr. Pagliati then went and stood by his bust, and Sir Frederick was constrained to admit: "There is a likeness distinctly to him in the bust."

After this demonstration of unanimity by the Royal Academy,

Sir Hardinge Giffard rose and said, "I now propose to call five or six eye-witnesses to the execution of the first bust by Mr. Belt." Russell objected strongly, but Baron Huddleston allowed this new evidence. First, however, he directed Belt to stand up where he was in the well of the Court, and Belt, pointing to the first Pagliati, said: "My hand alone touched that bust. My mind alone conceived the composition thereof." "This affirmation was given with a dramatic intonation and emphasis, and was greeted from the rear of the Court with a muffled murmur of applause."

Such was the evidence. Must the judgment of the Royal Academy be accepted as final? Baron Huddleston did not think so. "I give all due honour," he said, "to the gifts and character of those members of the Academy who gave unanimous testimony against the plaintiff, but it is only matter of opinion. They are but skilful experts, and while I would, if I were in doubt, hear and follow them, in a case where there is no doubt I would not yield my own opinion, founded on my own experience, to any number of Academicians, however distinguished they may be." On the fourth and last day of his summing-up the Judge re-told the tale of Belt's challenge to his enemy and its acceptance:

"Pagliati, the plaintiff's studio assistant and servant, was selected, as you all know, to be the subject of this test modelling, because the plaintiff had already executed one, not then denied to be the very work of the plaintiff. So a new Pagliati was done during the intervals between the daily hearings of the cause. On its production a cloud of Academicians were brought down, with their gifted and accomplished President at their head, himself eloquently scorning the finish and form of the new Pagliati, and with all his brother Academicians, sculptors as well as painters, concurring with him that the new Pagliati, the vulgar caricature, could not have been executed by the same hand as the old, which, with similar unanimity, they all belauded as an elegant, meritorious, and highly-finished delicate work of art. So much theoretic opinion, this. What do you think of it? Do you believe it? Can you allow yourselves to be governed by it in face of explicit testimony of fact? After this some witnesses were called who swore that, with respect to this 'old Pagliati', they had seen the plaintiff work upon it last autumn. Now this is direct evidence of fact, and if it be true, if you believe it to be true, what becomes of theoretic evidence to the contrary?"

The Judge's last words gave the jury their direction on the question of damages: "If you consider that the defendant has only just failed to substantiate his defence, and that practically some doubt as to the authenticity and originality of the plaintiff's work still exists, you will probably give your verdict for the plaintiff with only nominal damages. If, however, you are of the opinion, after your patient and intelligent review of the whole evidence, that this is an attempt, by an injurious libel, to blast the prospects and destroy the rising reputation of a young artist, and poison against him the foundation of his fortunes—the minds of those who are at once his rival compeers and his professional judges—by the instigation of false and wicked reports, then I unhesitatingly inform you that you are entitled to give the plaintiff, if you consider that this is a false and malicious attempt upon his character and fame, compensation for the outrage to which he has been subjected with no niggard hand. One word of caution and I cease. Whichever way you find, find clearly and without any comment (which often compromises and nullifies the verdict of juries) for one or the other of the parties to this suit. Consider your verdict."

No sooner had Baron Huddleston finished than the foreman of the jury rose and said "in very measured tones": "My Lord, before we retire to our duty, I wish, in view of many foolish and false observations which have been made in newspapers and elsewhere, that this trial has been unnecessarily protracted, and that your Lordship's summing up has been unduly prolonged, to give my opinion upon that matter at once. Although I am a juryman only now, I practised for many years as a solicitor. I remember Lord Abinger sitting in this Court, and am of opinion that we are all of us much indebted to your Lordship for the elaborate assistance which you have given us towards the discharge of our duty." His Lordship bowed a courteous acknowledgment.

Only half an hour later, "amid a silence almost as grave as that preceding a criminal verdict," the jury returned to their box with a verdict for the plaintiff for £5,000 damages.

"This finding was welcomed with an irrepressible burst of

applause in the Court, which no frowns from the Bench, nor hushings from the Ushers, could restrain, and which was at once re-echoed by a louder and deeper roar from the crowd without in Westminster Hall. On Mr. Belt's appearance in Westminster Hall, he was vociferously applauded and borne through the Hall, down through the great door, on the shoulders of his friends. So ended the trial of the last and longest libel case ever heard in Westminster Hall."

"There is," added *The Times*, "an appropriateness in the last of the causes at Westminster being tried by the last of the Lawyer Barons, but it is to be hoped that the Royal Courts of Justice will not be inoculated with the modern disease of prolonged trials."

Belt v. *Lawes* was not only the last trial in Westminster Hall. It was also the first case to be heard in the new Law Courts in the Strand. As soon as the Courts opened in January, 1883, the defendant applied for a new trial on the grounds that the verdict was against the weight of the evidence, that the Judge had misdirected the jury in his summing-up on the value of the evidence of the Royal Academicians and other matters, and that the damages were excessive. The appeal was heard before Lord Coleridge, the Lord Chief Justice, and Mr. Justices Denman and Manisty. It was the custom at that time for an appeal Court to read aloud the evidence which had been given at the hearing. In this case, a printed copy of the Judge's notes ran into 1,500 pages. The Court only wished to hear counsel's arguments on the Judge's supposed misdirections, but Sir Hardinge Giffard insisted that all the evidence be read, and Mr. Justice Manisty, as the junior Judge, began to do so, reading until he was tired, when Mr. Justice Denman took it up. The extraordinary thing is that, having demanded the reading of the evidence, both leading counsel then left the Court. When the Court came to the evidence about the statues they refused to have the exhibits in Court, Lord Coleridge declaring that he could not form a judgment on the evidence if he was also expected to form a judgment on the statues. So the reading of the evidence continued, until Mr. Justice Manisty's voice became so weak with fatigue that he was hardly audible. At last he could not help ejaculating pathetically, "What is the use of all this?" As he had only reached the third day of the trial, though half the day was spent, Lord Coleridge asked ironically, "Might it not be as well for all three of us to read different parts of the evidence together? It would certainly save time and would be very much the same thing in point of utility, and would perhaps be more lively. What do counsel say to that?" As their learned leaders were absent, the junior counsel did not feel that they could express an opinion, and, efforts to obtain the opinion of Sir Hardinge having failed, the reading continued until the end of the day, by which time some 1,000 or 1,200 pages still remained. In a modern appeal, evidence is read by counsel with the Judges following from transcripts of the shorthand note which is now taken at every High Court trial.

On the following morning Sir Hardinge consented to abandon the reading, and began to argue the case, referring only to the evidence which was relevant to his arguments. After a short time, however, he obtained permission for the reading of the summing-up. This was the duty of counsel, and every counsel in Court now took turns, until after two days of it, Lord Coleridge intervened: "We are desirous of avoiding what is really likely to become a public scandal. The reading of this summing-up seems now to have reached the point at which the reading of the evidence was stopped. Sir Hardinge Giffard told us, with an air of authority, that it was necessary to read the whole of the evidence. On consideration he found it was not necessary, and gave way to the remonstrances of the Court. He then told us, with the same air of authority, that it was absolutely necessary to read the whole of the summing-up. The reading of the summing-up has now extended over three days and we have only got to the seventy-fifth page out of 175. Now we feel that it is not doing us any good. Mere reading over of the summing-up without comment, and indeed in the absence of the leaders, so that if any question arises the junior counsel who are present cannot take any responsibility upon themselves in dealing with it, is becoming a rather serious and discreditable waste of time."

And so on the fourth day the appeal really began. In the end the Court said that it might like to look at the sculptures after all, and these were set out in a special room. The appeal lasted twelve days in all, and after a further delay the Court indicated that they were divided. The majority were of the opinion that there ought to be a new trial; on the other hand they were not agreed about their reasons for this, or on the issues upon which the new trial should be held. In fact, Manisty thought that the verdict and damages given by the jury should stand. Lord Coleridge thought there should be a new trial without conditions. Denman thought there should be no new trial, provided that the plaintiff agreed to a reduction in his damages, but he did not suggest by what amount. This was a hint to counsel to settle the action before the Court delivered judgment. There followed a further delay during which the parties failed to agree on a compromise, and eventually the Court delivered its judgment on the 17th December, 1883. There was to be a new trial, unless the plaintiff consented to reduce his damages to £500. Lord Coleridge's judgment makes an interesting contrast with what Baron Huddleston said at the trial and the Master of the Rolls was to say subsequently:

"Under ordinary circumstances, whether a public writer was or was not justified in saying of a man that he was not a sculptor, but an ingenious and successful sculpture-broker, who presents to the public, as his own, work which has been invariably designed and executed by other hands than his (for this is the real gist and substance of the alleged libel), this was a question hardly, in itself, worthy the expenditure of very large sums of money and forty-three days of the public time. But some of the very greatest names in the country have been involved, either personally or by reference, in the discussion. The Royal Academy has itself, so to say, been put upon its trial and the case has assumed proportions and an importance quite incommensurate with the issues that it alone necessarily raised. . . . I have already stated what I conceive to be the true question in this case; it is perhaps better that I should also state what I conceive it was not. It was not whether Mr. Belt could make a passable model, one which to an uneducated or uncultivated eye would pass muster as a piece of sculpture. Most men of the least dexterity of hand could do as much as this. The question was not this, but whether fine works of art, admitted on all hands to be so, were really his work or the works of other men; and as to this, again, not whether, in the long course of working upon them, he may not now and then have actually

handled the clay, or even carved the marble, but whether the
completed work, the art in them when they had art—what I
believe logicians call 'the formal cause' of them—that which
made them what they are, was Mr. Belt's work or another's. . . .
In sculpture, in the long and various process from the slight clay
sketch or drawing to the completed marble, there is so much
which is necessarily mechanical, and which a competent carving
mason can do just as well as a Phidias or Michaelangelo. Help,
therefore, up to a certain point, every sculptor from the highest
to the lowest, has, or may have, with absolute integrity; indeed
with universal knowledge and acceptance. But there comes a
point in modelling, and I should have supposed, but for what I
have heard of Flaxman, there comes a point in the carving too,
where mechanism ends and original art begins. I imagine that
this point is almost impossible to state in words with any approach
to accuracy. I certainly will make no attempt of the kind, for I
have no pretensions to, and disclaim altogether, any artistic knowledge. I have it not, and if I had it, I think I should have no business to apply it. The law has said that a jury who may know
nothing, and a judge who may know nothing too, are to determine, if necessary, as facts abstruse points of science or subtle and
delicate questions of art. . . . I deprecate the course of fine language to conceal cloudiness of thought; and if I seem to use it, it
is only because I despair, as I have said, of describing with any
accuracy a fact which is a fact, but which is to be felt rather than
expressed. Yet this fact, whether Mr. Belt had help which was
not honest, is cardinal to the cause. If he had not, if he had no
more help than every sculptor has or may have, then he is a real
sculptor, and, subject to a subordinate question as to the amount
of damages, he is entitled to keep his verdict. If the evidence
shows that he had such help, that the completed works which he
put forward as his own, were not his own in character nor in art,
then he is a mere sculpture-broker, the verdict is wrong and the
case should be tried again. I have said 'if the evidence shows' because I conceive the issue to be one of fact, but fact of a peculiar kind,
and that the evidence to establish it must likewise be evidence of a
peculiar kind. Now the character or genuineness of works of art is
not, in my judgment, a matter of opinion. Anything, no doubt, may

17

be said to be a matter of opinion as to which men will not take the trouble to inform themselves. But a knowledge of art is like a knowledge of science; it is a matter of education and experience; and it seems to me that you might almost as well disbelieve a body of astronomers, who tell you that the earth moves and the sun stands still, on the ground that very eminent members of society tell you, as a fact, they have seen the earth stand still and the sun rise in the East and go down in the West, as disbelieve a body of great artists who tell you that the same man did not make two works of art, because persons very high in the social scale, but with no knowledge or training in art, tell you as a fact that they saw the same man at work upon them. It is what I think (with deference) the fallacy of opposing 'fact' to 'opinion' in this matter that constitutes, to my mind, the error of summing-up of my learned brother, and which has led the jury to a conclusion against the weight of the evidence. I do not doubt that one fact is worth twenty opinions, 'fact' and 'opinion' being each used in its proper sense. But the words are not used in their proper sense if 'fact' is confined to the physical fact of working manually on a bust, and the scientific conclusion of a body of men as to an artistic fact is called 'opinion'. It is not 'opinion' at all; it is evidence of fact. No one has ever been honoured with the intimacy or enjoyed the society of artists but must be aware how many things we overlook in works of art which are before our eyes, which are there indeed, to be seen, but which it needs training or instruction to see. A copy and the original stand side by side and a man of ordinary education can see no difference between them. A great artist comes, decides at once which is which, and decides it on grounds which are conclusive to the man of ordinary education, but which, nevertheless, he would never have discovered by himself."

Belt agreed to take the course proffered by the Court, but the intractable Lawes was not satisfied, and decided to appeal from the Divisional Court to a still higher Court, the new Court of Appeal. The second appeal was heard in March, 1884, before the Master of the Rolls (Sir William Britt) and Lords Justices Baggallay and Lindley. Judgment was delivered after seven more days of argument: it was unanimous in favour of the plaintiff for the full amount of £5,000, given by the jury at the trial. "The libels," said the Master of the Rolls, "accuse the plaintiff of mean and dishonourable conduct as a professional sculptor. By what standard is the truth of these accusations to be tried? I answer by the standard which the majority of careful, simple, honest-minded men of ordinary intelligence and ordinary sensitiveness of right and wrong will apply. Such accusations are not to be determined by the sensitive delicacy of a high-minded profession, which is often too sensitive itself. They are not to be determined by a puritanism of honour, which belongs sometimes to minds of the highest order. They are to be decided by the ordinary standards of honour of ordinary honourable men. The mind of a single man may be too high-pitched, the minds of men of a different class might be too low-pitched; but the concurrent opinion of a jury, reasonably and fairly selected, is probably safe."

The wisest judges may differ, as the most learned philosophers differ, on what is the surest guide to truth. But English law, in the fullness of its wisdom, has decreed that this—the lodestar of all knowledge—is a question for the jury. And so Belt retained his judgment for £5,000 and his costs in all three Courts. Whether he received much of what was owing to him may be wondered, as Lawes took refuge in bankruptcy. It may well be, however, that he received as much as his deserts, since two years later he was convicted at the Old Bailey of obtaining money by false pretences and sentenced to twelve months' hard labour. The charge related to the sale of worthless jewellery for £8,000, and Sir Charles Russell, the new Attorney-General, appeared for the prosecution. But thereafter Belt lived to a ripe old age, and the statue of Queen Anne with attendant figures, which stands beneath the steps of St. Paul's, is proof that the Lord Mayor and the City Corporation had the courage to ignore the deadly libel which was laid before them, though whether it proves their artistic insight is matter, perhaps, for another jury.

ACKNOWLEDGMENTS

First and foremost my deepest thanks are due to Mr. Edward Wilfrid Fordham, Barrister-at-Law of the Inner Temple, and author of *Notable Cross-examinations* (Constable, 1951), who conceived the idea of this book and sustained me throughout the writing of it with many helpful recommendations and the most careful and constructive criticism of each Chapter as it was completed in draft. Of many other friends to whom I am grateful I should particularly like to thank Dr. Lawson, the Oxford Professor of International Law, for some useful suggestions, and also Bip Pares for her striking cover design. My clerk, Mr. Ernest Weston, kindly helped in the preparation of the index. I gratefully acknowledge the permission given to me by the Editor of *The Times Law Reports* to make free use of material contained in those invaluable columns, by the *Daily Express* to quote from their Verbatim Report of the Laski trial, and by the Chairman of the Incorporated Council of Law Reporting for England and Wales to summarise or quote extracts from the judgments in the following cases in the *Law Reports*:

The Capital and Counties Bank Ltd., *v.* George Henty and Sons (1880) 5 C.P.D. 514; (1882) 7 App. Cas. 741.

Byrne *v.* Deane [1937] 1 K.B. 818.

Australian Newspaper Co. Ltd. *v.* Bennett [1894] A.C. 284.

Ralston *v.* Ralston [1930] 2 K.B. 238.

E. Hulton and Co. *v.* Jones [1909] 2 K.B. 444; [1910] A.C. 20.

Cassidy *v.* Daily Mirror Newspapers Ltd. [1929] 2 K.B. 331.

Hough *v.* London Express Newspaper Ltd., [1940] 2 K.B. 507.

Newstead *v.* London Express Newspaper Ltd. [1940] 1 K.B. 377.

Monson *v.* Tussaud's Ltd. [1894] 1 Q.B. 671.

Tolley *v.* J. S. Fry and Sons Ltd. [1930] 1 K.B. 467; [1931] A.C. 33.

Hobbs *v.* Tinling (C. T.) and Co., Ltd. ⎱
Hobbs *v.* Nottingham Journal Ltd. ⎰ [1929] 2 K.B.1.

JOSEPH DEAN.

BIBLIOGRAPHY

References to or other accounts of the cases related in this book will be found in the following works:

Rex. *v.* Lord Alfred Douglas.   *The Life of Lord Alfred Douglas: by William Freeman (Herbert Joseph,* 1948).

Morris *v.* Associated Newspapers Ltd.
The Last Serjeant, The Memoirs of Serjeant A. M. Sullivan, Q.C. (Macdonald, 1952).
Behind the Bar, by A. E. Bowker (Staples Press, 1947).

Wright *v.* Lord Gladstone.   *Behind the Bar,* by A. E. Bowker.

Blennerhassett *v.* Novelty Sales Services Ltd.
Youssoupoff *v.* Metro-Goldwyn-Mayer Pictures Ltd.

Cases in Court, by Sir Patrick Hastings, K.C. (Heinemann, 1949).

Regina *v.* Ledger.   *Later Leaves,* by Montague Williams, Q.C. (Macmillan, 1891).

Hobbs *v.* Tinling (C.T.) & Co. Ltd.
Hobbs *v.* Nottingham Journal Ltd.

The Last Serjeant, The Memoirs of Serjeant A. M. Sullivan, Q.C.

Crowley *v.* Constable & Co. Ltd.
The Great Beast: by John Symonds (Rider, 1951).

Laski *v.* Newark Advertiser Co. Ltd.
Cases in Court, by Sir Patrick Hastings.
Harold Laski, by Kingsley Martin (Victor Gollancz, 1953).

Belt *v.* Lawes.   *Leaves of a Life,* by Montague
                                    Williams, Q.C. (Macmil-
                                    lan, 1890).
                                    The Life of Lord Russell of Killowen,
                                    by R. Barry O'Brien (Smith,
                                    Elder, 1901).
                                    The Earl of Halsbury, by A. Wilson
                                    Fox (Chapman & Hall, 1929).

Apart from legal textbooks and law reports, I have also consulted:

Westminster Hall, by Hilary St. George Saunders (Michael Joseph,
1951).

London's Open-Air Statuary, by Lord Edward Gleichen (Longman's
Green, 1928).

Oscar Wilde and the Black Douglas, by the Marquess of Queensberry
(Hutchinson, 1949).

Rasputin: his malignant influence and his assassination, by Prince
Youssoupoff, translated by O. Rayner (Jonathan Cape, 1927).

Aleister Crowley, by Charles Richard Cammell (The Richards
Press, 1951).

INDEX